Dodge &
Plymouth

MUSCLE CAR
RED BOOK

Second Edition

Peter C. Sessler

MOTORBOOKS

This edition published in 2001 by Motorbooks, an imprint of MBI
Publishing Company, Galtier Plaza, Suite 200, 380 Jackson Street,
St. Paul, MN 55101-3885 USA

The information in this book is true and complete to the best of our
knowledge. All recommendations are made without any guarantee
on the part of the author or Publisher, who also disclaim any
liability incurred in connection with the use of this data or specific
details.

We recognize, further, that some words, model names, and
designations mentioned herein are the property of the trademark
holder. We use them for identification purposes only. This is not an
official publication.

MBI Publishing Company titles are also available at discounts in
bulk quantity for industrial or sales-promotional use. For details
write to Special Sales Manager at MBI Publishing Company,
Galtier Plaza, Suite 200, 380 Jackson Street, St. Paul, MN 55101-
3885 USA

Library of Congress Cataloging-in-Publication Data
    Dodge & Plymouth muscle car red book / Peter C. Sessler—2nd ed.
      p. cm.
    ISBN-10: 0-7603-0801-2 (pbk. : alk. paper)
    ISBN-13: 978-0-7603-0801-1
    1. Dodge automobile. 2. Plymouth automobile. 3. Muscle
    cars—United States. I. Title.

  TL215.D6 S48 2000
  629.222'2—dc21   99-049629

On the front cover: A 1970 AAR Cuda 340 Six-Pack owned by
Alan Spry. *Steve Statham*

Printed in the United States of America

Contents

Introduction

The *Dodge and Plymouth Muscle Car Red Book* is designed to help the Dodge enthusiast determine the authenticity and originality of 1967–74 Dodge and Plymouth performance cars. This updated second edition now also includes the 1986–89 Shelby-modified Dodge front-drive cars and Dakota pickup truck. Also included is the 1992–2000 Dodge Viper and the 1997–2000 Plymouth Prowler.

Chapters on the 1968–69 Dart GTS, 1971–72 Demon 340, 1970–73 Valiant Duster 340, and the 1970–71 Sport Fury GT have been added as well.

Each chapter covers a single model year of production, listing production figures, the vehicle identification number (VIN) decoding information, engine codes, carburetor part numbers, exterior color codes, interior trim codes, options, pricing and selected facts. Certain chapters also include distributor part numbers.

Every effort has been made to insure the accuracy of the information presented here, and the information is applicable to the great majority of Dodge and Plymouth cars built. There are exceptions, however. Because of the nature of the automobile business, Chrysler (now known as DaimlerChrysler) deals with thousands of vendors who supply the thousands of parts that go into the making of a vehicle. The possibility of shortages, substitutions, deletions and the like is always there, which sometimes results in cars that don't quite fit published specifications. Most of the variations are relatively minor detail items that do not change the basic specifications of the car in question. Occasionally, however, some very interesting cars surface. For example, some factory original cars have surfaced over the years that weren't supposed to be equipped with the 426 Hemi engine (according to published specifications), yet somehow were.

The most important number on a vehicle is the VIN. From 1967 to 1974, the VIN is a 13-digit number, and from 1981 on up it was a 17-digit number. The VIN is stamped onto the car in various places, sometimes requiring disassembly to see it. For titling and registration purposes, there was one specific area where the manufacturer must affix the vehicle's VIN. For 1967 cars, this number is stamped on a plate and is attached to the left front door pillar. From 1968 to the present, the number is stamped on a plate and attached to the edge of the instrument panel and is visible through the windshield. The VIN can also be found on the body code plate, on which additional information is found.

Chrysler also took the trouble to stamp the VIN or the last eight digits, depending on manufacturing plant, on the engine block itself. On the 198 and 225 ci six-cylinder engines, this number is stamped on the right side, front of the block, near the coil mounting bracket. On the small-block V-8s (318, 340, and 360 ci), the number is stamped on the left side of the block, below the cylinder head. On big-block engines (383, 400, 426, and 440 ci), the number is stamped on the left rear side of the block near the oil pan flange. In addition, the VIN is also stamped on the transmission, whether it is a manual or an automatic. On manual transmissions, it is located below the centerline on the front portion of the right side. On automatics, it is on the left oil pan side rail.

The VIN can also be found in various places on the car itself. Common places include the radiator yoke top side or bottom and on the cowl. Naturally, the VIN must be the same in all locations for the car to be a "numbers matching car."

Beginning with 1970 models, the VIN is stamped on a label along with the date of manufacture, and attached to the rear face of the driver's door. This is known as the "vehicle certification label" and it certifies that the car conforms to federal safety regulations.

The color and interior trim codes listed in each chapter are correct according to published specifications. However, Chrysler built cars in colors and interiors that weren't normally listed. Cars with special-order paint will have the numbers 999 in place of the regular paint code on the body data plate and broadcast sheet. Special-order interiors are indicated by the numbers 888.

The option and price lists were obtained from various sources, mostly from dealers' files and from salespeople's data/price books. With the exception of 1971, all pricing is from the beginning of the model year. Mid-year options have been inserted according to their option number sequence and they are not listed separately. However, the possibility exists that some options were never installed in any car and some cars may have options or equipment that was never listed in any published factory literature. Some options may have been deleted during the model year and others added. In the same way, prices are often revised throughout the model year.

The production figures listed in each chapter may not match other published figures. I believe these are correct; they are taken from the original factory shipment reports that Chrysler provided for use in this book.

This book will help you establish authenticity and value for the cars covered in this book. In the final analysis, the information presented here will be weighed in with other factors—strong gut feelings or common sense—to make a judgment.

The Shelby Connection

Just as Carroll Shelby modified Ford Mustangs in the late 1960s, in the 1980s he did the same for Dodge. However, there is some confusion as to which cars are "true" Shelbys—those that he actually modified at his own facility in Whittier, California, versus those that only bear his name. The cars that were Shelby Dodge models were the 1983–87 Shelby Charger, the 1984–86 Omni GLH, the 1984–91 Dodge Daytona Shelby/Shelby Z, and the 1988–89 Dodge Lancer Shelby. There were also several "CS" option packages on the 1986–91 Dodge Daytona. The cars that are listed are just Shelby named, not true Shelbys (i.e., the ones he personally worked on).

The true Shelby cars were not Dodge vehicles officially, but Shelby cars instead. These are: 1986–87 Shelby GLHS, 1987 Shelby CSX, 1987 Shelby Lancer, 1988 Shelby CSX-T, 1989 Shelby CSX-VNT, and the 1989 Shelby Dakota pickup truck. You'll note that none of these have "Dodge" in their description.

Although every effort has been made to make sure that the information contained in The *Dodge and Plymouth Muscle Car Red Book* is correct, the author cannot assume any responsibility for any loss arising from the use of this book.

Chapter 1

1968 Dodge Dart GTS

Production

2 dr hardtop	7,699
2 dr convertible	403
Total	8,102

Serial numbers

LS23P8A100001
L—car line, Dodge Dart
S—price class (S-special)
23—body type (23-2 dr hardtop, 27-convertible)
P—engine code
8—last digit of model year
A—assembly plant code (B-Hamtramck, E-Los Angeles)
100001—consecutive sequence number
Serial number located on plate attached to left side of dash panel, visible through the windshield.

Engine codes

P—340 ci 4V V-8 275 hp
H—383 ci 4V V-8 300 hp

Head casting numbers

340 ci—2531894
383 ci—2843906

Carburetors

340 ci 4V—Carter AVS4424S/manual, AVS4425S/automatic, AVS4636S/automatic w/AC
383 ci 4V—Carter AVS4426S/manual, AVS4401S/automatic,

Distributors

340 ci—2875086 IBS-4015/manual, 2875140 IBS-4015A/automatic
383 ci—2875356/manual, 2875358/automatic

Option order codes and retail prices

LS23 2 dr hardtop	$3,163.00
LS27 2 dr convertible	3,383.00
351 Dart Radio Group (w/340 ci)	182.45
351 Dart Radio Group (w/383 ci)	102.10
355 Light Package (NA convertible)	22.15
355 Light Package (convertible)	14.50
393 Manual 4 speed transmission	NC
395 TorqueFlite automatic transmission	STD
62 383 ci 4V engine	35.40
408 Sure-Grip differential	42.35
411 Air conditioner (NA w/383 ci)	334.60
418 Rear window defogger (NA convertible)	21.30

421 Music Master AM radio	61.55
451 Power brakes	41.75
456 Power steering (NA w/383 ci)	80.35
479 Front disc brakes	72.95
481 Front bumper guards	14.05
482 Rear bumper guards	11.25
483 Front & rear bumper guards	23.10
486 Console	50.10
505 Pedal dress-up	3.75
517 Fender-mounted turn signals	10.50
521 Tinted glass—all windows (exc convertible backglass)	30.50
522 Tinted glass—windshield only	18.55
531 Left head restraint	21.95
532 Right head restraint	21.95
533 Left & right head restraints	43.90
536 Remote control outside left mirror	9.40
537 Manual outside right mirrors	6.55
550 Deluxe seatbelts, 2 front, 2 rear	10.50
557 Seatbelt, center pass. rear	6.50
568 Front shoulder belts	26.45
566 Rear shoulder belts (NA convertible)	26.45
571 Full-horn-ring steering wheel	9.35
573 Wood-grain steering wheel	25.95
577 Tachometer w/console only	51.10
579 Undercoating w/hood insulator pad	16.10
581 Deluxe wheel covers	21.30
587 Simulated Mag, 14 in.	45.10
589 Windshield wiper/washer package	10.30
591 46 amp alternator	11.00
627 59 amp battery (std w/383 ci)	8.10
628 Steering, fast manual (NA w/456)	14.05
708 Special Buffed Silver Metallic paint	17.60
Two-tone paint (NA convertible)	19.80
Bucket seats (convertible)	70.95
Vinyl roof	75.10
39 Tires—set of 5 (E70x14 WSW)	NC

Exterior color codes*

Buffed Silver Metallic	AA1
Black Velvet	BB1
Midnight Blue Metallic	EE1
Mist Green Metallic	FF1
Forest Green Metallic	GG1
Ember Gold Metallic	JJ1
Surf Turquoise Metallic	LL1
Turbine Bronze Metallic	MM1
Matador Red	P1
Electric Blue Metallic	QQ1
Burgundy Metallic	RR1
Sunfire Yellow	SS1
Avocado Green Metallic	TT1
Frost Blue Metallic	UU1

Sable White	WW1
Satin Beige	XX1
Sierra Tan Metallic	YY1

*First letter indicates top color, second letter indicates lower color, last number indicates one- or two-tone paint. Example: BB1-Black top/black bottom, 1-one-tone. BP2-Black top/Matador Red bottom, 2-two-tone

Interior trim codes

	Vinyl buckets	Split-bench convertible
Blue	S6B	P4B
Green	S6F	—
Red	S6R	P4R
Black	S6X	P4X
White/Black	—	P4W

Bumblebee stripe color codes

White	317
Black	310
Red	314

Vinyl roof color codes —hardtop only

Green	304
Black	306
White	307

Convertible top color codes

Green	300
Black	301
White	302

Facts

Whereas the Dart GT first appeared in 1965, the high-performance GTS model appeared in 1968. Setting it off from other Darts, the GTS came with a power bulge hood and GTS identification on the hood, front fenders and trunk lid. Bumblebee stripes were optional. The GTS was available as a two-door hardtop or convertible.

As it was the top of the line Dart, the GTS came with upgraded interior trim with standard bucket seats (bench on the convertible, with buckets optional).

The standard engine was the 340 ci small-block V-8 with the three-speed TorqueFlite automatic transmission. The only optional engine was the 383 ci big-block V-8. Optional on both engines, at no extra cost, was the four-speed manual transmission.

Heavy-duty torsion bars, springs, shocks and front sway bar characterized the GTS's suspension. Heavy-duty drum brakes were standard with front discs optional. Because of the 383's large size, power steering was not available with it.

A total of 80 Dart S/S models were built and powered by the 426 ci Hemi engine for drag racing.

The Dodge Dart GSS was a 440-ci-powered Dart. Only a small number of the Dart GSS models were built by Mr. Norm's Grand Spaulding Dodge in Chicago, Illinois.

Chapter 2

1969 Dodge Dart GTS

Production

2 dr hardtop 8 cyl	5,717
2 dr coupe 8 cyl	360
Total	6,077

Serial numbers

LS23P9A100001
L—car line, Dodge Dart
S—price class (S-special)
23—body type (23-2 dr hardtop, 27-convertible)
P—engine code
9—last digit of model year
A—assembly plant code (B-Hamtramck, E-Los Angeles)
100001—consecutive sequence number
Serial number located on plate attached to left side of dash panel, visible through the windshield.

Engine codes

P—340 ci 4V V-8 275 hp
H—383 ci 4V V-8 330 hp
M—440 ci 4V V-8 375 hp

Head casting numbers

340 ci—2531894
383 ci—2843906
440 ci—2843906

Carburetors

340 ci 4V V-8—Carter AVS4611S/manual, AVS4612S/automatic, AVS4639S/automatic w/AC
383 ci 4V V-8—Carter AVS4615S/manual, AVS/4616S/automatic
440 ci 4V V-8—Carter AVS4617S/manual, AVS4618S/automatic

Distributors

340 ci—2875782 IBS-4015B/manual, 2875779/automatic
383 ci—2875779 IBS-4016A/manual, 2875846 IBS-4016/automatic
440 ci—2875772 IBS-4014B/manual, 2875758/automatic

Option order codes and retail prices

LS23 2 dr hardtop V-8	$3,209.00
LS27 2 dr convertible V-8	3,402.00
A01 Dart Light Group (hardtop)	26.05
A01 Dart Light Group (convertible)	22.15
A04 Dart Radio Group (w/14 in. wheels & bucket seats)	189.05
A04 Dart Radio Group (w/14 in. wheels & bench seat)	197.35
A13 440 ci engine conversion package	NA
A35 Trailer Towing Package (w/D34, 340 ci w/o H51)	14.75
A35 Trailer Towing Package (w/D34, 340 ci w/H51)	4.25
B41 Front disc brakes	48.70
B51 Power brakes	42.95
C13 Front shoulder belts (convertible)	26.45
C14 Rear shoulder belts (hardtop)	26.45

C16 Console (w/bucket seats)	53.35
C25 Left head restraint	13.25
C28 Right head restraint	13.25
C31 Left & right head restraints	26.50
C92 Protective rubber floor mats	10.90
C65 Air foam front bench seat	8.30
D21 Manual 4 speed transmission (NA w/A3)	NC
D34 TorqueFlite automatic transmission	NC
D91 Sure-Grip differential	42.35
E63 383 ci 4V engine	35.40
E86 440 ci 4V engine	NA
F11 46 amp alternator	11.00
F25 59 amp battery (std w/383 ci)	8.40
G11 Tinted glass—all windows (exc convertible backglass)	32.75
G15 Tinted glass—windshield only	20.40
G31 Manual outside right mirror	6.85
G33 Remote control outside left mirror	10.45
H31 Rear window defogger (NA convertible)	21.90
H51 Air conditioner (NA w/E63, E86)	343.45
J25 Variable speed windshield wipers w/electric washers	10.60
J41 Pedal dress-up	3.90
J55 Undercoating w/hood insulator pad	16.60
L31 Fender-mounted turn signal	0.80
M05 Door edge protectors	4.65
M31 Bodyside belt moldings	13.60
N85 Tachometer (w/C16, NA w/H51)	50.15
R11 Music Master radio	61.55
R21 Solid-state AM/FM radio	134.95
S75 Steering, fast manual (NA w/S77)	14.45
S77 Power steering	85.15
S78 Full-horn-ring steering wheel	5.45
S81 Wood-grain steering wheel	26.75
W11 Deluxe wheel covers	21.30
Simulated Mag wheel covers	64.10
W23 Cast road wheels	100.10
Bucket seats	73.00
Two-tone paint (NA convertible)	22.65
Vinyl roof	78.65
Tires—set of 5 (replaces E70x14 Red Streak)	
T74 E70x14 WSW	26.45

Exterior color codes

Silver Metallic	A4
Light Blue Metallic	B3
Bright Blue Metallic	B5
Medium Blue Metallic	B7
Light Green	
Medium Green Metallic	F5
Dark Green Metallic	F8
Beige	L1
Bright Turquoise Metallic	Q5

Performance Red	R4
Red	R6
Light Bronze Metallic	T3
Copper Metallic	T5
Dark Bronze Metallic	T7
White	W1
Black	X9
Yellow	Y2
Cream	Y3
Gold	Y4

Interior trim codes

Color	Std bench seat convertible	Std buckets-hardtop	Opt buckets-convertible
Blue	P2B	P6B	P6B
Black	P2	P6X	P6X
Red	P2R	P6R	P6R
White	P2W	P6W	P6W
White/Blue	—	P6C	P6C
White/Gold	—	P6E	—
White/Green	—	P6F	P6F
Green	6G	P6G	—
Gold	—	P6Y	P6Y

Vinyl roof color codes

Antique Green	V1F
Saddle Bronze	V1T
Pearlescent White	V1W
Black	V1X

Convertible top color codes

Black	V3X
White	V3W

Bumblebee stripe color codes

Black	V8X
Red	V8R
White	V8W

Facts

Sharing the same body style as the 1968s, the 1969 GTS got a new grille and taillight panel. The hood had side facing simulated scoops which indicated engine size. The GTS's bumblebee stripe was changed to a different single band design.

Engine choice expanded with the availability of the 375 hp 440 ci V-8 during the later part of the model year. Exact production figures are unknown, but 30 are known to exist according to Galen Govier, Chrysler historian.

Standard engine was the 340 ci small-block V-8. There were 3,919 hardtops and 73 convertibles built with this engine.

The optional 383 ci V-8 was now rated at 330 hp. Like the 1968 version, power steering was not available.

Chapter 3

1971 Dodge Dart Demon 340

Production
2 dr sports hardtop 8 cyl   7,899

Serial numbers
LM29H1B100001
L—car line, Dodge Dart
M—price class (M-medium)
29—body type (29-2 dr sports hardtop)
H—engine code
1—last digit of model year
B—assembly plant code (B-Hamtramck)
100001—consecutive sequence number
Serial number located on plate attached to left side of dash panel,
visible through the windshield.

Engine code
H—340 ci 4V V-8 275 hp (net rating 235 hp)

Head casting number
340 ci—2531894

Carburetors
340 ci 4V V-8—Carter TQ4972S/manual, TQ4973S/automatic

Distributors
340 ci—3438522/manual, 3438517/automatic, 3656151/manual
w/electronic ignition, 3438986/automatic w/electronic ignition

Option order codes and retail prices*
LM29 2 dr sports hardtop	$2,721.00
A01 Dart Light Group	27.65
A04 Dart Radio Group (models w/bucket seats)	203.55
A04 Dart Radio Group (models w/bench seats)	211.75
A31 High-Performance Axle Package (NA w/H51)	61.40
A46 Dart Molding Group	7.45
A88 Interior Decor Group	13.85
B41 Front disc brakes	22.50
B51 Power brakes	41.55
C14 Rear shoulder belts	24.40
C16 Console (w/buckets & D34)	52.55
C65 Front foam seat cushion	8.20
D21 Manual 4 speed transmission	189.80
D34 TorqueFlite automatic transmission	214.40
D91 Sure-Grip differential	41.70
F11 50 amp alternator (std w/H51)	10.85
F23 59 amp battery	13.60
G11 Tinted windows	33.85

G15 Tinted windshield only	25.05
G31 Chrome outside right mirror (requires G33)	6.80
G33 Chrome outside left mirror	10.35
G36 Remote outside left racing mirrors & manual right color-keyed (w/A04)	15.55
G36 Remote outside left racing mirrors & manual right color-keyed (w/oA04)	25.75
G37 Remote outside left racing mirrors & manual chrome right (w/A04)	15.55
G37 Remote outside left racing mirrors & manual chrome right (w/oA04)	25.75
G41 Day-night inside mirror	7.05
H31 Rear window defogger	27.35
H51 Air conditioning	363.40
J25 Variable speed windshield wipers w/electric washer	10.60
J31 Dual horns	5.10
J41 Pedal dress-up	5.35
J45 Hood pins	15.20
J54 Hood scoops, includes black performance hood	44.45
J55 Undercoating w/hood insulator pad	20.80
J81 Aerodynamic rear spoiler	34.30
M05 Door edge protectors	4.60
M25 Custom sill molding	11.25
M31 Belt molding	13.40
M81 Front bumper guards	13.85
M83 Rear bumper guards	11.10
M85 Front & rear bumper guards	24.90
N25 Engine block heater	13.85
N85 Tachometer	49.45
N95 NOx exhaust emission control (Calif)	11.90
R11 Music Master radio AM	61.10
R26 AM radio w/stereo cassette player (NA w/C16)	201.60
R33 Microphone-tape recorder (w/R26)	10.75
S77 Power steering	94.75
S81 Deluxe steering wheel	9.90
S84 Tuff steering wheel (S77 req'd)	28.85
V3 Manual folding vinyl sunroof (NA w/vinyl roof)	229.50
W11 Deluxe wheel covers	25.15
W21 Rallye road wheels	54.25
High-impact paint colors	3.85
Bodyside stripes	25.50
Vinyl roof	7.45
Vinyl side molding	14.25
Deluxe cloth and vinyl bench seat	12.75
Vinyl bucket seat & carpeting	89.65
Tires (replaces E70x14 BSW P/F) T76 E70x14 RWL	38.25
*As of April 1, 1971	

Exterior color codes

Light Gunmetal Metallic	GA4
Light Blue Metallic	GB2

Bright Blue Metallic	GB5
Dark Blue Metallic	GB7
Light Green Metallic	GF3
Dark Green Metallic	GF7
Dark Bronze Metallic	GK6
Tan Metallic	GT5
Butterscotch	EL5
Bright Red	FE5
Bright White	GW3
Black	TX9
Gold Metallic	GY8
Dark Gold Metallic	GY9
Green Go	FJ6
Plum Crazy	F\C7
Hemi Orange	EV2
Citron Yella	GY3
Top Banana	FY1

Interior trim color codes

Color	Cloth & Vinyl bench	Vinyl bench	Vinyl buckets
Black	—	E2X9	M6X9
Blue	M1B7	E2B7	—
Green	M1F8	—	—
Tan	—	E2T5	—
Black/Orange	M1XV	—	M6XV
Black/White	M1XX	—	M6XW

Vinyl roof color codes

Black	V1X
White	V1W
Green	V1F
Gold	V1Y

Side stripe color codes

Black	V9X
White	V9W

Facts

Dodge's response to the Duster 340 was the Demon 340. Both cars shared the same body and differed only in front grille and taillight treatments. Demon decals appeared on the front fenders and on the taillight panel.

The standard and only engine available was the 275 hp 340 ci V-8 mated to a three-speed manual transmission. The four-speed manual and TorqueFlite automatic were optional.

In the interior, a bench seat was standard equipment; however, buckets were optional. A 150 mph speedometer was standard, and the 6000 rpm tachometer was optional.

Performance options included the Tuff steering wheel, performance hood with dual scoops, a rear spoiler, hood pins and Rallye wheels.

An interesting and rare option was the manual folding sunroof.

Chapter 4

1972 Dodge Dart Demon 340

Production
2 dr sports hardtop 8 cyl   8,739

Serial numbers
LM29H2B100001
L—car line, Dodge Dart
M—price class (M-medium)
29—body type (29-2 dr sports hardtop)
H—engine code
2—last digit of model year
B—assembly plant code (B-Hamtramck)
100001—consecutive sequence number
Serial number located on plate attached to left side of dash panel,
visible through the windshield.

Engine code
H—340 ci 4V V-8   240 hp

Head casting number
340 ci—3418915

Carburetors
340 ci 4V V-8—Carter TQ6138S/manual, TQ6139S/automatic

Distributors
3656278/manual, 3656283/manual & automatic

Option order codes and retail prices
LM29 2 dr sports hardtop	$2,759.00
A01 Light Package	30.50
A04 Basic Group	119.35
A21 Custom Exterior Package	21.10
A25 Interior Convenience Group	19.55
A88 Interior Decor Group (w/L1, C4, C6 trim)	19.85
A88 Interior Decor Group (others)	38.25
B41 Power disc brakes	65.95
B51 Power drum brakes	42.80
C16 Console (buckets & D34 req'd)	54.00
D21 Manual 4 speed transmission	195.25
D34 TorqueFlite automatic transmission	220.55
D91 Sure-Grip differential	43.05
F23 59 amp battery1	4.10
G11 Tinted glass, all windows	37.95
G15 Tinted windshield	25.80
G31 Chrome manual outside right mirrors (G33 req'd)	7.00
G33 Chrome remote control outside left mirror (std w/A04)	12.30
G36 Dual racing mirrors, remote left, manual right (body color w/ A04)	14.30
G36 Dual racing mirrors, remote left, manual right (body color w/o A04)	26.60

G37 Remote outside left racing mirrors & chrome manual right (w/A04)	14.30
G37 Remote outside left racing mirrors & chrome manual right (w/oA04)	26.60
G41 Day-night inside mirror (std w/A04)	7.25
H31 Rear window defogger	28.10
H51 Air conditioning	374.40
J11 Glove box lock (std w/A04)	4.20
J25 Variable speed wipers w/electric washers (std w/A04)	10.95
J52 Inside hood release	10.05
J55 Undercoating w/hood insulator pad	21.45
M05 Door edge protectors	4.80
M31 Belt molding	13.80
M85 Front & rear bumper guards	25.65
N23 Electronic ignition system	32.55
N95 Emission control system & testing (req'd Calif)	27.05
R11 Solid-state AM radio	62.90
R21 AM/FM radio, w/A04	8.95
R21 AM/FM radio (w/oA04)	131.80
R31 Rear seat speaker	14.25
S77 Power steering	97.65
S84 Tuff steering wheel (NA w/A25, S77 req'd)	29.65
S84 Tuff steering wheel (w/A25, S77 req'd)	19.50
V21 Performance hood paint	18.35
W11 Deluxe wheel covers	25.95
W21 Rallye road wheels, set of 4 w/std spare (w/A04)	30.00
W21 Rallye road wheels, set of 4 w/std spare (w/oA04)	55.90
High-impact paint colors	14.25
Two-tone paint	29.35
Vinyl roof	79.85
Sunroof (NA w/vinyl roof)	236.40
Vinyl side molding	14.75
Vinyl bench seat	24.40
Vinyl split back bench seat w/center armrest and carpet	78.90
Vinyl bucket seat & carpeting	127.25
Tires (replaces E70x14 BSW Bias belted)	
T76 E70x14 RWL	39.50

Exterior color codes

Light Gunmetal Metallic	GA4
Super Blue	GB3
Light Blue	HB1
Red	FE5
Light Green Metallic	GF3
Dark Green Metallic	GF7
Bright Blue Metallic	HB5
Medium Tan Metallic	GT6
Dark Tan Metallic	GT8
Eggshell White	GW1
Light Gold	GY5
Gold Metallic	GY8

Dark Gold Metallic	GY9
Black	TX9
Hemi Orange	EV2
Top Banana	FY1

Interior trim codes

Color	Vinyl buckets	Vinyl bench	Cloth & vinyl bench
Blue	—	F4B5	F3B5
Green	—	F4F6	F3F6
Black	C6X9	F4X9	F3X9
Gold	—	F4Y3	—
Black/White	C6XW	—	—

Vinyl roof color codes

Black	V1X
White	V1W
Gold	V1Y
Green	V1F

Tape stripe codes

| Black | V6X |
| White | V6W |

Facts

Besides some minor grille and parking light refinements, the Demon remained unchanged.

The 340 ci V-8 engine was rated at 240 hp due to a compression ratio drop from 10.5:1 to 8.5:1. The 340 ci engine now used cylinder heads from the 360, which had a smaller intake valve, 1.88 in. The 340 also came with the Carter Thermoquad carburetor and electronic ignition.

Suspension and brakes were unchanged from 1971.

Dodge chose not to use the Demon name for 1973. The car was renamed the Dodge Dart 340 Sport. In 1974, the 340 ci V-8 engine was dropped and replaced by the 360 ci V-8, and accordingly it was named the Dart 360 Sport. The Dart 360 Sport would continue until mid-1976 when it was replaced by the Dodge Aspen.

Chapter 5

1964 Plymouth Barracuda

Production
Hardtop coupe 6 cyl	2,647
Hardtop coupe 8 cyl	20,796
Total	23,443

Serial numbers
18V2100001
1 — car line, Valiant
8 — Barracuda
V — model year, 1964
2 — assembly plant code (2-Detroit)
100001 — consecutive sequence number
   Serial number located on plate attached to left front door hinge post.

Engines
170 ci 1V 6 cyl 101 hp
225 ci 1V 6 cyl 145 hp
273 ci 2V V-8 180 hp

Head casting number
273 ci — 2465315

Option order codes and retail prices
149 Barracuda Series Six	$2,365.00
V49 Barracuda Series V-8	2,496.00
02 225 ci engine	47.35
322 Basic Group	96.30
323 Basic Radio Group	159.00
343 Manual 4 speed transmission (6 cyl)	186.25
(8 cyl)	179.20
345 TorqueFlite (6 cyl)	171.55
(8 cyl)	181.00
351 Power steering	82.05
352 Power brakes	42.60
361 Transaudio radio	58.50
381 Air conditioning — single unit w/heater	364.00
383 Air conditioning — single unit wo/heater	289.60
385 Heater w/defroster	74.40
414 3 spoke wood-grain steering wheel	17.30
415 Padded dash	16.35
419 2 retractable front seatbelts	7.05
423 Back-up lights	10.70
428 Dual-jet windshield washer	11.80
429 Variable-speed windshield wipers	5.05
431 Tinted glass — all windows	28.45
432 Tinted glass — windshield only	14.30

443	Front & rear bumper guards	11.45
457	Simulated bolt-on wheel covers	34.15
481	Manual outside left mirrors	5.05
482	Remote outside left mirrors	12.00
492	Inside Day/Nite rearview mirrors	4.20
522	Sure-Grip differential	38.35
570	Trailer Towing Package (8 cyl only)	62.60
578	48 amp battery (170 engine only)	7.60
611	Undercoating w/underhood pad	12.85
616	PCV system (Calif only)	5.05
617	Antifreeze (6 cyl)	3.95
	(8 cyl)	3.95

Tires — set of 5

11	7.00x13 BSW (std 8 cyl)	12.85
12	6.50x13 WSW (6 cyl only)	29.10
13	7.00x13 WSW (6 cyl only)	44.95
13	7.00x13 WSW (8 cyl only)	32.20

Exterior color codes*

Barracuda Gold Metallic	AA1
Valiant Black	BB1
Valiant Light Blue	CC1
Valiant Medium Blue Metallic	DD1
Valiant Dark Blue Metallic	EE1
Valiant Light Turquoise	JJ1
Valiant Medium Turquoise Metallic	KK1
Valiant Medium Gray Metallic	MM1
Valiant Red	PP1
Signet Royal Red	TT1
Valiant White	WW1
Valiant Light Tan	XX1
Valiant Medium Tan Metallic	YY1

*First letter of code indicates top color, second letter indicates bottom color, end number indicates one- or two-tone paint. Examples: BB1-Black top, Black bottom, one-tone paint; BP2-Black top, Bright Red bottom, two-tone paint.

Interior trim codes

Color	Vinyl
Blue	P5B
Red	P5R
Black	P5X
Gold	P5Y

Facts

Introduced in May 1964, the Barracuda was in reality a 1964½ model. Compared with other Detroit offerings, the Barracuda's fastback design, which incorporated a large rear window, stood out. Relying heavily on the 106 in. wheelbase Valiant platform, the Barracuda shared the same suspension, engines and driveline components. The only sheet metal differences occurred over the beltline.

Bucket seats were standard equipment. The major interior feature that was heavily promoted was the fold-down rear seat. The Barracuda fastback was out a good four months earlier than the Mustang fastback, which came available only in September 1964. Even so, the public was so enthralled by the Mustang that the Barracuda's sales were negligible in comparison.

Two six-cylinder engines and one V-8 engine were available. The 101 hp 170 ci six-cylinder was standard. More desirable was the 145 hp 225 ci six-cylinder and the 180 hp 273 ci V-8. Standard transmission was a three-speed manual. Optional on the larger six-cylinder and 273 ci V-8 was Chrysler's four-speed manual transmission.

Power drum brakes were used on all Barracudas. Disc brakes were not available. Suspension was typical Valiant, with torsion bars in the front and leaf springs in the rear. This configuration continued until 1974, when Barracuda production ceased.

1964 Plymouth Barracuda

Chapter 6

1965 Plymouth Barracuda

Production
Hardtop coupe 6 cyl	18,567
Hardtop coupe 8 cyl	41,601
Total	60,168

Serial numbers
18A2500001
1 — car line, Valiant (1-6 cyl, V-8 cyl)
8 — model, Barracuda
A — model year, 1965
2 — assembly plant code (2-Hamtramck)
500001 — consecutive sequence number
    Serial number located on plate attached to left front door hinge post.

Engines
225 ci 1V 6 cyl 145 hp
273 ci 2V V-8 180 hp
273 ci 4V V-8 235 hp

Head casting number
273 ci — 2465315

Option order codes and retail prices
V89 Barracuda Series Six	$2,502.00
V89 Barracuda Series V-8	2,586.00
31 Commando 273 8 cyl 2 bbl engine	99.40
284 Racing stripes	31.25
321 Basic Group	84.45
322 Formula S Package (8 cyl only)	258.00
325 Performance Group (NA 6 cyl)	95.90
326 Rear seatbelts (delete)	(14.90)
333 Sport Group (6 cyl only)	80.55
(8 cyl only)	83.65
363 Manual 4 speed transmission (6 cyl)	179.20
(8 cyl)	179.20
365 TorqueFlite (6 cyl)	171.55
(8 cyl)	181.00
401 Air conditioner (requires code 436)	325.00
406 Heater (delete; NA w/401)	(70.80)
410 Power steering	82.05
411 Power brakes	42.60
436 Cigar lighter	3.75
441 Transaudio radio	58.50
464 3 spoke simulated-wood-grain steering wheel	17.30
465 Padded instrument panel	16.35
468 Tachometer (8 cyl only)	49.70
473 Back-up lights	10.70

478 2 front, 2 rear retractable seatbelts	9.85
485 Custom wheel covers w/spinners, 13 in.	12.50
488 Sports bolt-on-design wheel covers, 13 in.	34.15
14 in.	36.30
493 Front & rear bumper guards	11.45
511 Manual outside left mirrors	5.05
512 Remote outside left mirrors	12.00
522 Inside Day/Nite rearview mirrors	4.20
539 Windshield washer & variable-speed wipers	16.70
541 Tinted glass — all windows	28.45
542 Tinted glass — windshield only	14.30
592 Sure-Grip differential	38.35
611 Undercoating w/underhood pad	15.70
616 PCV system (Calif only — mandatory)	5.05
630 Shock Absorber & Suspension Package	17.15
634 Firm Ride shock absorbers	3.30
639 Suspension Package	13.85
696 Fast manual steering (NA power steering)	13.50
704 Special buffed paint	17.10
Vinyl roof	63.85
Tires — set of 5	
03 6.50x13 WSW (6 cyl only)	29.10
10 7.00x13 BSW (std 8 cyl)	12.85
12 7.00x13 WSW (6 cyl only)	44.95
(8 cyl only)	32.20
50 6.95x14 BSW (6 cyl only)	20.45
(8 cyl only)	7.75
52 6.95x14 WSW (6 cyl only)	52.65
(8 cyl only)	39.90

Exterior color codes

Light Blue	CC1
Medium Blue Metallic	DD1
Dark Blue Metallic	EE1
Light Turquoise	JJ1
Medium Turquoise Metallic	KK1
Light Tan	XX1
Medium Tan Metallic	YY1
White	WW1
Black	BB1
Ruby	PP1
Medium Red Metallic	TT1
Ivory	SS1
Gold Metallic	AA1
Copper Metallic	HH1
Barracuda Silver	NN1

Interior trim codes

Color	Vinyl
Blue	P4B
Red	P4R
Black	P4X
Gold	P4Y

Vinyl roof color codes

Black	306
White	307

Racing stripe colors

Black
Medium Blue
Gold
Ruby
White

Facts

Styling changes for 1965 were minimal. The Valiant name was deleted from the rear deck lid panel. In the interior, the dash was redesigned using three round instrument pods: one large pod on each side of the steering column and a smaller pod in the center. A floor-mounted transmission shift lever replaced the dash-mounted push buttons for automatic-equipped Barracudas.

Engine choice was juggled slightly. The 170 ci was dropped and a more powerful version of the 273 ci V–8 was added—a four-barrel version rated at 235 hp. It could have produced more power had Chrysler elected to equip it with dual exhausts.

Several options groups were added to the line-up. The most important was the Formula S Package. It consisted of the 235 hp engine; the Suspension Package with heavy-duty springs, shocks and front sway bar; a tachometer; 6.95x14 Blue Streak tires on 14 in. wheels; and 14 in. bolt-on-design wheel covers.

The Performance Group, which was not available with the Formula S Package, consisted of the bigger 273 ci engine and the Suspension Package.

The Sport Group, again not available with the Formula S Package, was strictly a cosmetic package. It contained a three-spoke simulated-wood steering wheel, bolt-on wheel covers and whitewall tires.

The racing stripes, available in five colors, were an option and not part of the Formula S Package.

1965 Plymouth Barracuda

Chapter 7

1966 Plymouth Barracuda

Production
Hardtop coupe 6 cyl   10,645
Hardtop coupe 8 cyl   25,536
   Total   36,181

Serial numbers
BP29B62100001
B — car line, Barracuda
P — price class, premium
29 — body type, 2 dr sports hardtop
B — engine code
6 — last digit of model year
2 — assembly plant code (2-Detroit)
100001 — consecutive sequence number
   Serial number located on plate attached to left front door hinge post.

Engine codes
B — 225 ci 1V 6 cyl 145 hp
C — 273 ci 2V V-8 180 hp
C — 273 ci 4V V-8 235 hp

Head casting number
273 ci — 2536178

Carburetors
273 ci 2V V-8 — Carter BBD4113S
273 ci 4V V-8 — Carter AFB4119S

Option order codes and retail prices
BP29 Barracuda Six	$2,556.00
BP29 Barracuda V-8	2,637.00
32 Commando 273 8 cyl 4 bbl engine (3 speed manual transmission)	97.30
294 Paint — racing stripes	30.65
306 Vinyl roof	62.60
352 Basic Group	68.35
359 Sport (6 cyl)	94.55
(8 cyl)	82.10
367 Formula S Package (8 cyl only — NA w/359 or 368)	257.75
368 Suspension Package (NA w/367)	13.60
393 Manual 4 speed transmission (8 cyl)	175.45
395 TorqueFlite (6 cyl)	167.95
(8 cyl)	177.20
408 Sure-Grip differential	37.60
411 Air conditioner (NA 273 ci w/3 speed manual transmission)	318.50
416 Heater (delete; NA w/411)	(69.30)
421 Transaudio AM radio	57.35

451 Power brakes	41.75
456 Power steering	80.35
471 Cleaner Air Package (6 cyl; Calif only)	18.00
(8 cyl; Calif only)	25.00
479 Disc Brake Package	81.95
483 Front & rear bumper guards	17.45
486 Console (NA 3 speed transmission)	48.70
521 Tinted glass — all windows	27.90
522 Tinted glass — windshield only	14.05
534 Day-Night inside rearview	4.15
536 Remote outside left mirrors	6.85
557 2 front, 2 rear retractable seatbelts	9.65
573 3 spoke simulated-wood-grain steering wheel	17.00
577 Tachometer (8 cyl only)	48.70
578 Trailer Towing Package (6 cyl)	55.70
(8 cyl)	36.85
(8 cyl w/Formula S)	23.30
579 Undercoating w/underhood pad	15.40
583 Bolt-on-design wheel covers, 13 in.	33.50
14 in.	35.60
628 Fast manual steering (NA w/456)	13.25
638 Firm Ride shock absorbers	3.25
646 Emergency flasher (mandatory NY state)	12.60
708 Special buffed paint	16.80

Tires — set of 5
(6 cyl replaces 6.50x13 BSW)

03 6.50x13 WSW	28.55
11 7.00x13 BSW	12.60
13 7.00x13 WSW	44.05
16 7.00x13-8 PR BSW nylon	59.05
18 7.00x13-8 PR WSW nylon	90.55
21 6.95x14 BSW	20.05
23 6.95x14 WSW	51.60
28 Special Blue Streak 6.95x14 (requires 368)	66.85

Tires — set of 5
(8 cyl replaces 7.00x13 BSW)

13 7.00x13 WSW	31.60
16 7.00x13-8 PR BSW nylon	46.55
18 7.00x13-8 PR WSW nylon	78.05
21 6.95x14 BSW	7.60
23 6.95x14 WSW	39.10
28 Special Blue Streak 6.95x14 (requires 368)	54.35

Exterior color codes

Silver Metallic	AA1	Dark Red Metallic	QQ1
Black	BB1	Yellow	RR1
Light Blue	CC1	Soft Yellow	SS1
Light Blue Metallic	DD1	White	WW1
Dark Green Metallic	GG1	Beige	XX1
Light Turquoise Metallic	KK1	Bronze Metallic	YY1
Dark Turquoise Metallic	LL1	Citron Metallic	ZZ1
Bright Red	PP1	Light Mauve Metallic	661

Interior trim codes

Color	Vinyl
Blue	P4B
Red	P4H
Black	P4X
Citron	P4Y
Tan & White	P4V

Sport stripe color codes

Black	311
Dark Blue	315
Red	312
White	313
Bronze	314
Citron Gold	316

Vinyl roof color codes

Black	306
White	307

Facts

Receiving its first facelift in 1966, the Barracuda got a new grille, restyled taillights and fender-mounted turn signal indicators. In the interior, the dash was again redesigned, new bucket seats replaced those of 1965 and a longer console (incorporating a storage compartment and ashtray) was optional.

An oil pressure gauge replaced the previous warning lights. Cars equipped with the optional tachometer also came with a vacuum gauge.

Engine and transmission choice remained the same. A welcome addition was the front disc brakes, available with or without vacuum assist.

Chapter 8

1967 Plymouth Barracuda

Production

2 dr hardtop 6 cyl	10,483	2 dr sport coupe 6 cyl	5,603
2 dr hardtop 8 cyl	16,277	2 dr sport coupe 8 cyl	22,425
Convertible 6 cyl	859	Total	58,791
Convertible 8 cyl	3,144		

Serial numbers

BH23B72100001

B — car line, Plymouth Barracuda

H — price class, high

23 — body type (23-2 dr hardtop, 29-2 dr fastback, 27-convertible)

B — engine code

7 — last digit of model year

2 — assembly plant code (2-Hamtramck)

100001 — consecutive sequence number

Serial number located on plate attached to left front door hinge post.

Engine codes

B — 225 ci 1V 6 cyl 145 hp

D — 273 ci 2V V-8 180 hp

E — 273 ci 4V V-8 235 hp

H — 383 ci 4V V-8 280 hp

Head casting numbers

273 ci — 2658920

383 ci — 2406516

V-8 Carburetors

273 ci 2V — Carter BBD4113S, BBD4115S/manual, BBD4114S, BBD4116/automatic

273 ci 4V — Carter AFB4294S/manual, AFB4304S/manual w/CAP, AFB4295S/manual, AFB4305S/automatic w/CAP

383 ci 4V — Carter AFB4298S/manual, AFB4309S/manual w/CAP, AFB4299S/automatic, AFB4310S/automatic w/CAP

Distributors

383 ci 4V — 2642949/manual, 2642248/all, 2642745/automatic w/CAP

Option order codes and retail prices

Barracuda Six

BH23 2 dr hardtop	$2,449.00
BH27 Convertible	2,779.00
BH29 2 dr fastback	2,639.00

Barracuda V-8

BH23 2 dr hardtop	2,530.00
BH27 Convertible	2,860.00
BH29 2 dr fastback	2,720.00
32 273 ci 4V engine	97.30
62 383 ci 4V engine (requires 367 & 479)	52.30
294 Paint — Sport stripe	30.65
306 Vinyl roof	75.10
351 Basic Group (wo/bucket seat, NA w/62)	153.15
(w/bucket seats, NA w/62)	142.65
358 Sport (convertible only)	94.30
(fastback only)	105.35
(hardtop only)	126.65
359 Trailer Towing Package (6 cyl wo/479 or 411)	55.70
(6 cyl w/479 or 8 cyl wo/411)	36.85
(6 cyl w/411 & 479 or 8 cyl w/411)	27.15
(6 cyl w/411)	45.95
(8 cyl wo/411, 367 required)	23.20
(8 cyl w/411, 367 required)	13.60
360 Decor Group	40.40
367 Formula S Package (8 cyl only — NA 3 speed manual)	177.50
393 Manual 4 speed transmission (8 cyl)	179.15
395 TorqueFlite (6 cyl)	189.05
(273 ci)	202.05
(383 ci)	216.20
408 Sure-Grip differential	41.45
411 Air conditioner (NA 273 ci w/3 speed transmission or 62)	318.50
416 Heater (delete)	(69.30)
418 Rear window defogger	20.20
421 Transaudio AM radio	57.35
451 Power brakes	41.75
456 Power steering (NA w/628 or 62)	80.35
471 Cleaner Air Package (Calif 6 cyl)	18.00
471 Cleaner Air Package (Calif 8 cyl)	25.00
479 Front disc brakes	69.50
483 Front & rear bumper guards	22.00
486 Console (NA 3 speed transmission)	48.70
509 Glovebox lock	3.95
521 Tinted glass — all windows	27.90
522 Tinted glass — windshield only	14.05
531 Left headrests (w/bucket seats only)	20.95
532 Right headrests (w/bucket seats only)	20.95
533 Left and right headrests (w/bucket seats only)	41.90
536 Remote outside left mirrors	6.85
537 Manual outside right mirrors	6.35
544 Sill molding	17.45
551 Foam front seat cushion	10.50
556 Center passenger front lap belt	9.10
557 Center passenger rear lap belt	9.10
568 2 front shoulder belts	26.45

571 Full-horn-ring steering wheel		5.25
573 Deluxe wood-grain steering wheel		25.95
574 Vacuum gauge		15.30
577 Tachometer (8 cyl only)		48.70
579 Undercoating w/underhood pad		15.40
581 Deluxe wheel covers		21.30
583 Bolt-on-design wheel covers (fastback or w/358)		30.00
583 Bolt-on-design wheel covers (exc fastback)		51.10
588 Wheelhouse liners		44.80
589 Variable-speed windshield wipers		4.95
591 46 amp alternator (6 cyl wo/411)		14.05
591 46 amp alternator (6 cyl w/411 & 8 cyl)		10.50
621 70 amp-hr battery (w/359 only)		7.70
624 HD suspension		13.60
628 Fast manual steering (NA w/456)		13.25
638 Firm Ride shock absorbers		3.25
708 Special buffed paint		16.80
Vinyl bucket seats		32.35

Tires — set of 5

23 6.95x14 WSW	31.60
28 D70x14 Red Streak	63.35

Exterior color codes

Buffed Silver Metallic	AA1	Turbine Bronze Metallic	MM1
Black	BB1	Bright Red	PP1
Light Blue Metallic	DD1	Dark Red Metallic	QQ1
Dark Blue Metallic	EE1	Yellow	RR1
Bright Blue Metallic	881	Soft Yellow	SS1
Dark Green Metallic	GG1	Medium Copper Metallic	TT1
Dark Copper Metallic	HH1	White	WW1
Light Turquoise Metallic	KK1	Beige	XX1
Dark Turquoise Metallic	LL1	Light Tan Metallic	YY1
		Gold Metallic	ZZ1

Interior trim codes

Color	Vinyl bench seats	Vinyl bucket seats
Blue	H5B	H6B
Red	H5R	H6R
Black	H5X	H6X
Tan	H5T	H6T
Copper	H5K	H6K
White & Blue	H5C	H6C
White & Red	H5V	H6V
White & Black	H5W	H6W

Vinyl roof color codes

White	307
Black	306
Green	304

Racing stripe color codes

White	313
Black	311
Red	312
Blue	315
Green	316

Convertible top color codes

Green	300
Black	301
White	302

Facts

The Barracuda could no longer be considered a Valiant spin-off. Totally new styling was now incorporated on its three body styles—fastback, hardtop and convertible. It was also a larger, heavier car, as wheelbase increased by 2 in., to 108 in. Overall length increased by 5 in.

The interior was also redesigned. A bench seat was standard equipment, except on the convertible, where the optional buckets were standard equipment.

Four engines were now available: the 225 ci six-cylinder, a two-barrel version of the 273 ci V-8 rated at 180 hp, the 235 hp 273 ci carried over from 1966 and the 383 ci big-block rated at 280 hp.

The 383 ci V-8, the Commando 383, was available only with the Formula S Package. Rated at 280 hp, its output was limited by restrictive exhaust manifolds. The regular manifolds would not fit in the Barracuda's tight engine compartment. Other victims of the small engine compartment were power steering, power brakes and air conditioning. The lack of these options made 383 ci equipped Barracudas suitable for straight-line driving only. Manual disc brakes were mandatory with the 383. Production figures indicate that only 1,871 Barracudas got the 383 ci engine.

Mandatory with the 383 ci engine was either the four-speed manual transmission or the TorqueFlite automatic transmission. Also mandatory were the front console and bucket seats.

The Formula S Package was similar to previous S packages. Available on the four-barrel engines, it consisted of heavy-duty suspension components, front sway bar, D70x14 Red Streak tires and front fender Formula S medallions. The Formula S Package was available on the fastback body style only.

The Decor Trim Package consisted of wood-grain panels on the instrument panel and doors, bright pedal frames, a 150 mph speedometer and rear armrests with ashtrays.

1967 Plymouth Barracuda

Chapter 9

1968 Plymouth Barracuda

Production

2 dr hardtop 6 cyl	7,402	2 dr sport coupe 6 cyl	3,290
2 dr hardtop 8 cyl	11,155	2 dr sport coupe 8 cyl	16,055
Convertible 6 cyl	551	Total	40,497
Convertible 8 cyl	2,044		

Serial numbers

BH23B8B100001

B — car line, Plymouth Barracuda

H — price class, high

23 — body type (23-2 dr hardtop, 29-2 dr fastback, 27-convertible)

B — engine code

8 — last digit of model year

B — assembly plant code (B-Hamtramck)

100001 — consecutive sequence number

    Serial number located on plate attached to left side of dash panel, visible through windshield.

Engine codes

B — 225 ci 1V 6 cyl 145 hp

F — 318 ci 2V V-8 230 hp

P — 340 ci 4V V-8 275 hp

H — 383 ci 4V V-8 300 hp

Head casting numbers

318 ci — 2843675

340 ci — 2531894

383 ci — 2843906

V-8 carburetors

318 ci 2V — Carter BBD4420S/manual, BBD4421S/automatic

340 ci 4V — Carter AVS4424S/manual, AVS4425S/manual, AVS4636S/automatic w/AC

383 ci 4V — Carter AVS4426S/manual, AVS4401S/automatic, AVS46358/automatic w/AC

Distributors

340 ci — 2875086 IBS-4015/manual, 2875105 IBS-4015A/automatic

383 ci — 2875356/manual, 2875358/automatic

Option order codes and retail prices

Barracuda Six

BH23 2 dr hardtop	$2,605.00
BH27 Convertible	2,907.00
BH29 2 dr fastback	2,762.00

Barracuda V-8

BH23 2 dr hardtop	2,711.00
BH27 Convertible	3,013.00
BH29 2 dr fastback	2,868.00

Hemi Barracuda

BO29 Hemi Barracuda Super Stock	5,214.00
304 Vinyl roof	75.10
306 Vinyl roof	75.10
307 Vinyl roof	75.10
351 Basic Group (NA w/383 ci)	161.60
(w/383 ci)	81.25
355 Light Package	28.55
358 Sport Package	53.20
359 Trailer Towing Package (NA w/manual transmission, w/367, NA w/225 ci & AC)	
(6 cyl wo/disc brakes)	58.50
(6 cyl w/disc brakes or 8 cyl wo/AC)	38.70
(8 cyl w/AC)	28.55
360 Decor Group (hardtop)	90.45
(fastback)	105.00
(convertible)	82.40
362 Rallye cluster	6.10
367 Formula S Package (w/340 ci)	186.30
(w/383 ci)	221.65
393 Manual 4 speed transmission (8 cyl)	179.15
395 TorqueFlite (6 cyl)	189.05
(318 ci)	202.05
(340 ci)	216.20
(383 ci; requires console & bucket seats)	227.05
408 Sure-Grip differential	42.35
411 Air conditioner (NA w/383 ci)	334.60
418 Rear window defogger	21.30
421 Solid-state AM radio	61.55
451 Power brakes	41.75
463 Luggage rack	32.35
456 Power steering (NA w/fast manual steering)	80.35
479 Front disc brakes	72.95
483 Front & rear bumper guards	23.10
484 Clock (NA w/performance gauge or tachometer)	16.05
486 Console	53.35
509 Glovebox lock	3.95
521 Tinted glass — all windows	30.50
522 Tinted glass — windshield only	18.55
529 Custom sill molding	21.15
531 Left head restraints	21.95
532 Right head restraints	21.95
533 Left & right head restraints	43.90
536 Remote outside left mirrors	9.40
537 Manual outside right mirrors	6.65
538 Gas cap lock	4.25
540 Belt molding (std w/vinyl roof)	13.20
551 Foam front seat cushion (w/bench seat)	8.30
566 2 rear shoulder belts	26.45
568 2 front shoulder belts	26.45
571 Full-horn-ring steering wheel	9.35

573 Sport simulated-wood-grain steering wheel	25.95
574 Performance gauge	16.05
577 Tachometer (8 cyl only)	48.70
579 Undercoating w/underhood pad	16.10
581 Deluxe wheel covers	21.30
583 Bolt-on-design wheel covers	44.90
583 Wire wheel covers	64.10
588 Wheelhouse liners	46.55
589 Deluxe windshield wiper/washer package	10.30
591 46 amp alternator (6 cyl wo/411)	14.70
(6 cyl w/411 & 8 cyl)	11.00
624 HD suspension (6 cyl)	14.35
(318 ci)	11.00
627 59 amp battery (std w/383 ci)	8.10
628 Fast manual steering	14.05
638 Firm Ride shock absorbers	3.45
708 Special buffed paint	17.60
Accent stripes	14.05
Bench seats	NC
Paint — Sport stripe	20.40
Tires — set of 5	
23 6.95x14 WSW	31.60
26 D70x14 BSW	24.30
27 D70x14 WSW	55.70
38 E70x14 Red Streak	69.60
39 E70x14 WSW	69.60

Exterior color codes

Buffed Silver Metallic	AA1	Electric Blue Metallic	QQ1
Black Velvet	BB1	Burgundy Metallic	RR1
Midnight Blue Metallic	EE1	Sunfire Yellow	SS1
Mist Green Metallic	FF1	Avocado Green Metallic	TT1
Forest Green Metallic	GG1	Frost Blue Metallic	UU1
Ember Gold Metallic	JJ1	Sable White	WW1
Surf Turquoise Metallic	LL1	Satin Beige	XX1
Turbine Bronze Metallic	MM1	Sierra Tan Metallic	YY1
Matador Red	PP1		

Interior trim codes

Color	Vinyl bench seats	Vinyl bucket seats	Vinyl luxury
Frost Blue	H5B	H6B	D6B
Forest Green	—	H6F	D6F
Burgundy	—	H6R	D6R
Black	H5X	H6X	D6X
Ember Gold	—	—	D6Y
White/Burgundy	H5V	H6V	D6V
White/Blue	H5C	H6C	D6C
White/Black	H5W	H6W	D6W
White/Green	H5D	H6W	D6D
White/Gold	—	—	D6E

Vinyl roof color codes*

Green	304
Black	306
White	307

*Hardtop coupe only.

Convertible top color codes

Green	300
Black	301
White	302

Sport stripe color codes

White	313
Black	311
Red	312
Blue	315
Green	316

Accent stripe color codes

Black	31B
Bright Blue	31C
Bright Red	31H
Green	31P
White	31W

Facts

Minor changes characterized the interior. An optional instrument-panel-mounted clock was available, the optional Rallye instrument cluster included a 150 mph speedometer and woodgrain trim was offered.

Engine line-up changed. The 225 ci six-cylinder, still rated at 145 hp, was standard equipment. A 318 ci two-barrel engine, rated at 230 hp, replaced the 273 ci V-8. Optional was the Commando 340 ci 4V V-8 rated at 275 hp. The largest engine available was the Super Commando 383 ci V-8, which was rated at 300 hp, thanks to a better intake manifold and cylinder heads. As with the 1967 version, power brakes, steering and air conditioning were not available. The total number of 383 powered Barracudas built was 1,270.

The 340 and 383 engines included the Formula S Package, which was now available in all three body styles. Similar to the 1967 option, it upgraded the tire size to E70x14 Red Streaks. Only the four-speed manual or TorqueFlite automatic transmission was available with the 340 or 383 ci engine.

Fast manual steering was optional. It had a 16:1 ratio and 3.6 turns lock to lock. It was not recommended with the 383 engine.

The Interior Decor Group included luxury bucket front seats, wood-grain door panels, map pouches on the doors, bright pedal trim, rear armrests with ashtrays and carpeted wheelhouses on the fastback.

Red wheelhouse liners were optional only on the hardtop and fastback.

A nice, three-spoke simulated-wood-grain steering wheel with padded hub was optional on all body styles.

Seventy Hemi Barracuda Super Stock models were built. These were all constructed by Hurst Performance and were powered by the 426 ci Hemi engine. Intended for drag race use only, they were all painted white at the factory. All these cars had the letter M in the VIN to indicate engine size.

Chapter 10

1969 Plymouth Barracuda

Production

2 dr hardtop 6 cyl	4,203	2 dr sport coupe 6 cyl	2,163
2 dr hardtop 8 cyl	7,548	2 dr sport coupe 8 cyl	12,205
Convertible 6 cyl	300	Total	27,392
Convertible 8 cyl	973		

Serial numbers

BH23B9B100001

B — car line, Plymouth Barracuda

H — price class, high

23 — body type (23-2 dr hardtop, 29-2 dr fastback, 27-convertible)

B — engine code

9 — last digit of model year

B — assembly plant code (B-Hamtramck)

100001 — consecutive sequence number

Serial number located on plate attached to left side of dash panel, visible through windshield.

Engine codes

B — 225 ci 1V 6 cyl 145 hp
F — 318 ci 2V V-8 230 hp
P — 340 ci 4V V-8 275 hp
H — 383 ci 4V V-8 330 hp
M — 440 ci 4V V-8 375 hp

Head casting numbers

318 ci — 2843675
340 ci — 2531894
383 ci — 2843906
440 ci — 2843906

Carburetors

318 ci 2V V-8 — Carter BBD4607S/manual, BBD4608S/automatic

340 ci 4V V-8 — Carter AVS4611S/manual, AVS4612S & 4639S/automatic

383 ci 4V V-8 — Carter AVS4615S & 4711S/manual, AVS4616S & 4638S/automatic

440 ci 4V V-8 — Carter AVS4618S & 4640S/automatic

Distributors

340 ci — 2875782 IBS-4015B/manual, 2875779/automatic

383 ci — 2875779 IBS-4016A/manual, 2875846 IBS-4016/automatic

440 ci — 2875772 IBS-4014B/manual, 2875758/automatic

Option order codes and retail prices

Barracuda Six

BH23 2 dr hardtop	$2,674.00
BH27 Convertible	2,976.00
BH29 2 dr fastback	2,702.00

Barracuda V-8

BH23 2 dr hardtop	2,780.00
BH27 Convertible	3,082.00
BH29 2 dr fastback	2,813.00
A01 Light Group	32.90
A04 Basic Group (w/solid-state AM radio)	167.75
(w/solid-state AM/FM radio)	241.15
A06 Sport Group (NA w/'Cuda)	50.75
A13 440 ci Engine Conversion Package	
A35 Trailer Towing Package (NA w/manual transmission,	
NA w/383 ci, 440 ci, NA w/225 ci & H51)	
(6 cyl wo/B41)	60.25
(6 cyl w/B41)	39.90
(w/318 ci)	26.05
(w/318 ci & H51)	15.60
(w/340 ci)	14.75
(w/340 ci & H51)	4.25
A53 Formula S Package (w/340 ci)	186.30
(w/340 ci — convertible)	162.15
(w/383 ci)	221.65
(w/383 ci — convertible)	197.55
A56 'Cuda 340	309.35
A57 'Cuda 383	344.75
A62 Rallye cluster	6.30
A86 Interior Decor Group (NA w/'Cuda — hardtop)	93.30
(w/'Cuda — hardtop)	166.30
(requires C73 — fastback)	108.35
(requires C73 w/'Cuda — fastback)	181.35
(convertible)	85.05
B41 Front disc brakes	48.70
B51 Power brakes	42.95
C13 Front shoulder belts	26.45
C14 Rear shoulder belts	26.45
C16 Console (required w/383 ci & TorqueFlite)	53.35
C65 Foam front seat cushions (w/bench seat)	8.30
C73 Fold-down rear seat (required w/A86)	65.35
C92 Carpet protection mats	10.90
D21 Manual 4 speed transmission (8 cyl)	187.90
D34 TorqueFlite (6 cyl)	189.05
(318 ci)	202.05
(340 ci)	216.20
(340 ci w/'Cuda)	28.45
(383 ci)	227.05
(383 ci w/'Cuda)	39.30
D53 Opt 3.23 axle ratio (NC w/D91, A35 or B41)	
(6 cyl w/D34)	6.55
(318 ci w/D34)	6.55
D91 Sure-Grip differential	42.35
E55 340 ci engine (hardtop & fastback)	141.00
E55 340 ci engine (convertible)	116.70
E63 383 ci engine (see Formula S or 'Cuda 383)	
F11 46 amp alternator (6 cyl wo/H51)	14.70

F11 46 amp alternator (6 cyl w/H51 & 8 cyl)	11.00
F23 59 amp battery (std w/383 ci)	8.40
G11 Tinted glass — all windows	32.75
G15 Tinted glass —windshield only	20.40
G33 Remote control outside left mirrors	10.45
G33 Manual outside right mirrors	6.85
H31 Rear window defogger	21.90
H51 Air conditioner (NA w/383 ci & 225 ci w/trailer towing)	343.45
J11 Glovebox lock	4.10
J21 Clock (NA w/performance gauge or tachometer)	16.50
J25 Variable-speed wipers w/electric washers	10.60
J35 Wheelhouse liners	52.65
J46 Locking gas cap	4.40
J55 Undercoating w/underhood pad	16.60
M05 Door edge protectors	4.65
M25 Custom sill moldings (NA w/'Cuda)	21.75
M31 Bodyside belt moldings	13.60
M85 Front & rear bumper guards	23.80
N78 Performance gauge	16.50
N85 Tachometer (8 cyl only)	50.15
R11 Solid-state AM radio	61.55
R21 Solid-state AM/FM radio	134.95
S13 HD suspension (std w/340 ci & 383 ci)	14.75
(w/318 ci)	11.45
S25 Firm Ride shock absorbers	3.55
S75 Fast manual steering	14.45
S77 Power steering (NA w/fast manual steering)	85.15
S78 Full-horn-ring steering wheel	9.60
S81 Sport simulated-wood-grain steering wheel	22.70
W11 Deluxe wheel covers	21.30
W15 Deep-dish wheel covers	44.90
W18 Wire wheel covers	64.10
Accent paint stripe (NA w/Sport stripe)	15.15
Floral interior trim (w/'Cuda)	112.95
Floral interior trim (hardtop)	40.00
Floral vinyl roof	96.40
Paint — Sport stripe	25.30
Vinyl bench seat (w/'Cuda)	73.00
Vinyl bench seat (w/fold-down center armrest (w/'Cuda)	73.00
Vinyl roof	83.96
Tires — set of 5	
(w/225 ci & 318 ci — replaces 6.95x14 BSW)	
T12 6.95x14 WSW	31.60
T14 C78x14 WSW fiberglass-belted	57.95
T61 D70x14 BSW	24.30
T62 D70x14 WSW	55.70
T72 E70x14 WSW (requires HD suspension)	69.60
T73 E70x14 RSW (requires HD suspension)	69.60
T74 E70x14 WSW fiberglass-belted (requires HD suspension)	95.95

T75 E70x14 RSW fiberglass-belted (requires HD suspension)	95.95

Tires — set of 5
(w/Formula S or 'Cuda — replaces E70x14 RSW)

T72 E70x14 WSW	NC
T74 E70x14 WSW fiberglass-belted	26.45
T75 E70x14 RSW fiberglass-belted	26.45

Tires — set of 5
(w/340 ci or convertible w/318 ci replaces D70x14 BSW)

T62 D70x14 WSW	31.60
T72 E70x14 WSW (HD suspension required on convertible w/318 ci)	45.45
T73 E70x14 RSW	45.45
T74 E70x14 WSW fiberglass-belted (HD suspension required on convertible w/318 ci)	71.80
T75 E70x14 RSW fiberglass-belted (HD suspension required on convertible w/318 ci)	71.80

Exterior color codes

Silver Metallic	A4	Scorch Red	R6
Ice Blue Metallic	B3	Honey Bronze Metallic	T3
Blue Fire Metallic	B5	Bronze Fire Metallic	T5
Jamaica Blue Metallic	B7	Saddle Bronze Metallic	T7
Frost Green Metallic	F3	Alpine White	W1
Limelight Metallic	F5	Black Velvet	X9
Ivy Green Metallic	F8	Sunfire Yellow	Y2
Seafoam Turquoise Metallic	Q5	Yellow Gold	Y3
Performance Red	R4	Spanish Gold Metallic	Y4

Interior trim codes

Color	Vinyl bench seats	Vinyl bucket seats
Blue	H4B (L2B)*	H6B (D6B)†
Black	H4X (L2X)*	H6X (D6X)†
White/Black	H4W	H6W
White/Red	H4V	H6V
White/Blue	H4C	H6C
White/Green	H4F	H6F
Red	— (L2R)*	H6R (D6R)†
Tan/Green	—	— (D6U)†
Yellow/Black	—	— (D6P)†
Tan	—	— (D6T)†
Tan/Black	—	— (D6U)†
Yellow/Black	—	— (F6P)†
Floral Yellow/Green	—	— (F6J)†

*Parentheses indicate with 340 and 383 ci engines.
†Parentheses indicate luxury bucket seats.

Vinyl roof color codes

Green	1F
Tan	1T
White	1W
Black	1X
Floral	1P

Convertible top color codes

Black	3X
White	3W

Sport stripes color codes		Accent stripe color codes	
White	V6W	Blue	V7B
Black	V6X	Green	V7F
Red	V6R	Red	V7R
		White	V7W
		Black	V7X

Facts

In the Barracuda's third year, its three body styles received minor restyling. The divided front grille got checkered-pattern argent inserts, or black inserts on Formula S and 'Cuda models. In the rear, an argent rear deck appliqué with Barracuda lettering and emblem was used. The rear deck panel was painted black with Formula S models and had corresponding Formula S identification. The rear deck was painted red above and below the appliqué. Side marker lights were still rectangular, but larger than those used in 1968.

Engine line-up was the same as in 1968, but the 383 ci engine was rated at 330 hp. Late in the model year, a 440 ci engine, rated at 375 hp, became available on the 'Cuda hardtop and fastback. An unknown number were built, and according to Galen Govier, six of each body style were known to exist in 1990.

Total production for 383 ci equipped Barracudas amounted to only 683 units.

The 'Cuda 340 or 'Cuda 383 option was available only on the hardtop and fastbacks. External features included simulated black hood scoops, black hood tape stripes, black lower-body tape stripes, 'Cuda 340 or 'Cuda 383 callouts and chrome exhaust tips. Mechanically, the 340 or 383 ci engine with the four-speed manual, heavy-duty suspension and E70x14 Red Line tires could be had. Bench seats were standard.

The Formula S Package was not available with the 'Cuda 340 or 383. It included the 340 or 383 ci engine, dual exhausts with chrome tips, heavy-duty suspension, E70x15 Red Streak tires and Formula S identification.

The Sport Package included the simulated-wood-grain steering wheel; custom sill moldings, with the car painted black below the moldings; and the Rallye instrument panel.

1969 Plymouth Barracuda

Chapter 11

1970 Plymouth Barracuda

Production

2 dr hardtop 6 cyl	5,668	Convertible 8 cyl	1,169
2 dr hardtop 8 cyl	17,819	Convertible Gran Coupe 6 cyl	34
2 dr hardtop Gran Coupe 6 cyl	210	Convertible Gran Coupe 8 cyl	518
2 dr hardtop Gran Coupe 8 cyl	7,184	Convertible 'Cuda 8 cyl	550
2 dr hardtop 'Cuda 8 cyl	17,242	Total	50,617*
Convertible 6 cyl	223		

*Includes 2,724 All American Racers (AAR) 'Cudas.

Serial numbers

BH23B0B100001

B — car line, Plymouth Barracuda
H — price class (H-high, P-premium, S-special)
23 — body type (23-2 dr hardtop, 27-convertible)
B — engine code
0 — last digit of model year
B — assembly plant code (B-Hamtramck)
100001 — consecutive sequence number
    Serial number located on plate attached to left side of dash panel, visible through windshield.

Engine codes

C — 225 ci 1V 6 cyl 145 hp
G — 318 ci 2V V-8 230 hp
H — 340 ci 4V V-8 275 hp
J — 340 ci 3x2V V-8 290 hp
L — 383 ci 2V V-8 290 hp
L — 383 ci 4V V-8 330 hp
N — 383 ci 4V V-8 335 hp
R — 426 ci 2x4V V-8 425 hp
U — 440 ci 4V V-8 375 hp
V — 440 ci 3x2V V-8 390 hp

Head casting numbers

318 ci — 2843675
340 ci — 2531894
340 ci 3x2V — 3418915
383 ci — 2843906
426 ci — 2780559
440 ci — 2843906

Carburetors

318 ci 2V V-8 — Carter BBD4721S/manual, BBD4723S/manual w/ECS, BBD4722S/automatic, BBD4724S/automatic w/ECS, BBD4895S/automatic w/AC
340 ci 4V V-8 — Carter AVS4933S/manual, AVS4936S/manual w/ECS, AVS4934S/automatic, AVS4935S/automatic w/AC, BBD4937S/automatic w/ECS
340 ci 3x2V V-8 — Holley R4789A/front, R4790A/rear, R4791A/center manual, R4792A/center automatic

383 ci 2V V-8 — Carter BBD4726S/manual, BBD4725S/manual, Holley R4372A/manual w/ECS, Carter BBD4727S/manual w/ECS, BBD4894S/automatic w/AC, BBD4728S/automatic w/AC, Holley R4371A/automatic w/AC

383 ci 4V V-8 — Holley R4736A/manual w/Ram Air, R4738A/manual w/ECS w/Ram Air, R4737A/automatic w/Ram Air, R4739A/automatic w/ECS w/Ram Air, R4367A/manual, R4217A/manual w/ECS, R4368A/automatic, R4369A/automatic w/AC, Carter AVS4736S/automatic, AVS4732A/automatic w/AC, AVS4734S/automatic w/ECS

426 ci 2x4V V-8 — Carter AFB4742S/front, AFB4745S/rear manual, AFB4746S/rear automatic

440 ci 4V V-8 — Carter AVS4737S/manual, AVS4739S/manual w/ECS, AVS4738S/automatic, AVS4741A/automatic w/AC, AVS4740S/automatic w/ECS

440 ci 3x2V V-8 — Holley R4382A/front, R4175A/all w/ECS, R4374A/center manual, R4375A/manual w/ECS, R4144A/center automatic, R4376A/automatic w/ECS, R4365A/rear, R4383A/all w/ECS

Distributors

340 ci — 3438317/manual, 3438325/automatic

340 ci 3x2V — 3438521/manual, 3438523/automatic

383 ci 2V — 3438231

383 ci 4V — 3438233 (interchanges w/3438433)

440 ci — 3438222

440 ci 3x2V — 3438312/manual up to approx 01/01/70, 3438348/manual after approx 01/01/70, 2875982/automatic up to approx 01/01/70, 3438349/automatic after approx 01/01/70

426 ci — 2875989 — IBS-4014F/automatic, 2875987/manual

Option order codes and retail prices

Barracuda Six	
BH23 2 dr hardtop	$2,764.00
BH27 Convertible	3,034.00
Barracuda V-8	
BH23 2 dr hardtop	2,865.00
BH27 Convertible	3,135.00
Gran Coupe Six	
BP23 2 dr hardtop	2,934.00
BP27 Convertible	3,160.00
Gran Coupe V-8	
BP23 2 dr hardtop	3,035.00
BP27 Convertible	3,260.00
'Cuda V-8	
BS23 2 dr hardtop	3,164.00
BS27 Convertible	3,433.00
AAR 'Cuda	
BS23 AAR 'Cuda 2 dr hardtop	3,966.00
A01 Light Package	36.00

A04 Basic Group (NA w/A62, w/440 ci 3x2V & 426 ci)	182.15
(w/A62, 440 ci 3x2V & 426 ci)	171.55
A21 Elastomeric Front Bumper Group (Barracuda	
w/A04)	66.50
(others w/A04)	53.00
(Barracuda wo/A04)	81.50
(others wo/A04)	68.00
A22 Elastomeric Front & Rear Bumper Group (NA w/M46;	
G36 w/A21)	
(Barracuda w/A04)	121.30
(Gran Coupe w/A04)	107.75
('Cuda w/A04)	94.90
(Barracuda wo/A04)	136.40
Gran Coupe wo/A04)	122.85
('Cuda wo/A04)	110.00
A31 High Performance Axle Package (NA w/AC or	
trailer towing	
available w/340 & 383 4V engines w/D21 & D34)	102.15
A32 Super Performance Axle Package (NA w/AC	
or trailer towing)	
(w/440 ci & D34)	250.65
(w/426 ci & D34)	221.40
A33 Track Package (NA w/AC, w/440 ci 4V, 440 ci 6V,	
426 ci w/D21)	142.85
A34 Super Track Pak (NA w/AC, w/440 ci 4V,	
440 ci 6V, 426 ci w/D21)	235.65
A35 Trailer Towing Package (w/318 & 383 2V engines)	48.70
(w/340 & 383 4V engines)	34.80
(w/440 4V engine)	14.05
A36 Performance Axle Package (NA w/Trailer Towing	
Package)	
(w/340 ci or 383 ci 4V w/D21 or D34)	102.15
(w/440 ci 4V or 440 ci 6V w/D34)	92.25
(w/426 ci & D34)	64.40
A46 Exterior Trim Group (NA w/A36 or A22)	51.30
A62 Rallye instrument cluster (w/440 6 bbl & 426)	79.75
(all other V-8s)	90.30
B11 HD drum brakes	22.65
B41 Disc brakes (requires B51)	27.90
B51 Power brakes	42.95
C13 Front shoulder belts (convertible)	26.45
C14 Rear shoulder belts (NA convertible)	26.45
C15 Deluxe seatbelts	13.75
C16 Console (w/bucket seats only)	53.35
C62 Comfort Position 6 way seat adjuster	
(left bucket only)	33.30
C92 Color-keyed accessory floor mats	10.90
D21 Manual 4 speed transmission (NA 225 ci &	
383 ci 2V)	194.85
D34 TorqueFlite (6 cyl)	190.25
(318 ci)	202.05

(340 ci & 383 ci 2V)	216.20
(383 ci 4V, 440 ci 4V, 440 ci 6V, 426 ci 8V)	227.05
D51 Opt 2.76 axle ratio (w/383 ci 4V & D34)	10.35
D53 Opt 3.23 axle ratio (w/225 ci, 318 ci, 383 ci 2V & D34)	10.35
D91 Sure-Grip differential (std w/performance axle packages)	42.35
E55 340 ci 4V engine (w/'Cuda)	NC
E61 383 ci 2V engine (requires D34, NA w/'Cuda)	69.75
E63 383 ci 4V engine	137.55
E74 426 ci 8V engine (requires W34 — 'Cuda only)	871.45
E86 440 ci 4V engine ('Cuda only)	130.55
E87 440 ci 6V engine ('Cuda only)	249.55
F11 50 amp alternator	11.00
F25 70 amp battery	12.95
G11 Tinted glass — all windows	32.75
G15 Tinted glass — windshield only	20.40
G31 Chrome outside right racing mirror (requires G33)	10.95
G33 Chrome outside left racing mirror	15.15
G36 Color-keyed remote outside left & manual right racing mirrors (NA w/A04 & A21)	26.10
(w/A04 & A21)	10.95
H31 Rear window defogger	26.25
H51 Air conditioning	357.65
J11 Glovebox lock	4.10
J21 Electric clock	16.50
J25 Variable-speed wipers w/electric washers	10.60
J55 Undercoating w/underhood pad	16.60
L42 Headlight time delay & warning signal	18.20
M05 Door edge protectors	4.65
M26 Wheel lip molding	7.60
M31 Belt molding	13.60
M46 Quarter panel air scoop & black lower paint (NA w/A22 & A46)	35.80
M81 Front bumper guards (NA w/A21, A22)	14.05
M91 Deck lid luggage rack	32.35
N88 Automatic speed control (8 cyl only, NA w/340 ci, 440 ci 6V & 426 ci)	57.95
N95 Evaporative emission control (Calif)	37.85
N96 Shaker Hood Fresh Air Package (w/440 ci 6V)	97.30
N97 Noise Reduction Package (required in Calif w/440 ci 6V & 426 ci)	NC
P31 Power windows	105.20
P37 Power convertible top lift	52.85
R11 Solid-state AM radio (wo/A04)	61.55
R22 Solid-state AM radio w/stereo tape player (wo/A04)	196.25
(w/A04)	134.75
R31 Rear seat speakers, single (requires R11)	14.05
dual (requires R22 or R35)	25.90
R35 Multiplex AM/FM radio (wo/A04)	213.60
(w/A04)	152.20

S13 HD suspension (std w/383 4V & 340 engines)	14.75
S15 Extra HD Handling Package (w/383 4V & 340 engines)	18.25
S25 Firm Ride shock absorbers (std w/S15)	3.55
S77 Power steering	90.35
S83 3 spoke Rim Blow steering wheel	24.60
W08 Regular spare tire (convertible only, NA w/60 Series)	NC
W34 Collapsible spare tire (required w/15 in. tires)	12.95
Cloth & vinyl bucket seat (NA convertible)	(48.25)
Deluxe bucket seat (Gran Coupe)	(48.25)
Floral vinyl roof	96.40
High-impact paint colors	14.05
Leather bucket seat	118.90
Leather bucket seat (convertible)	64.75
Sport stripe ('Cuda only)	25.90
Two-tone paint (NA convertible)	31.70
Vinyl bench seat w/center armrest (NA Gran Coupe)	16.50
Vinyl bodyside insert protection molding	29.45
Vinyl roof	83.95
Wheels & wheel covers (models wo/A46)	
W11 Deluxe wheel covers	21.30
W15 Wire wheel covers	64.10
W21 Rallye road wheels, 14 or 15 in.	43.10
W23 Chrome styled road wheels, 14 in. only	86.15
Wheels & wheel covers (w/A46)	
W15 Wire wheel covers	42.85
W21 Rallye road wheels, 14 or 15 in.	21.95
W23 Chrome styled road wheels, 14 in. only	64.95
Tires	
(w/225 or 318 engines, replaces E78x14 BSW tires)	
T26 E78x14 WSW	26.45
T34 F78x14 WSW	44.55
T35 F78x14 BSW	15.40
T86 F70x14 WSW (requires B11 or B41 & S13)	65.35
T87 F70x14 RWL (requires B11 or B41 & S13)	65.35
Tires	
(w/383 engine, replaces F78x14 BSW tires)	
T34 F78x14 BSW	29.25
T86 F70x14 WSW (requires B11 or B41, S13 required w/383 ci 2V)	50.10
T87 F70x14 RWL (requires B11 or B41, S13 required w/383 ci 2V)	50.10
Tires	
('Cuda only, NA w/426 ci, replaces F70x14 RWL tires)	
T86 F70x14 WSW	NC
U82 E60x15 RWL (requires W34, NA convertible, w/440 engine & AC)	47.95

Exterior color codes

Ice Blue Metallic	EB3	In Violet Metallic	FC7*
Blue Fire Metallic	EB5*	Rallye Red	FE5*†
Jamaica Blue Metallic	EB7	Lime Green Metallic	FF4

Exterior color codes

Ivy Green Metallic	EF8*	Black Velvet	TX9*
Lime Light	FJ5*	Lemon Twist	FY1*
Vitamin C Orange	EK2	Yellow Gold	DY3
Deep Burnt Orange		Citron Mist Metallic	FY4
Metallic	FK5*	*Elastomeric colored bumpers	
Sandpebble Beige	BL1	available.	
Burnt Tan Metallic	FT6	†Rear elastomeric bumper	
Tor-Red	EV2	(A22) is limited to color FE5	
Alpine White	EW1*	only.	

Interior trim codes

Color	Gran Coupe vinyl deluxe bucket seats	Gran Coupe cloth & vinyl deluxe bucket seats	Barracuda, Gran Coupe, 'Cuda leather deluxe bucket seats	Barracuda, 'Cuda vinyl bench seats	Barracuda, 'Cuda vinyl bucket seats
Black	—	P5X9	PRX9	—	H6X9
Blue	P6B5	—	—	H4B5	H6B5
Black Frost	P6A8	—	—	—	—
Red	P6E4	—	—	—	H6E4
Green	P6F8	—	—	H4F8	H6F8
Burnt Orange	P6K4	P5K4	—	—	—
Tan	P6T5	—	PRT5	—	H6T5
White/ Blue	P6BW	—	—	H4BW	H6BW
White/ Red	P6EW	—	—	—	H6EW
White/ Green	P6FW	—	—	H4FW	H6FW
White/ Black	P6XW	—	PRXW	H4XW	H6XW
Gold/ Black	P6XY	—	—	—	—

Vinyl roof color codes

Green	V1F
Gator Grain	V1G
Yellow Floral	V1P*
Blue/Green Floral	V1Q*
White	V1W
Black	V1X

*Includes Mod Top decals on rear windows.

Convertible top color codes

White	V3W
Black	V3X

Sport stripes color code*

Black	V6X

*'Cuda only.

Facts

The second and last major restyle of the Barracuda resulted in two body styles (hardtop and convertible) available in three model series (Barracuda, Gran Coupe and 'Cuda). Wheelbase remained at 108 in. but width increased by 5 in. Whereas the previous Barracudas were a compromise in terms of design, the new Barracuda featured the long hood, short deck that the Mustang had popularized several years earlier.

Standard on the Barracuda was the 225 ci six-cylinder, still rated at 145 hp, mated to a three-speed manual transmission. Optional engines were the 230 hp 318 ci V-8, a 290 hp 383 ci V-8 and a 330 hp four-barrel version of the 383 rated at 330 hp. Unlike earlier big-block-powered Barracudas, the 1970 model had power steering and power brakes available. A four-speed manual transmission was optional only on the 330 hp 383 ci engine. The Torque-Flite three-speed automatic was optional on all engines.

The same powertrain line-up was available on the luxury Gran Coupe. Leather bucket seats were standard, as was an overhead console that housed several warning lights (low fuel, door ajar and fasten seatbelt). Cloth seats were optional only on the Gran Coupe.

The performance 'Cuda came with a 335 hp version of the 383 ci V-8. Optional engines were a 375 hp 440 ci 4V, the 440 ci 3x2V rated at 390 hp and the dual-quad 426 ci Hemi rated at 425 hp. Optional, at no cost, was the 275 hp 340 ci V-8 carried over from 1969.

The 440 3x2V engine came with some improvements over the 1969 version. For improved durability, the connecting rods were changed to increase the beam cross section, the camshaft was faced with Lubrite to prevent scuffing and the oil control rings had increased tension. As a cost-saving measure, a cast-iron intake manifold replaced the aluminum Edelbrock unit.

Other standard 'Cuda features were a performance hood with simulated hood scoops, which was optional on the Barracuda and Gran Coupe; hood pins; blacked-out rear taillight panel; hockey-stick side stripes with callouts giving engine size—except with the 426, when they read Hemi; and front road lamps.

The Shaker hood scoop, standard on the Hemi-equipped 'Cuda, was optional with the 440 engines. Later in the model year, it became optional with the 340 and 383 engines as well, and was also made available on the Barracuda and Gran Coupe. The Shaker was painted red with Rallye Red (FE5) cars and black with all other colors. The J25 wiper option was mandatory when the Shaker was ordered with a 340 ci engine. By the end of the model year, the Shaker was available in blue for (EB5 cars) and argent (Astrotone Silver).

Shaker production for the 'Cuda was 719 on hardtops and eight on convertibles. For the Hemi 'Cuda, it was 284 on hardtops with the four-speed, 366 on hardtops with the TorqueFlite, five on convertibles with the four-speed and nine on convertibles with the automatic.

Other midyear options were back window louvers and a rear spoiler.

Standard wheels on the 'Cuda were the 14 in. Magnum road wheels. Optional were the Rallye wheels in 14 or 15 in. size. Hemi-equipped 'Cudas came with the 15x7 in. Rallye wheels and F60x15 RWL tires. Standard tires with the 383 or 440 'Cuda were F70x14 RWLs. The E60x15 RWL tires came standard on the 340 ci powered 'Cuda.

Body-colored elastomeric bumpers were available for the front or the front and rear together on all 1970 Barracuda models. The front bumpers could be had in nine different colors, but the front and rear bumpers were available only in Rallye Red. In each case, the bumpers came with painted body-color rearview mirrors.

Drum brakes were standard equipment on all Barracudas. 'Cuda models came with heavy-duty drums. Power front disc brakes were optional.

The Rallye Instrument Cluster Group, optional on all Barracudas, included variable-speed wipers, tachometer, electric clock, heater control floodlight, 150 mph speedometer with trip odometer, oil pressure gauge and wood-grain applique.

The AAR 'Cuda was a midyear introduction. AAR stood for Dan Gurney's All American Racers team, and the AAR 'Cuda was designed to compete in the Trans-Am series against such cars as the Boss 302 Mustangs, Z-28 Camaros and AMC Javelins. Standard equipment included a special version of the 340 ci engine with 3x2V induction, four-speed manual transmission, Sure-Grip differential, heavy-duty shocks and suspension, front and rear sway bars, power disc brakes, and Rallye wheels with E60x15 front and G60x15 rear Goodyear Polyglas RWL tires. The AAR also sported a unique side exhaust system; flat-black paint treatment on the hood, cowl and fender tops; a front and rear ducktail-type spoiler; and a black 23 piece side tape treatment.

Production of 440 ci 3x2V equipped 'Cuda models was 1,755 hardtops and 29 convertibles.

Production of 426 ci Hemi equipped 'Cuda models was 652 hardtops (368 with the TorqueFlite and 284 with a four-speed) and 14 convertibles (nine with an automatic and five with a four-speed).

1970 Plymouth Barracuda

Chapter 12

1971 Plymouth Barracuda

Production

2 dr hardtop 6 cyl	1,555	2 dr hardtop 'Cuda 8 cyl	5,314
2 dr hardtop 8 cyl	6,846	Convertible 6 cyl	132
2 dr hardtop Gran Coupe 6 cyl	—	Convertible 8 cyl	721
2 dr hardtop Gran Coupe 8 cyl	1,298	Convertible 'Cuda 8 cyl	293
		Total	16,159

Serial numbers

BH23B1B100001

B — car line, Plymouth Barracuda
H — price class (H-high, P-premium, S-special)
23 — body type (21-2 dr coupe, 23-2 dr hardtop, 27-convertible)
B — engine code
1 — last digit of model year
B — assembly plant code (B-Hamtramck)
100001 — consecutive sequence number

Serial number located on plate attached to left side of dash panel, visible through windshield.

Engine codes

B — 198 ci 1V 6 cyl 125 hp (105 hp net)
C — 225 ci 1V 6 cyl 145 hp (110 hp net)
G — 318 ci 2V V-8 230 hp (155 hp net)
H — 340 ci 4V V-8 275 hp (235 hp net)
L — 383 ci 2V V-8 275 hp (190 hp net)
N — 383 ci 4V V-8 300 hp (250 hp net)
R — 426 ci 2x4V V-8 425 hp (350 hp net)
U — 440 ci 3x2V V-8 390 hp (330 hp net)

Head casting numbers

318 ci — 2843675
340 ci — 2531894
383 ci — 3462346
426 ci — 2780559
440 ci — 3462346

Carburetors

318 ci 2V V-8 — Carter BBD4957S/manual, BBD4958S/automatic
340 ci 4V V-8 — Carter TQ4972S/manual, TQ4973S/automatic
383 ci 2V V-8 — Carter BBD4962S/automatic
383 ci 4V V-8 — Holley R4667A/manual, R4668A/automatic, R4734A/manual w/fresh air, R4735A/automatic w/fresh air
426 ci 2x4V V-8 — Carter AFB4971S/front, AFB4969S/rear manual, AFB4970S/rear automatic
440 ci 3x2V V-8 — Holley R4671A/front, R4669A/center manual, R4670A/center automatic, R4672A/rear

Distributors

340 ci — 3438522/manual, 3438517/automatic, 3656151/manual
  w/electronic ignition, 3438986/automatic w/electronic ignition
383 ci — 3438534, 3438544 w/NOx
383 ci 4V — 3438690
426 ci — 2875987/manual, 3438579/automatic, 3438891/manual
  w/electronic ignition, 3438893/automatic w/electronic ignition
440 ci — 3438694
440 ci 3x2V — 3438577

Option order codes and retail prices*

Barracuda Six

BH21 2 dr coupe	$2,633.00
BH23 2 dr hardtop	2,745.00
BH27 Convertible	3,002.00
Barracuda V-8	
BH21 2 dr coupe	2,759.00
BH23 2 dr hardtop	2,846.00
BH27 Convertible	3,103.00
Gran Coupe V-8	
BP23 2 dr hardtop	3,008.00
'Cuda V-8	
BS23 2 dr hardtop	3,134.00
BS27 Convertible	3,391.00
A01 Light Package	35.75
A04 Basic Group (NA w/A62, w/440 ci 3x2V & 426 ci)	183.20
(w/A62, 440 ci 3x2V & 426 ci)	172.60
A21 Elastomeric front bumper	40.70
A22 Elastomeric front & rear bumpers	81.40
A28 Noise Reduction Package (required in Calif w/440 ci 6V)	33.55
A31 High Performance Axle Package (NA w/AC or trailer towing available w/340 ci & 383 ci 4V w/D21 & D34)	75.25
A33 Track Package (NA w/AC, w/440 ci 6V, 426 ci w/D21)	137.80
A34 Super Track Pak (NA w/AC, w/440 ci 6V, 426 ci w/D21)	201.75
A35 Trailer Towing Package (NA w/225 ci, 426 ci or 440 ci 6V)	
(w/318 or 383 2V engines)	48.70
(w/340 or 383 4V engines)	34.80
(w/440 4V engines)	14.05
A36 Performance Axle Package	
(w/440 ci 6V & D34)	75.25
(w/426 ci & D34)	41.70
A45 Aerodynamic Spoiler Package	54.65
A62 Rallye instrument cluster (w/440 ci 6 bbl & 426 ci)	76.75
(all other V-8s)	87.30
A67 Backlight Louver Package (w/A04)	156.10
(wo/A04)	171.00
B11 HD drum brakes (w/318 ci & 383 ci)	21.40

B41 Disc brakes (requires B51)	22.50
B51 Power brakes	41.55
C13 Front shoulder belts (convertible)	24.40
C14 Rear shoulder belts (NA convertible)	24.40
C16 Console (w/bucket seats only)	53.05
C62 Comfort Position 6 way seat adjuster (left bucket only)	32.20
D21 Manual 4 speed transmission (NA 198 ci, 225 ci,	
318 ci, 383 ci 2V)	198.10
D34 TorqueFlite (6 cyl)	209.00
(318 ci, 383 ci 2V)	209.00
(340 ci, 383 ci 4V, 426 ci, 440 ci)	229.35
D51 Opt 2.76 axle ratio (w/318 ci & manual	
transmission)	12.55
(w/340 ci & D34)	12.55
D53 Opt 3.23 axle ratio (w/225 ci, 318 ci, 383 ci 2V	
& D34)	12.55
D91 Sure-Grip differential (NA 6 cyl models)	41.70
E24 225 ci 6 cyl (BH21 only, std other 6 cyl models)	39.00
E55 340 ci 4V engine ('Cuda only)	44.35
E61 383 ci 2V engine (requires D34, NA w/'Cuda)	70.80
E65 383 ci 4V engine (Barracuda, Gran Coupe)	139.60
E74 426 ci 8V engine (requires W34 — 'Cuda only)	883.90
E87 440 ci 6V engine ('Cuda only)	253.20
F11 50 amp alternator	10.85
F25 70 amp battery	13.60
G11 Tinted glass — all windows	36.85
G15 Tinted glass — windshield only	25.05
G31 Chrome outside right racing mirror (requires G33)	10.80
G33 Chrome outside left racing mirror	14.95
G36 Color-keyed remote outside left & manual right	
racing mirrors (wo/A04)	25.75
(w/A04)	10.80
G41 Day-night inside mirror (BH21 only, std all others)	7.05
H31 Rear window defogger	28.90
H51 Air conditioning	370.15
J11 Glovebox lock	4.05
J15 Cigar lighter (BH21 only, std all others)	4.00
J21 Electric clock (std w/A62)	16.10
J25 Variable-speed wipers w/electric washers	10.60
J31 Dual horns (BH21 only, std all others)	5.10
J45 Hood pins	15.20
J54 Performance hood	20.25
J55 Undercoating w/underhood pad	20.80
J81 Aerodynamic rear spoiler (S13 required w/E22,	
E24, E44 or E61)	34.35
L34 Road lights (NA w/M85)	21.05
M05 Door edge protectors	6.00
M26 Wheel lip molding (Barracuda only)	7.45
M31 Belt molding (Barracuda only)	13.45
M85 Front & rear bumper guards	27.40
M91 Deck lid luggage rack	31.30

N95 NOx Exhaust emission control (Calif)	11.95
N96 Shaker Hood Fresh Air Package ('Cuda)	94.00
(w/383 ci 4V, NA w/H51)	114.20
N97 Noise Reduction Package (required in Calif	
w/440 ci 6V & 426 ci)	NC
P31 Power windows (NA BH21)	101.30
P37 Power convertible top lift	48.70
R11 Solid-state AM radio (wo/A04)	61.10
R26 Solid-state AM radio w/stereo tape player (wo/A04)	201.60
AM radio w/stereo tape (w/A04)	140.60
R31 Rear seat speakers, single (requires R11)	13.85
R32 Rear seat speakers, dual (requires R26, R35 or R36)	25.05
R33 Tape recorder microphone (w/R26 or R36)	10.75
R35 AM/FM stereo radio (wo/A04)	196.60
(w/A04)	135.60
R36 AM/FM stereo radio w/stereo tape player (wo/A04)	337.05
(w/A04)	276.05
S13 HD suspension (std w/383 ci 4V, 340 ci, 440 ci, 446 ci)	14.30
S25 Firm Ride shock absorbers	4.80
S77 Power steering	96.55
S83 3 spoke Rim Blow steering wheel	28.60
W08 Regular spare tire (convertible only, NA w/15 in. tires)	NC
W11 Deluxe wheel covers, 14 in.	25.15
W12 Wheel trim rings, 14 or 15 in. (w/hubcaps only)	25.15
W15 Wire wheel covers, 14 in.	64.55
W21 Rallye road wheels, 14 or 15 in. (15 in. required W34)	54.25
W23 Chrome styled road wheels, 14 in. only w/std spare	83.30
W34 Collapsible spare tire (required w/15 in. tires,	
R32 & H31)	12.55
Bodyside tape stripe (Barracuda)	28.50
Bodyside tape stripe (Gran Coupe)	14.25
Cloth & vinyl bucket seat (coupe)	(44.40)
Cloth & vinyl bucket seat (NA convertible)	16.00
Deluxe vinyl bucket seat (coupe)	(44.40)
High-impact paint colors	13.85
Leather bucket seat ('Cuda)	62.55
Two-tone paint (NA convertible)	29.20
Vinyl bench seat w/center armrest (NA coupe, convertible)	16.00
Vinyl bodyside insert protection molding (Barracuda)	28.50
Vinyl bodyside insert protection molding (Gran Coupe)	14.25
Vinyl roof (std w/A67)	82.40

Tires

(w/198, 225 & 318 engines, replaces 7.35x14 BSW tires)

T22 7.35x14 WSW	26.85
T26 E78x14 WSW	51.00
T34 F78x14 WSW	68.90
T35 F78x14 BSW	39.55
T86 F70x14 WSW (requires S13)	88.00
T87 F70x14 RWL (requires S13)	99.50
U82 E60x15 RWL (requires S13, B11 or B41 & W34)	139.65

Tires

(w/383 engine, replaces F78x14 BSW tires)

T34 F78x14 BSW		29.40
T86 F70x14 WSW (requires S13)		48.50
T87 F70x14 RWL (requires S13)		59.95
U82 E60x15 RWL (requires S13, B11 or B41 & W34, NA w/AC)		100.10

Tires

(replaces F70x14 WSW tires; NA 426 ci)

T34 F78x14 WSW (w/340 ci or 383 ci 4V only — 'Cuda)		NC
T87 F70x14 RWL ('Cuda only)		11.50
U82 E60x15 RWL (NA w/AC & 383 ci 4V combination)		51.65
*April 1, 1971, revision.		

Exterior color codes

Color	Code	Color	Code
Winchester Gray Metallic	GA4	Formal Black	TX9
Glacial Blue Metallic	GB2	Gold Leaf Metallic	GY8
True Blue Metallic	GB5	Tawny Gold Metallic	GY9
Evening Blue Metallic	GB7	In Violet	FC7
Amber Sherwood		Sassy Grass Green	FV6
Metallic	GF3	Bahama Yellow	EG5
Sherwood Green Metallic	GF7	Tor-Red	EV2
Autumn Bronze Metallic	GK6	Curious Yellow	GY3
Tunisian Tan Metallic	GT2	Lemon Twist	FY1
Sno White	GW3		

Interior trim codes

Color	Std vinyl bucket seats	Opt Barracuda & 'Cuda hardtops split bench seats	Gran Coupe vinyl bucket seats	Opt Gran Coupe cloth & vinyl bucket seats
Black	H6X9	H4X9	P6X9	P5X9
Blue	H6B5	H4B5	P6B5	—
Green	H6F8	H4F8	P6F8	—
Tan	H6T5	H4T5	P6T5	—
White/				
Black	H6XW	H4XW	—	—
Gold	—	—	P6Y4	—
Black/				
Orange	H6XV	—	—	—

Color	Opt Barracuda, 'Cuda hardtops cloth & vinyl bucket seats	Std Gran Coupe leather bucket seats	Opt 'Cuda leather bucket seats
Black	H5X9	PRX9	SRX9
Black/Orange	H5XV	—	—
Tan	—	PRT5	SRT5
Gold	—	PRY4	—

Vinyl roof color codes

Black	V1X	Green	V1F
White	V1W	Gold	V1Y

Convertible top color codes

Black	V3X
White	V3W

Facts

Some change occurred on the 1971 Barracuda. The front grille was restyled. Four headlights were used and the center area had six rectangular grille openings, commonly referred to as the cheese-grater grille. The taillight panel got redesigned taillights using separate housings for brake and turn signal lights and back-up lights.

'Cuda models got front fender air extractors and a large "billboard" rear quarter panel and door tape treatment in black or white.

The 440 ci 4V engine was dropped. The rating of the 383 ci 2V was reduced to 275 hp, and the rating of the 383 ci 4V engine went down to 300 hp. The 335 hp 383 ci was no longer available. The 440 ci 3x2V also lost 5 hp, but the Hemi remained unchanged. The downgraded horsepower ratings were due to a compression ratio reduction. Transmission choice remained unchanged.

Base engine on the 'Cuda was the 300 hp 383 ci. This engine was the largest one available on the Barracuda and Gran Coupe. It was also the smallest engine that could be had with a four-speed manual transmission.

As the AAR 'Cuda was no longer produced, the 290 hp version of the 340 engine was also no longer available.

A new engine did join the line-up—a 198 ci version of the six-cylinder rated at 125 hp. It was available only on the Barracuda two-door coupe model.

The year 1971 was the last for the Barracuda convertibles.

The Backlight Louver Package continued as an option on all three Barracuda models. Not available on Pennsylvania-bound cars, the package included a black vinyl roof, black backlight moldings and racing mirrors.

The front road lights were optional on all Barracuda models.

Beginning with February 1, 1970, all 'Cuda 340s ordered with power steering (S77) got the 1970 AAR fast-ratio steering. However, if the Basic Group (A04) was ordered, the regular power steering was installed. The fast-ratio version was available only by itself and the A04 options had to be ordered separately.

The AM/FM cassette tape system had provision for an optional microphone. The unit could record off the radio or could be used for dictation.

Shaker hood production for the 'Cuda was 683 on hardtops and 19 on convertibles. For the Hemi 'Cuda, it was 284 on hardtops with four-speed, 366 on hardtops with TorqueFlite, five on convertibles with four-speed and nine on convertibles with TorqueFlite.

'Cuda 440 ci 3x2V production was 237 hardtops and 17 convertibles.

Hemi 'Cuda production, in its last year, was only 108 hardtops (48 with TorqueFlite and 60 with four-speed) and seven convertibles (five with TorqueFlite and two with four-speed).

Chapter 13

1972 Plymouth Barracuda

Production

2 dr hardtop 6 cyl	809	2 dr hardtop 'Cuda 8 cyl	6,382
2 dr hardtop 8 cyl	8,951	Total	16,142

Serial numbers

BH23B2B100001

B — car line, Plymouth Barracuda
H — price class (H-high, S-special)
23 — body type (23-2 dr hardtop)
B — engine code
2 — last digit of model year
B — assembly plant code (B-Hamtramck)
100001 — consecutive sequence number

Serial number located on plate attached to left side of dash panel, visible through windshield.

Engine codes

C — 225 ci 1V 6 cyl 110 hp
G — 318 ci 2V V-8 150 hp
H — 340 ci 4V V-8 240 hp

Head casting numbers

318 ci — 2843675
340 ci — 3418915

Carburetors

318 ci 2V V-8 — Carter BBD6149S/manual, BBD6151/manual w/NOx, BBD6150S/automatic, BBD6151S/automatic w/NOx
340 ci 4V V-8 — Carter TQ6138S/manual, TQ6139S/automatic

Option order codes and retail prices

BH23 2 dr hardtop 6 cyl	$2,848.00
BH23 2 dr hardtop V-8	2,952.00
BS23 2 dr hardtop 'Cuda V-8	3,105.00
A01 Light Package	37.05
A04 Basic Group	199.95
A36 Performance Axle Package (w/340 ci only)	63.45
A51 Sport Decor Package (w/340 ci)	50.55
(wo/340 ci)	71.40
B41 Front power disc brakes	65.95
C16 Console	54.60
D21 Manual 4 speed transmission (w/340 ci only)	204.10
D34 TorqueFlite transmission	215.30
(w/340 ci)	236.30
D51 2.76 axle ratio (w/340 ci & D34; NC w/D91)	12.95
D53 3.23 axle ratio (w/225 ci & 318 ci w/D34)	12.95
D91 Sure-Grip differential (std w/A36, NA 6 cyl)	43.05
E55 340 ci 4V engine (Barracuda)	292.70
('Cuda)	221.90

F25 70 amp battery	14.10
G11 Tinted glass — all windows	37.95
G15 Tinted windshield	25.80
G35 Chrome outside left racing mirror	15.45
G36 Body-color remote left, manual right dual racing	
mirrors (w/A04)	11.15
(wo/A04)	26.60
G37 Chrome remote outside left & manual right racing	
mirrors (w/A04)	11.15
(wo/A04)	26.60
H31 Rear window defogger	29.80
H51 Air conditioning (NA 6 cyl, NA w/3 speed manual)	386.00
J11 Glovebox lock	4.20
J21 Electric clock (std w/J97)	16.65
J25 Variable-speed wipers w/electric washers (std w/J97)	10.95
J52 Inside hood release	10.05
J54 Sport hood (std w/340 ci & w/A51)	20.85
J55 Undercoating w/hood insulator pad	21.45
J97 Rallye instrument panel (w/8 cyl engines w/A04)	79.05
(w/8 cyl engines wo/A04)	89.95
M05 Door edge protectors	6.15
M26 Wheel lip molding (Barracuda only)	7.70
M51 Power-operated sunroof w/vinyl roof	459.25
M85 Bumper guards, front & rear rubber inserts	28.20
N23 Electronic ignition system (w/318 ci, std w/340 ci)	32.55
N95 Emission control system & testing (required Calif)	27.05
R11 Solid-state AM radio (wo/A04)	62.90
R26 Solid-state AM radio w/stereo tape player (wo/A04)	207.65
AM radio with stereo tape (w/A04)	144.80
R31 Rear seat speakers, single (requires R11)	14.25
R32 Rear seat speakers, dual (w/R35 or R36)	25.80
R35 AM/FM stereo radio (wo/A04)	202.55
(w/A04)	139.70
S13 HD suspension (std w/340 ci)	14.80
S77 Power steering (std w/A04)	110.15
V21 Performance hood paint	18.35
W11 Deluxe wheel covers	25.95
W21 Set of 4 Rallye road wheels w/std spare	55.90
W23 Set of 4 chrome style road wheels w/std spare	85.85
Dual bodyside tape stripes (std w/A51)	29.40
High-impact paint colors	14.25
Vinyl roof	84.90
Vinyl side molding	29.40
Tires	
(w/198, 225 & 318 engines, replaces 7.35x14 BSW tires)	
T22 7.35x14 WSW	27.65
T34 F78x14 WSW	71.05
T86 F70x14 WSW (requires S13)	90.75
T87 F70x14 RWL (requires S13)	102.60
Tires	
(w/340 engine, replaces F70x14 WSW tires)	
T34 F78x14 BSW	NC
T87 F70x14 RWL	11.95

Exterior color codes

Winchester Gray Metallic	GA4
Blue Sky	HB1
Basin Street Blue	TB3
True Blue Metallic	GB5
Rallye Red	FE5
Amber Sherwood Metallic	GF3
Mojave Tan Metallic	HT6
Chestnut Metallic	HT8
Spinnaker White	EW1
Honeydew	GY4
Gold Leaf Metallic	GY8
Tawny Gold Metallic	GY9
Formal Black	TX9
Tor-Red	EV2
Lemon Twist	FY1

Interior trim codes

Blue	A6B5
Green	A6F6
Black	A6X9
White	A6XW
Gold	A6Y3

Vinyl roof color codes

Black	V1X
White	V1W
Gold	V1Y
Green	V1F

Side stripes codes

Black	V6X
White	V6W

Facts

The 1972 Barracuda reverted to single headlights, and once again, the taillight panel was changed, this time incorporating four round taillights.

Model choice was reduced to just two alternatives, a hardtop and the performance 'Cuda. No convertibles were available.

Standard engine was the trusty 225 ci six-cylinder mated to a three-speed manual. Optional was a 318 ci two-barrel. The 340 ci 4V was optional on the Barracuda and standard equipment on the 'Cuda. The four-speed manual was optional only with the 340 ci engine. The TorqueFlite automatic was available on all engines.

The 340 ci engine now used the same cylinder head as did Chrysler's 360 ci V-8. This cylinder head came with smaller intake valves, 1.88 versus 2.02 in. on 1968–71 340s. Exhaust valve size was the same as in 1968–71 at 1.60 in. However, the real culprit for lower horsepower ratings was the 8.5:1 compression ratio.

Most performance options were deleted, such as 60 Series tires, 15 in. wheels, all the big-block V-8 engines, front and rear spoilers and the Shaker hood.

Manual front disc brakes became standard equipment on all Barracuda models.

The 'Cuda's suspension included front and rear sway bars.

In the interior, redesigned bucket seats were available, in five colors and only in vinyl.

A total of 490 Barracudas came with the 340 ci engine, and 5,864 'Cuda 340s were built.

Chapter 14

1973 Plymouth Barracuda

Production

2 dr hardtop 8 cyl	9,976
2 dr hardtop 'Cuda 8 cyl	9,305
Total	19,281

Serial numbers

BH23G3B100001
B — car line, Plymouth Barracuda
H — price class (H-high, S-special)
23 — body type (23-2 dr hardtop)
G — engine code
3 — last digit of model year
B — assembly plant code (B-Hamtramck)
100001 — consecutive sequence number
    Serial number located on plate attached to left side of dash panel, visible through windshield.

Engine codes

G — 318 ci 2V V-8 150 hp
H — 340 ci 4V V-8 240 hp

Head casting numbers

318 ci — 2843675
340 ci — 3671587

Carburetors

318 ci 2V V-8 — Carter BBD6316S/manual, BBD6343S/manual Calif, BBD6317S/automatic, BBD6344S/automatic Calif
340 ci 4V V-8 — Carter TQ6318S/manual, TQ6339S/manual Calif, TQ6321S/automatic, TQ6342S/automatic Calif

Option order codes and retail prices

BH23 2 dr hardtop V-8	$2,848.00
BS23 2 dr hardtop 'Cuda V-8	3,033.00
A01 Light Package	35.00
A04 Basic Group	188.45
A36 Performance Axle Package (w/340 ci only)	59.90
A51 Sport Decor Package (w/340 ci)	47.70
(wo/340 ci)	67.40
B41 Front power disc brakes (required w/340 ci)	40.45
C16 Console	51.60
D21 Manual 4 speed transmission (w/340 ci only)	192.85
D34 TorqueFlite transmission (w/318 ci)	203.45
(w/340 ci)	223.30
D53 3.23 axle ratio (w/318 ci w/D34)	12.20
D91 Sure-Grip differential (std w/A36, NA 6 cyl)	40.65
E55 340 ci 4V engine (Barracuda)	245.85
('Cuda)	179.00
F23 375 amp battery	13.30

G11 Tinted glass — all windows	35.85
G35 Chrome outside left racing mirror	14.60
G36 Body-color remote left, manual right dual racing mirrors (w/A04)	10.50
(wo/A04)	25.10
G37 Chrome remote outside left & manual right racing mirrors	
(w/A04)	10.50
(wo/A04)	25.10
H31 Rear window defogger	28.15
H51 Air conditioning (NA w/3 speed manual, required B41)	364.80
J21 Electric clock (std w/J97)	15.70
J25 3 speed windshield wipers w/electric washers	10.35
J52 Inside hood release	9.50
J54 Sport hood (std w/A51 & w/340 ci)	19.70
J55 Undercoating w/hood insulator pad	20.25
J97 Rallye instrument panel (w/A04)	74.70
(wo/A04)	85.00
M25 Sill molding (std w/A51)	12.50
M26 Wheel lip molding (std w/A51)	7.25
N95 Emission control system & testing (required Calif)	25.55
R11 Solid-state AM radio (wo/A04)	59.40
R26 Solid-state AM radio w/stereo tape player (wo/A04)	196.25
AM radio w/stereo tape (w/A04)	136.85
R31 Rear seat speakers, single (requires R11)	13.45
R32 Rear seat speakers, dual (w/R35 or R36)	24.35
R35 AM/FM stereo radio (wo/A04)	191.40
(w/A04)	132.00
S13 HD suspension (std w/340 ci)	13.95
S77 Power steering (std w/A04)	104.10
W11 Deluxe wheel covers	24.50
W21 Rallye road wheels	52.80
W23 Chrome styled road wheels	81.10
Bodyside tape stripe (std w/A51)	27.75
High-impact paint colors	13.45
Vinyl roof	80.20
Vinyl side molding	27.75
Tires	
(replaces 5 7.35x14 tires — extra charge)	
T22 7.35x14 WSW (std w/Barracuda 318)	26.10
T34 F78x14 WSW	67.15
T86 F70x14 WSW (requires S13)	85.75
T87 F70x14 RWL (requires S13)	96.95
Tires	
(replaces 5 F70x14 WSW tires — extra charge)	
T34 F78x14 BSW	NC
T87 F70x14 RWL	11.25

Exterior color codes

Silver Frost Metallic	JA5	True Blue Metallic	GB5
Sky Blue	HB1	Rallye Red	FE5
Basin Street Blue	TB3	Mist Green	JF1

Exterior color codes

Forest Green Metallic	JF8
Autumn Bronze Metallic	GK6
Sahara Beige	HL4
Honey Gold	JY3
Golden Haze Metallic	JY6
Tahitian Gold Metallic	JY9
Spinnaker White	EW1
Formal Black	TX9
Lemon Twist	FY1
Amber Sherwood Metallic	GF3

Vinyl roof color codes

Black	V1X
White	V1W
Gold	V1Y
Green	V1F

Side stripes codes

Black	V6X
White	V6W

Interior trim codes

Blue	A6B5
Green	A6F6
Black	A6X9
White	A6XW

Facts

Styling changes were minimal for 1973. Most noticeable were the front and rear bumper guards. The front bumpers were designed to accept a 5 mph impact without damage. A new side tape treatment was available in black or white.

The 225 ci six-cylinder was dropped. Engine choice was now limited to just two V–8s—the 318 ci 2V and the 340 ci 4V, which was standard with the 'Cuda model.

Electronic ignition was standard on both engines, as were induction-hardened exhaust valve seats, allowing the engines to run on unleaded fuel.

A total 6,583 'Cuda 340s were built.

1973 Plymouth Barracuda

Chapter 15

1974 Plymouth Barracuda

Production
2 dr hardtop 8 cyl	6,745
2 dr hardtop 'Cuda 8 cyl	4,989
Total	11,734

Serial numbers
BH23G4B100001

B — car line, Plymouth Barracuda
H — price class (H-high, S-special)
23 — body type (23-2 dr hardtop)
G — engine code
4 — last digit of model year
B — assembly plant code (B-Hamtramck)
100001 — consecutive sequence number
    Serial number located on plate attached to left side of dash panel, visible through windshield.

Engine codes
G — 318 ci 2V V-8 150 hp
J — 360 ci 4V V-8 245 hp

Head casting numbers
318 ci — 2843675
360 ci — 3671587

Carburetors
318 ci 2V V-8 — Carter BBD6464S/manual, BBD6465S/automatic, BBD6467S/automatic Calif, BBD8018S/automatic Calif, BBD8028S/automatic Calif
360 ci 4V V-8 — Carter TQ6452S/manual, TQ6454S/manual Calif, TQ6453S/automatic, TQ6455S/automatic Calif

Option order codes and retail prices
BH23 2 dr hardtop V-8	$3,067.00
BS23 2 dr hardtop 'Cuda V-8	3,252.00
A01 Light Package	36.60
A04 Basic Group	196.00
A36 Performance Axle Package (w/360 ci only)	62.85
A51 Sport Decor Package (w/360 ci)	70.55
(wo/360 ci)	49.85
B41 Front power disc brakes (required w/360 ci)	42.55
C16 Console	54.25
D21 Manual 4 speed transmission (w/360 ci only)	203.05
D34 TorqueFlite transmission (w/318 ci)	214.20
(w/360 ci)	235.05
D53 3.23 axle ratio (w/318 ci w/D34)	12.75
D91 Sure-Grip differential (std w/A36)	42.70
E58 360 ci 4V engine (Barracuda)	258.85
('Cuda)	188.50

F23 375 amp battery	13.90
G11 Tinted glass — all windows	37.35
G54 Chrome remote control left racing mirror (w/A04)	15.35
G74 Chrome remote outside left & manual right racing	
mirrors (w/A04)	11.05
(wo/A04)	26.40
G75 Body-color remote left, manual right dual racing	
mirrors (w/A04)	11.05
(wo/A04)	26.40
H31 Rear window defogger	29.55
H51 Air conditioning (NA w/3 speed manual,	
required B41)	384.05
J21 Electric clock (std w/J97)	17.35
J25 3 speed windshield wipers w/electric washers	10.85
J52 Inside hood release	9.90
J54 Sport hood (std w/A51 & w/340 ci)	20.70
J55 Undercoating w/hood silencer pad	21.30
J97 Rallye instrument panel (w/A04)	78.65
(wo/A04)	89.45
M25 Sill molding (std w/A51)	13.30
M26 Wheel lip molding (std w/A51)	7.55
N95 Emission control system & testing (required Calif)	26.85
R11 Solid-state AM radio (std w/A04)	62.55
R31 Rear seat speakers, single (requires R11)	14.10
R32 Rear seat speakers, dual (w/R35)	25.60
R35 AM/FM stereo radio (wo/A04)	201.50
(w/A04)	138.95
S13 HD suspension (std w/360)	14.65
S42 Front sway bar (required w/radial tires, std w/S13)	9.40
S77 Power steering (std w/A04)	107.25
W11 Deluxe wheel covers	25.75
W21 Rallye road wheels	55.50
W23 Chrome styled road wheels	85.30
Vinyl side molding (NA w/body tape stripes)	29.10
Vinyl roof	84.35
Bodyside tape stripe (std w/A51)	29.10
Tires	
(replaces 5 7.35x14 tires — extra charge)	
T22 7.35x14 WSW (std w/Barracuda 318)	27.45
T34 F78x14 WSW	70.50
T36 FR78x14 WSW (requires S13 or S42)	180.25
T86 F70x14 (requires S13)	88.90
T87 F70x14 RWL	100.65
Tires	
(replaces 5 F70x14 WSW tires — extra charge)	
T34 F78x14 BSW	NC
T36 FR78x14 WSW (requires S13, or S42)	91.40
T87 F70x14 RWL	11.75

Exterior color codes

Powder Blue	KB1	Burnished Red Metallic	GE7
Lucerne Blue Metallic	KB5	Frosty Green Metallic	KG2
Rallye Red	FE5	Deep Sherwood Metallic	KG8

Exterior color codes

Avocado Gold Metallic	KJ6
Sahara Beige	HL4
Dark Moonstone Metallic	KL8
Sienna Metallic	KT5
Spinnaker White	EW1
Formal Black	TX9
Golden Fawn	KY4
Yellow Blaze	KY5
Golden Haze Metallic	JY6
Tahitian Gold Metallic	JY9

Interior trim codes

Blue	A6B6
Green	A6G6
Black	A6X9
White	A6XW

Vinyl roof color codes

Black	V1X
White	V1W
Gold	V1Y
Green	V1G

Upper bodyside, tape stripes codes

Black	V6X
White	V6W

Facts

The major change for the last year of the Barracuda was the substitution of a 360 ci 4V V-8 in place of the 340 ci engine.

1974 Plymouth Barracuda

Chapter 16

1970 Dodge Challenger

Production

2 dr hardtop 6 cyl	9,929	2 dr hardtop R/T	
2 dr hardtop 8 cyl	39,350*	8 cyl	13,796
2 dr sports hardtop		2 dr sports hardtop	
6 cyl	350	R/T 8 cyl	3,753
2 dr sports hardtop		Convertible R/T 8 cyl	963
8 cyl	5,873	Total	76,935
Convertible 6 cyl	378	*Includes 2,399 Challenger	
Convertible 8 cyl	2,543	T/As.	

Serial numbers

JH23B0B100001

J — car line, Dodge Challenger

H — price class (H-high, S-special)

23 — body type (23-2 dr hardtop, 27-convertible, 29-2 dr sports hardtop)

B — engine code

0 — last digit of model year

B — assembly plant code (B-Hamtramck)

100001 — consecutive sequence number

Serial number located on plate attached to left side of dash panel, visible through windshield.

Engine codes

B — 198 ci 1V 6 cyl 101 hp

C — 225 ci 1V 6 cyl 145 hp

G — 318 ci 2V V-8 230 hp

H — 340 ci 4V V-8 275 hp

J — 340 ci 3x2V V-8 290 hp

L — 383 ci 2V V-8 290 hp

L — 383 ci 4V V-8 330 hp

N — 383 ci 4V V-8 335 hp

R — 426 ci 2x4V V-8 425 hp

U — 440 ci 4V V-8 375 hp

V — 440 ci 3x2V V-8 390 hp

Head casting numbers

318 ci — 2843675

340 ci — 2531894

340 ci 3x2V — 3418915

383 ci — 2843906

426 ci — 2780559

440 ci — 2843906

V-8 carburetors

318 ci 2V — Carter BBD4721S/manual, BBD4722S/automatic, BBD4723S/manual w/ECS, BBD4724S/automatic w/ECS

340 ci 4V — Carter AVS4936S/manual, AVS4936S/manual w/ECS, AVS4934S/automatic, AVS4935S/automatic w/AC, AVS4937A/automatic w/ECS

340 ci 3x2V — Holley R4789A/front, R4790A/rear, R4791A/center manual, R4792A/center automatic

383 ci 2V — Carter BBD4725S, BBD4726S/manual, Holley R4372/manual w/ECS, Carter BBD4747S/manual w/ECS, BBD4894S/automatic w/AC, Holley R4317A/automatic w/AC, Carter BBD4728S/automatic w/AC

383 ci 4V — Holley R4367A/manual, R4217A/manual w/ECS, R4368A/automatic, R4737/automatic w/fresh air, R4218A/automatic w/ECS, R4369A/automatic w/AC, Carter AVS4736S/automatic, AVS4732S/automatic w/AC, AVS4734S/automatic w/ECS

426 ci 2x4V — Carter AFB4742S/front, AFB4745S/rear manual, AFB4746S/rear automatic

440 ci 4V — Carter AVS4737S/manual, AVS4739S/manual w/ECS, AVS4738S/automatic, AVS4741/automatic w/AC, AVS4740S/ automatic w/ECS

440 ci 3x2V — Holley R4382A/front, R4175A/front all w/ECS, R4374A/center manual, R4375A/center manual, R4144A/center automatic, R4376A/center automatic w/ECS, R4365A/rear all, R4383A/rear all w/ECS

Distributors

340 ci — 3438317/manual, 3438325/automatic

340 ci 3x2V — 3438521/manual, 3438523/automatic

383 ci — 3438231

383 ci 4V — 3438233 (interchanges w/3438433)

426 ci — 2875987/manual, 2875989 IBS-4014F/automatic

440 ci — 3438222

440 ci 3x2V — 3438314/manual up to approx 01/01/70, 3438348/manual after approx 01/01/70, 2875982/automatic up to approx 01/01/70, 3438349/automatic after approx 01/01/70

Option order codes and retail prices

Challenger Six

JH23 2 dr hardtop	$2,851.00
JH27 Convertible	3,120.00
JH29 2 dr sports hardtop Special Edition	3,083.00
Challenger V-8	
JH23 2 dr hardtop	2,953.00
JH27 Convertible	3,222.00
JH29 2 dr sports hardtop Special Edition	3,185.00
Challenger R/T	
JS23 2 dr hardtop	3,266.00
JS27 Convertible	3,535.00
JS29 2 dr sports hardtop Special Edition	3,498.00
A01 Light Package (NA w/340 ci & NA R/T)	41.15
(w/340 ci on Challenger)	30.35
A04 Radio Group (w/14 in. wheels, NA w/A62, NA R/T)	198.95
(w/15 in. wheels, NA w/A62, NA R/T)	177.65
(w/14 in. wheels, A62 required w/Challenger)	188.35
(w/15 in. wheels, A62 required w/Challenger)	167.05
A05 Challenger Protection Group (w/340 ci on Challenger)	43.25
(NA R/T)	57.90
A31 High Performance Axle Package (NA w/AC or trailer towing available w/340 & 383 4V engines w/D21 & D34)	102.15

A32 Super Performance Axle Package (NA w/AC or trailer towing)	
(w/440 ci & D34)	250.65
(w/426 ci & D34)	221.40
A33 Track Package (NA w/AC, w/440 ci 4V, 440 ci 6V, 426 ci w/D21)	142.85
A34 Super Track Pak (NA w/AC, w/440 ci 4V, 440 ci 6V, 426 ci w/D21)	235.65
A35 Trailer Towing Package (w/318 & 383 2V engines)	48.70
(w/340 & 383 4V engines)	34.80
(w/440 4V engine)	14.05
A36 Performance Axle Package (NA w/Trailer Towing Package)	
(w/340 ci or 383 ci 4V w/D21 or D34)	102.15
(w/440 ci 4V or 440 ci 6V w/D34)	92.25
(w/426 ci & D34)	64.40
A44 Back Window Louvers Package (hardtop only)	91.10
A45 Front/Rear Spoiler Package	55.65
A53 Challenger T/A Package	865.70
A62 Rallye instrument panel cluster (V-8s only, std R/T)	90.30
A63 Molding Group A (std SE)	37.20
A66 Challenger 340 4V Engine Package (NA R/T, W21 & W34 required)	258.90
B11 HD drum brakes	22.65
B41 Disc brakes (requires B51)	27.90
B51 Power brakes	42.95
C13 Front shoulder belts (convertible)	26.45
C14 Rear shoulder belts (NA convertible)	26.45
C16 Console (w/bucket seats only)	53.35
C62 Comfort Position 6 way seat adjuster (left bucket only)	33.30
C92 Color-keyed accessory floor mats	10.90
D21 Manual 4 speed transmission (NA 225 ci & 383 ci 2V)	194.85
D34 TorqueFlite (6 cyl)	190.25
(318 ci)	202.05
(340 ci & 383 ci 2V)	216.20
(383 ci 4V, 440 ci 4V, 440 ci 6V, 426 ci 8V)	227.05
D51 Opt 2.76 axle ratio (w/383 ci 4V & D34)	10.35
D53 Opt 3.23 axle ratio (w/225 ci, 318 ci, 383 ci 2V & D34)	10.35
D91 Sure-Grip differential (std w/performance axle packages)	42.35
E55 340 ci 4V (NA R/T — see A66)	
E61 383 ci 2V engine (requires D34, NA R/T)	69.75
E63 383 ci 4V engine (std/R/T)	137.55
E74 426 ci 8V engine (A33 or A34 required w/4 speed R/T only)	778.75
E86 440 ci 4V engine (R/T only)	130.55
E87 440 ci 6V engine (R/T only)	249.55
F11 50 amp alternator	11.00
F25 70 amp battery	12.95

G11 Tinted glass — all windows (exc convertible backglass)	32.75
G15 Tinted glass — windshield only	20.40
G31 Chrome manual outside right mirror (requires G33)	10.95
G32 Painted manual outside right mirror	10.95
G33 Chrome remote control outside left mirror	15.15
G34 Painted remote control outside left mirror	15.15
H31 Rear window defogger	26.25
H51 Air conditioning	357.65
J21 Electric clock	16.50
J25 Variable-speed wipers w/electric washers	10.60
J41 Pedal dress-up	5.45
J45 Hood tie-down pins (w/340 Engine Package on Challenger & R/T)	15.40
J46 Locking gas cap	4.40
J55 Undercoating w/underhood pad	16.60
J78 Front spoiler (T/A)	20.95
J81 Rear spoiler	34.80
L42 Headlight time delay and warning signal (wo/A01)	18.20
(w/A01)	13.00
M05 Door edge protectors	4.65
M25 Sill molding	21.75
M51 Sunroof (incl vinyl roof, hardtops only, NA SE)	461.45
M85 Bumper guards, front & rear rubber inserts	23.80
M91 Deck lid luggage rack	32.35
N88 Automatic speed control (8 cyl only, NA w/340 ci, 440 ci 6V & 426 ci)	57.95
N95 Evaporative emission control (Calif)	37.85
N96 Shaker Hood Fresh Air Package (w/440 ci 6V & 426 ci 8V)	97.30
N97 Noise Reduction Package (required in Calif w/440 ci 6V & 426 ci)	NC
P31 Power windows	105.20
P37 Power convertible top lift	52.85
R11 Music Master AM radio (wo/A04)	61.55
R22 Music Master AM radio w/stereo tape player (wo/A04)	196.25
AM radio w/stereo tape player (w/A04)	134.75
R31 Rear seat speakers, single (requires R11)	14.05
dual (requires R22 or R35)	25.90
R35 Multiplex AM/FM radio (wo/A04)	213.60
(w/A04)	152.20
S13 HD suspension (std w/383 4V & 340 engines)	14.75
S15 Extra HD Handling Package (w/383 4V & 340 engines)	18.25
S25 Firm Ride shock absorbers (std w/S15)	3.55
S77 Power steering	90.35
S79 Partial-horn-ring steering wheel	5.45
S83 3 spoke Rim Blow steering wheel	24.60
S84 Tuff steering wheel	19.15
V21 Hood performance paint (w/340 Challenger & R/T)	24.30
W08 Regular spare tire (convertible only, NA w/60 Series)	NC
Bumblebee paint stripe (w/340 Challenger & R/T)	NC

Cloth & vinyl bucket seat (hardtops, NA SE)	16.50
Cloth & vinyl bucket seat (SE)	(48.25)
High-impact paint colors	14.05
Leather bucket seat (std SE)	64.75
Longitudinal tape stripe (R/T)	NC
Two-tone paint (hardtops only, NA SE models)	31.70
Vinyl bench seat w/center armrest (Challenger hardtop & D34 required)	16.50
Vinyl bodyside insert protection molding	29.45
Vinyl roof, (std w/SE)	83.95

Wheels and wheel covers
(models wo/A04)

W11 Deluxe wheel covers	21.30
W13 Deep-dish 14 in.	44.90
W15 Wire, 14 in.	64.10
W21 Rallye road wheels, 14 or 15 in.	43.10
W23 Chrome road wheels w/trim ring, 14 in. only	86.15

Wheels & wheel covers
(models w/A04)

W13 Deep-dish, 14 in.	23.75
W15 Wire, 14 in.	42.85
W21 Rallye road wheels, 14 or 15 in.	21.95
W23 Chrome road wheels w/trim ring, 14 in. only	64.95
W34 Collapsible spare tire (required w/15 in. tires)	12.95

Tires
(w/225 or 318 engines, replaces E78x14 BSW tires, NA R/T)

T26 E78x14 WSW	26.45
T34 F78x14 WSW	44.55
T35 F78x14 BSW	15.40
T86 F70x14 WSW (requires B11 or B41 & S13)	65.35
T87 F70x14 RWL (requires B11 or B41 & S13)	65.35

Tires
(w/383 engine, replaces F78x14 BSW tires, NA R/T)

T34 F78x14 BSW	29.25
T86 F70x14 WSW (requires B11 or B41, S13 required w/383 ci 2V)	50.10
T87 F70x14 RWL (requires B11 or B41, S13 required w/383 ci 2V)	50.10

Tires
(R/T only, w/383 ci 4V, 440 ci 4V, 440 ci 6V, replaces F70x14 RWL tires)

T86 F70x14 WSW	NC
U82 E60x15 RWL (requires W34, NA convertible w/440 engine & AC)	47.95

Exterior colors

Light Blue Metallic	EB3	Dark Burnt Orange	FK5
Bright Blue Metallic	EB5	Beige	BL1
Dark Blue Metallic	EB7	Dark Tan Metallic	FT6
Rallye Red	FE5	White	EW1
Light Green Metallic	FF4	Black	TX9
Dark Green Metallic	EF8	Cream	DY3

Exterior colors

Light Gold Metallic	FY4	Go-Mango	EK2
Plum Crazy	FC7	Hemi Orange	EV2
Sublime	FJ5	Banana	FY1

Interior trim codes

Color	Vinyl	Cloth & vinyl	Leather	Vinyl bench seats
Tan	H6T5	H5F8	HRT5	—
Burnt Orange	H6K4	H5X9	HRK4	H4X9
Black	H6X9	H5X9	HRX9	—
White	H6XW	—	—	—
Red	H6E4	—	—	—
Blue	H6B7	H5B5	—	H4B5
Green	H6F8	—	—	—
Black/White	L6X9			—
Black	L6XW			—

Vinyl roof color codes

Green	V1F
Gator Grain	V1G
White	V1W
Black	V1X

Sport stripes color codes

Black	V6X (V6H)*
White	V6W

*Parentheses indicate T/A stripe.

Convertible top color codes

White	V3W
Black	V3X

Facts

Similar to Plymouth's Barracuda, the Challenger was Dodge's first pony car. Although both cars shared the same drivetrain and suspension components, the Challenger was built on a longer, 110 in., wheelbase versus the 108 in. wheelbase for the Barracuda. Four headlights were used, and on the rear was a full-length taillight panel.

Three models were offered: Challenger Six, Challenger V-8 and Challenger R/T. Standard engine on the base model was the 225 ci six-cylinder mated to a three-speed manual transmission. Standard engine on the Challenger V-8 was the 230 hp 318 ci 2V. Optional engines were the 340 ci, 383 ci 2V and 4V engines, all with a three-speed manual, except for the 290 hp 383 ci 2V, which was available only with the TorqueFlite. The four-speed manual was optional on all engines except the 225 ci six-cylinder and 383 ci 2V V-8.

The 340 ci V-8 that was optional on the Challenger came with 15x7 in. Rallye wheels and E60x15 tires. Late in the model year, the shaker hood became available for the 340.

Standard engine on the performance Challenger R/T was the 335 hp 383 ci Magnum. Standard transmission was a three-speed manual. Optional R/T engines were the 375 hp 440 ci Magnum, the

440 ci Six-pack rated at 390 hp and the 425 hp 426 ci Hemi. The 426 Hemi came with a hydraulic camshaft for 1970. On the 440 and 426 engines, transmission choice was either a four-speed manual or a TorqueFlite automatic. All R/Ts came with a performance hood with two hood scoops and either longitudinal side stripes or bumblebee rear wraparound stripes.

The functional Shaker hood was optional on the 440 Six-Pack and 426 Hemi engines. It was painted Red (FE5) on red-colored cars, Blue on Blue (EB5) cars and Astrotone Silver (argent) or Black Oragnisol with all other colors. Later in the model year, the Shaker was made available on all four-barrel-equipped V-8s. Some Challengers got the Challenger T/A fiberglass hood instead of the Shaker during the time when a shortage of Shakers occurred.

Shaker production, as provided by John Sloan, was 164 on Challenger R/T hardtops, 15 on Challenger R/T Special Editions (SEs) and five on Challenger R/T convertibles.

All R/Ts, except those powered by the 426, came with 14 in. wheels and F70x14 tires. Hemi-powered R/Ts got 15x7 in. Rallye wheels and F60x15 tires.

R/T Challengers came with the Rallye instrument cluster—which included a 150 mph speedometer, an 8000 rpm tachometer and an oil pressure gauge.

The Special Edition Challengers came with a vinyl roof, a smaller rear window, an overhead interior console that housed three warning lights (door ajar, low fuel and seatbelts) and leather bucket seats. Cloth and vinyl buckets could be substituted as a credit option.

Air conditioning was not available with the 440 4V engine with manual transmission, the 440 Six-Pack and the 426 Hemi.
Suspension on the R/T was heavy-duty with heavy-duty drum brakes all around. Front discs were optional.

Two midyear introductions appeared, one memorable and one not. Most significant was the Challenger T/A. The T/A was built so that Dodge could race the Challenger in the Trans-Am series. The Challenger T/A Package consisted of a special 340 ci V-8 with 3x2V induction rated at 290 hp, power front disc brakes, heavy-duty shocks and suspension, fiberglass hood with Fresh Air Package, 15x7 in. Rallye wheels with E60x15 front and G60x15 rear tires, rear ducktail spoiler, remote control left mirror and locking fliptop gas cap. The T/A could also be identified by its T/A longitudinal side stripes, 340 Six-Pack front fender decals, flat-black painted hood and side exhaust system.

The T/A came with front and rear sway bars, fast-ratio steering, an optional front spoiler and the choice of either a four-speed manual or the TorqueFlite automatic transmission.

A version of the T/A available to West Coast dealers was known as the Western Special. It came with a rear-exit exhaust system and Western Special identification on the rear deck lid, and some examples came with a vacuum-operated trunk release system.

Less exciting was the midyear introduction of the Challenger Deputy.

Chapter 17

1971 Dodge Challenger

Production

2 dr hardtop 6 cyl	1,672	Convertible 8 cyl	1,774
2 dr hardtop 8 cyl	18,956	2 dr hardtop R/T 8 cyl	3,814
Convertible 6 cyl	83	Total	26,299

Serial numbers

JH21B1B100001

J — car line, Dodge Challenger

H — price class (H-high, S-special)

21 — body type (21-2 dr coupe, 23-2 dr hardtop, 27-convertible)

B — engine code

1 — last digit of model year

B — assembly plant code (B-Hamtramck)

100001 — consecutive sequence number

   Serial number located on plate attached to left side of dash panel, visible through windshield.

Engine codes

B — 198 ci 1V 6 cyl 125 hp (105 hp net)

C — 225 ci 1V 6 cyl 145 hp (110 hp net)

G — 318 ci 2V V-8 230 hp (155 hp net)

H — 340 ci 4V V-8 275 hp (235 hp net)

L — 383 ci 2V V-8 275 hp (190 hp net)

N — 383 ci 4V V-8 300 hp (250 hp net)

R — 426 ci 2x4V V-8 425 hp (350 hp net)

U — 440 ci 3x2V V-8 390 hp (330 hp net)

Head casting numbers

318 ci — 2843675

340 ci — 2531894

383 ci — 3462346

426 ci — 2780559

440 ci — 3462346

V-8 carburetors

318 ci 2V — Carter BBD4957S/manual, BBD4858S/automatic

340 ci 4V — Carter TQ4972S/manual, TQ4973S/automatic

383 ci 2V — Carter BBD4961S/manual, BBD4962S/automatic

383 ci 4V — Holley R4734A/manual w/fresh air, R4667A/wo/fresh air, R4735A/automatic w/fresh air, R4668A/automatic wo/fresh air

426 ci 2x4V — Carter AFB4971S/front, AFB4970S/rear automatic, AFB4969S/rear manual

440 ci 4V — Carter AVS4967S/manual, AVS4968S/automatic

440 ci 3x2V — Holley R4671A/front all, R4669A/center manual, R4670A/center automatic, R4672A/rear all

Distributors

340 ci — 3438522/manual, 3438517/automatic, 3656151/manual w/electronic ignition, 3438986/automatic w/electronic ignition

383 ci — 3438534, 3438544/w/NOx
383 ci 4V — 3438690
426 ci — 2875987/manual, 3438579/automatic, 3438891/manual
   w/electronic ignition, 3438579/automatic w/electronic ignition
440 ci — 3438694
440 ci 3x2V — 3438577

Option order codes and retail prices*

Challenger Six

JH21 2 dr coupe	$2,727.00
JH23 2 dr hardtop	2,848.00
JH27 Convertible	3,105.00
Challenger V-8	
JH21 2 dr coupe	2,853.00
JH23 2 dr hardtop	2,950.00
JH27 Convertible	3,207.00
Challenger R/T	
JS23 2 dr hardtop	3,273.00
A01 Light Package	30.20
A04 Basic Group (NA w/A62, or N96, NA R/T)	193.60
(w/A62, N96, required w/R/T & convertible)	183.00
A21 Front Elastomeric Bumper Group (NA R/T)	50.05
A22 Front & Rear Elastomeric Bumper Group (NA R/T)	94.00
A28 Noise Reduction Package (440 ci 6V w/D34,	
required in Calif)	33.55
A31 High Performance Axle Package (NA w/AC or	
trailer towing available w/340 & 383 4V engines	
w/D21 & D34)	75.25
A33 Track Package (NA w/H51, w/440 ci 6V,	
426 ci w/D21)	137.80
A34 Super Track Pak (NA w/H51, w/440 ci 6V,	
426 ci w/D21)	201.75
A36 Performance Axle Package (w/340 ci or 383 ci 4V	
w/D34 or D21)	75.25
(w/440 ci 6V & D34)	75.25
(w/426 ci & D34)	41.70
A44 Louver Package (w/A04)	73.70
(wo/A04)	8.65
A45 Front & rear spoiler (NA 6 cyl, 2V V-8s & w/A78)	54.65
A46 Molding Group	35.10
A62 Rallye instrument cluster (8 cyl only,	
wo/N96, std R/T)	87.30
(8 cyl only, w/N96, std R/T)	76.75
A78 Formal Roof Package (NA w/A44)	127.50
B11 HD drum brakes (w/318 ci & 383 ci)	21.40
B41 Disc brakes (requires B51)	22.50
B51 Power brakes	41.55
C13 Front shoulder belts (convertible)	24.40
C14 Rear shoulder belts (NA convertible)	24.40
C16 Console (w/bucket seats only)	53.05
C62 Comfort Position 6 way seat adjuster	
(left bucket only)	32.20

D21 Manual 4 speed transmission (NA 198 ci, 225 ci, 318 ci, 383 ci 2V)	198.10
D34 TorqueFlite (6 cyl)	209.00
(318 ci, 383 ci 2V)	209.00
(340 ci, 383 ci 4V, 426 ci, 440 ci)	229.35
D51 Opt 2.76 axle ratio (w/318 ci & manual transmission)	12.55
(w/340 ci or 383 ci 4V & D34)	12.55
D53 Opt 3.23 axle ratio (w/225 ci, 318 ci, 383 ci & D340)	12.55
D91 Sure-Grip differential (NA 6 cyl models)	41.70
E24 225 ci 6 cyl (JH21 only, std other 6 cyl models)	39.00
E55 340 ci 4V engine (NA coupe, R/T)	252.50
(R/T only)	44.35
E61 383 ci 2V engine (requires D34, NA w/R/T)	70.80
E65 383 ci 4V engine (std R/T)	139.60
E74 426 ci 8V engine (requires W34 — R/T only)	789.95
E87 440 ci 6V engine (R/T only)	253.20
F11 50 amp alternator	10.85
F25 70 amp battery	13.60
G11 Tinted glass — all windows (exc convertible backglass)	36.85
G15 Tinted glass — windshield only	25.05
G31 Chrome outside right racing mirror (requires G33)	10.80
G33 Chrome outside left racing mirror	14.95
G36 Color-keyed remote outside left & manual right racing mirrors (wo/A04)	25.75
G41 Day-night inside mirror (coupe only, std all others)	7.05
H31 Rear window defogger	28.90
H51 Air conditioning	370.15
J15 Cigar lighter (coupe only)	4.00
J21 Electric clock (std w/A62 & R/T)	16.10
J25 Variable-speed wipers w/electric washers	10.60
J31 Dual horns (coupe only, std all others)	5.10
J41 Pedal dress-up	5.40
J45 Hood pins	15.20
J46 Locking fliptop gas cap	7.75
J55 Undercoating w/underhood pad	20.80
J64 Wood-grained instrument panel (NA w/A62, NA R/T)	5.70
J81 Spoiler, rear only (NA 6 cyl or 2V V-8s, NA w/A78)	34.35
L31 Fender-mounted turn signals (NA R/T)	10.70
M05 Door edge protectors	6.00
M25 Sill moldings	21.05
M28 Wide grille surround molding (NA w/A21, A22)	16.30
M51 Power sunroof, incl vinyl roof (NA w/A78)	445.85
M71 Elastomeric front bumper (R/T only)	40.70
M73 Elastomeric front & rear bumpers (R/T only)	81.40
M85 Front & rear bumper guards (NA w/A21, A22)	27.40
M91 Deck lid luggage rack	31.30
N25 Engine block heater	14.30
N94 Fiberglass hood w/Fresh Air Package (NA w/6 cyl & 2V engines w/340 engine on Challenger & all R/Ts)	152.95
(NA w/340 engine, NA w/R/T)	173.20

N95 NOx exhaust emission control (Calif)	11.95
N96 Shaker Hood Fresh Air Package (w/340 Challenger & R/T)	94.00
(w/383 ci 4V, NA w/H51)	114.20
N97 Noise Reduction Package (required Calif w/440 ci 6V & 426 ci 8V & 4 speed manual)	NC
P31 Power windows (NA w/coupe)	101.30
P37 Power convertible top lift	48.70
R11 Music Master AM radio	61.10
R26 Music Master AM radio w/stereo tape player	201.60
R31 Rear seat speakers, single (requires R11)	13.85
R32 Rear seat speakers, dual (requires R26, R35 or R36)	25.05
R33 Tape recorder microphone (w/R26 or R36)	10.75
R35 Multiplex AM/FM stereo radio	196.60
R36 Multiplex AM/FM stereo radio w/stereo tape player	337.05
S13 Rallye suspension w/sway bar (std w/340 ci, 383 ci 4V & R/T)	14.30
S25 Firm Ride shock absorbers (std w/340 ci, 383 ci 4V & R/T)	4.80
S77 Power steering	96.55
W08 Regular spare tire (convertible only, NA w/15 in. tires)	NC
W11 Deluxe wheel covers, 14 in.	25.15
W12 Wheel trim rings, 14 or 15 in. (w/hubcaps only)	25.15
W15 Wire wheel covers, 14 in.	64.55
W21 Rallye road wheels, 14 or 15 in. (15 in. requires W34)	54.25
W23 Chrome styled road wheels, 14 in. only w/std spare	83.30
W34 Collapsible spare tire (required w/15 in. tires, R32 & H31)	12.55
Bodyside lacquer paint stripe (coupe only)	14.65
Bodyside perf. tape stripe (coupe only)	28.50
Bodyside tape stripe (replaces paint stripe)	14.25
Cloth & vinyl bucket seat (NA convertible & coupe)	16.00
High-impact paint colors	13.85
Leather bucket seat (NA coupe)	62.55
Vinyl bench seat w/center armrest (NA coupe, convertible)	16.00
Vinyl bodyside insert protection molding (coupe only)	28.50
Vinyl bodyside insert protection molding (replaces stripe)	14.25
Vinyl roof	82.40

Tires

(w/198, 225 & 318 engines, replaces 7.35x14 BSW tires)

T22 7.35x14 WSW	26.85
T26 E78x14 WSW	51.00
T34 F78x14 WSW	68.90
T35 F78x14 BSW	39.55
T86 F70x14 WSW (requires S13)	88.00
T87 F70x14 RWL (requires S13)	99.50
U82 E60x15 RWL (requires S13, B11 or B41 & W34)	139.65

Tires

(w/383 engine, replaces F78x14 BSW tires)

T34 F78x14 BSW		29.40
T86 F70x14 WSW (requires S13)		48.50
T87 F70x14 RWL (requires S13)		59.95
U82 E60x15 RWL (requires S13, B11 or B41 & W34, NA w/H51)		100.10

Tires

(w/340 on Challenger & all R/Ts, replaces F70x14 WSW tires)

T34 F78x14 WSW (w/340 ci or 383 ci 4V only)		NC
T87 F70x14 RWL		11.50
U82 E60x15 RWL (NA w/H51 & 383 ci 4V combination)		51.65

*April 1, 1971, revision.

Exterior color codes

Light Gunmetal Metallic	GA4	Bright White	GW3
Light Blue Metallic	GB2	Black	TX9
Bright Blue Metallic	GB5*	Butterscotch	EL5
Dark Blue Metallic	GB7	Citron Yella	GY3*
Dark Green Metallic	GF7	Hemi Orange	EV2*
Light Green Metallic	GF3	Green Go	FJ6*
Gold Metallic	GY8	Plum Crazy	FC7
Dark Gold Metallic	GY9	Top Banana	FY1
Dark Bronze Metallic	GK6	*Colors available for elasto-	
Tan Metallic	GT5	meric bumpers.	
Bright Red	FE5		

Interior trim codes

Color	Vinyl	R/T vinyl	Cloth & vinyl bucket seats	Leather	Vinyl bench seats
Blue	L6B7	H6B7	—	—	—
Green	L6F8	H6F8	H5F8	—	H4F8
Tan	L6T5	H6T5	—	—	—
Black	L6X9	H6X9	H5X9	HRX9	H4X9
Black/White	L6XW	H6XW	H5XX	—	—
Gold	—	H6Y3	—	—	—
Green/White	—	—	L5FW	—	—

Vinyl roof color codes

Black	V1X
White	V1W
Green	V1F
Gold	V1Y

Convertible top color codes

Black	V3X
White	V3W

Side stripes codes

Black	V9X
White	V9W

Facts

The 1971 Challengers got a new split grille insert that was painted silver, except on the R/T, where it was painted black. The taillight arrangement changed too, with two rectangular lamps on each side. Simulated brake scoops were located in front of the rear wheels on R/Ts. The R/Ts also got new bodyside tape stripes.

The model line-up changed as well. The SE model was deleted, as were the convertibles from the R/T. Challengers could be had in six-cylinder or V–8 form or with the V–8 powered R/Ts. The bottom of-the-line Challenger was the 198 ci six-cylinder-powered coupe with fixed rear side windows.

Standard engine available for the Challenger hardtops was the 225 ci six-cylinder mated to a three-speed transmission. Optional engines were the 318 2V, 340 4V, 383 2V and 383 4V. Standard transmission was the three-speed manual. The optional four-speed manual was available only on 4V equipped engines. The TorqueFlite automatic could be had with all engines except the 198 ci six-cylinder.

R/T engine line-up was modified by the deletion of the 375 hp 440 ci engine. Horsepower ratings were slightly lower due to a compression ratio reduction. The suspension was basically unchanged as well, with the exception of the addition of a rear sway bar. Standard brakes were still heavy-duty drums, but front discs were available.

Shaker production was 72 on base Challengers, 11 on Challenger convertibles and 141 on Challenger R/Ts.

Challenger 340 production amounted to 1,057 hardtops and 176 convertibles. The R/T 340 figures are not available.

Only 250 Challenger R/Ts got the 440 Six-Pack engine.

The 426 Hemi engine was installed in only 71 Challenger R/Ts (12 w/a TorqueFlite and 59 with a four-speed).

1971 Dodge Challenger

Chapter 18

1992 Dodge Viper

Production
RT/10 Roadster   285

Serial numbers
1B3BR65EXNV100001
1—country, U.S.A.
B—make, Dodge
3—vehicle type, passenger car
B—restraint system, manual seatbelts
R—vehicle line, Viper RT/10
6—series, Sport
5—body style (convertible, open body)
E—engine, EWB, 8.0l 10 cyl
X—check digit, 0 thru 9 or X
N—model year, 1992
V—assembly plant code (V-New Mack)
100001—consecutive sequence number

Engine code
E—8.0l V-10 400 hp

Options and retail prices
SRDS27 2 dr Roadster $50,000.00
EWB 8.0l V-10   Std
DEC Manual 6 speed transmission   Std

Exterior color code
Viper Red   PRN

Interior trim code
Gray leather   MLXD

Facts
    The Viper was originally introduced as a concept show car at
the Detroit North American International Auto Show in January
1989. A year later, in May 1990, Chrysler decided to go ahead with
a production version of the Viper, and a year after that the Viper
was the official Pace Car at the 1991 Indianapolis 500 race.
    In January 1992, the Viper RT/10 became officially available.
The RT/10 was powered by an all-aluminum V-10 rated at 400 hp at
4600 rpm with 465 ft.-lbs. torque at 3600 rpm. The only transmission available was a Borg-Warner T-56 six-speed manual. A 3.07:1
axle ratio was used on the limited-slip rear axle. Power steering and
power four-wheel disc brakes were standard equipment as well.
    The Viper used a tubular space frame design and composite
body panels with a fiber reinforced skin. The only color listed

was Viper Red with a gray leather interior. However, there was one green, one yellow and one black car built, and there was also one car built with a black interior. Total production amounted to 285 units—236 for the U.S. market, 14 Canadian units and 35 for export.

Three-spoke silver wheels with a six-bolt mounting flange were used on the Viper. The front wheels measured 17x10 in., while the rears were 17x13 in. The tires used were Michelin XGTZ radials measuring P275/40ZR17 on the front and P335/35ZR17 at the rear.

The Viper did not have side windows; the standard black folding top included plastic zipper-windowed side curtains. The rear window was removable. Other standard features included an AM/FM cassette stereo system, side exhausts and fog lamps with removable lens covers.

The 1992 Vipers have an externally mounted radio antenna on the driver side rear fender. They also have the battery mounted in the center of the trunk between the frame rails.

Chapter 19

1993 Dodge Viper

Production

RT/10 Roadster   1,043

Serial numbers

1B3BR65EXPV100001
1—country, U.S.A.
B—make, Dodge
3—vehicle type, passenger car
B—restraint system, manual seatbelts
R—vehicle line, Viper RT/10
6—series, Sport
5—body style, (5-convertible, open body, 9-coupe)
E—engine, EWB, 8.0l 10 cyl
X—check digit, 0 thru 9 or X
P—model year, 1993
V—assembly plant (New Mack)
100001—consecutive sequence number

Engine code

E—8.0l V-10 400 hp

Options and retail prices

SRDS27 2 dr Roadster	$50,000.00
EWB 8.0l V-10	Std
DEC Manual 6 speed transmission	Std
HCD Air conditioning	1,200.00
VK-8 Removable hardtop	2,500.00

Exterior color codes

Viper Red	PRN
Viper Black	PX3

Interior trim code

Gray leather	MLXD

Facts

Changes were minimal to the 1993 model Viper. An additional color, Viper Black, became available. An indeterminate amount of Vipers were 1992 carry-over cars as they have the rear-mounted radio antenna and trunk-mounted battery. All other Vipers were equipped with a windshield-mounted antenna, and the battery was relocated to the left frame rail.

The front and rear bumpers were made of a composite material. Air conditioning became available as an option as did a removable hardtop.

Of the 1,043 units built, 938 were for the U.S. market, 39 for Canada and 66 for export. According to the Viper Club (www.viperclub.org), 115 Vipers were painted Viper Black and approximately 928 were painted Viper Red.

Chapter 20

1994 Dodge Viper

Production
RT/10 Roadster   3,083

Serial numbers
1B3BR65EXRV100001
1—country, U.S.A.
B—make, Dodge
3—vehicle type, passenger car
B—restraint system, manual seatbelts
R—vehicle line, Viper RT/10
6—series, Sport
5—body style (5-convertible, open body, 9-coupe)
E—engine, EWB, 8.0l 10 cyl
X—check digit, 0 thru 9 or X
R—model year, 1994
V—assembly plant (New Mack)
100001—consecutive sequence number

Engine code
E—8.0l V-10 400 hp

Options and retail prices
SRDS27 2 dr Roadster $54,000.00
EWB 8.0l V-10   Std
DEC Manual 6 speed transmission   Std
HCD Air conditioning   1,200.00
VK8 Removable hardtop   2,500.00

Exterior color codes   **Interior trim codes**
Viper Red   PRN   Gray/Black leather   MLXD
Viper Black   PX3   Tan/Black leather   MLXK
Viper Emerald Green   PGQ
Viper Bright Yellow   PJE

Facts
Once again changes to the Viper RT/10 were minimal for 1994. Mesh map pockets were added to the seats along with a grab handle for the interior side of the passenger door. On the underside of the hood, a heat shield/EMI protector was added.

Two new exterior colors were added: Viper Emerald Green and Viper Bright Yellow. In some Dodge literature, the yellow is also referred to as Dandelion Yellow. In the interior, a new color combination was added, tan/black.

Of the 3,083 units built, 2,394 were sold in the U.S., 246 in Canada and 443 were exported. Most Vipers were painted red; Viper Club estimates are 2,189 in Viper Red, 678 in Viper Black, 133 in Viper Emerald Green and 83 in Viper Bright Yellow.

Chapter 21

1995 Dodge Viper

Production
RT/10 Roadster   1,577

Serial numbers
1B3AR65EXSV100001
1—country, U.S.A.
B—make, Dodge
3—vehicle type, passenger car
A—restraint system, air bag
R—vehicle line, Viper RT/10
6—series, Special/Sport
5—body style (convertible, open body)
E—engine, EWB, 8.0l 10 cyl
X—check digit, 0 thru 9 or X
S—model year, 1995
V—assembly plant (New Mack)
100001—consecutive sequence number

Engine code
E—8.0l V-10 400 hp

Options and retail prices
SRDS27 2 dr Roadster	$56,000.00
EWB 8.0l V-10	Std
DEC Manual 6 speed transmission	Std
HAA Air conditioning	1,200.00
VK-8 Removable hardtop	2,500.00

Exterior color codes
Viper Red	PRN
Viper Black	PX3
Viper Emerald Green	PGQ
Viper Bright Yellow	PJE

Interior trim codes
Gray/Black leather	MLXD
Tan/Black leather	MLXK

Facts
Exterior and interior color choices were unchanged from 1994. The major change for 1995 was the use of a new one-piece cast intake manifold.

Of the total 1,577 units built, 1,422 were for the U.S. market, 114 for Canada and 41 for export. Exterior color choice was divided as follows: 514 in Viper Black, 458 in Viper Red, 307 in Viper Green and 298 in Viper Bright Yellow. There were 1,005 cars fitted with the Gray/Black interior and 572 with the tan/black combination.

Chapter 22

1996 Dodge Viper

Production

RT/10 Roadster	721
GTS Coupe	1,166
Total	1,887

Serial numbers

1B3AR65ETV100001
1—country, U.S.A.
B—make, Dodge
3—vehicle type, passenger car
A—restraint system, air bag
R—vehicle line, Viper
6—series, Special/Sport
5—body style (5-convertible, open body, 9-coupe)
E—engine, EWB, 8.0l 10 cyl
X—check digit, 0 thru 9 or X
T—model year, 1996
V—assembly plant (Conner Ave.)
100001—consecutive sequence number

Engine code

E—8.0l V-10 415/450 hp

Options and retail prices

SRDS27 2 dr Roadster	$58,600.00
SRDS29 2 dr GTS Coupe	66,000.00
EWB 8.0l V-10	Std
DEC Manual 6 speed transmission	Std
HAA Air conditioning (RT/10)	1,200.00
VK-7 Removable hardtop (RT/10)	2,500.00

Exterior color codes

Viper Red	PRN
Viper Black	6SX
Stone White	6SW
Viper Blue	6SB

Interior trim codes

Black/Black leather	MLX9

Facts

The Viper received considerable changes for the 1996 model year. The chassis was modified so that it became torsionally stiffer. A new dual outlet tip exhaust system replaced the previous side-exhaust which exited at the rear. The new exhaust system provided 20 percent less back pressure which helped to increase output to 415 hp at 5,200 rpm and torque to 488 ft.-lbs. at 3,600 rpm. For added durability, a power steering cooler was added. Other changes included a windage tray for the engine, and a stronger differential and driveshafts.

The suspension was also improved through the use of cast aluminum control arms and knuckles; the previous units were made of steel and cast-iron. This helped reduce weight by 60 lbs. Besides the use of these components, the suspension mounting points were changed, and stiffer springs (18 percent front, 12 percent rear), along with recalibrated shock absorbers, made the Viper handle better than previous models.

The RT/10 also got much-needed sliding glass side-windows to replace the previous curtains. These can be retrofitted to earlier Viper RT/10 models.

Five-spoke wheels, the same ones used on the 1993 GTS show cars, were also used on the RT/10 along with new Michelin Pilot SX-MXX3 tires. Wheel and tire size remains unchanged from 1995.

Exterior colors for the RT/10 were Viper Red, Viper Black and Stone White. Interior color choice was limited to black leather. However, there were three cars built with gray leather and two with tan leather interiors.

The big news for 1996 was the addition of a coupe to the Viper line. This was the GTS. Although the front of the GTS looked similar to the RT/10, the rear was different. The hood had a large NACA duct, louvers above both front wheels, and right behind the passenger door is a race-type aluminum quick-fill gas cap. The roof of the car also has twin bulges to improve interior head room.

The GTS interior is also different from the RT/10s. The instrument panel layout is revised, and the GTS also includes dual air bags. The standard stereo system includes a CD player, and the leather seats have a pump-up lumbar feature.

The V-10 engine was also redesigned for the GTS. New head and block castings, along with a revised cooling system, resulted in an engine that weighs 80 lbs. less, but also produces 450 hp at 5200 rpm and 490 ft.-lbs. torque at 3,700 rpm. The compression ratio increased to 9.6:1.

Exterior color of the GTS coupe was limited to Viper Blue for 1996. However, of the total 1,166 1996 Vipers, five cars were actually white. All but five GTS coupes were equipped with polished wheels; five were equipped with white painted wheels.

*1996 Dodge Viper
GTS Coupe*

Chapter 23

1997 Dodge Viper

Production

RT/10 Roadster	117
GTS Coupe	1,671
Total	1,788

Serial numbers

1B3AR65EVV100001
1—country, U.S.A.
B—make, Dodge
3—vehicle type, passenger car
A—restraint system, air bag
R—vehicle line, Viper
6—series, Special/Sport
5—body style (5-convertible, open body, 9-coupe)
E—engine, EWB, 8.0l 10 cyl
X—check digit, 0 thru 9 or X
V—model year, 1997
V—assembly plant (Conner Ave.)
100001—consecutive sequence number

Engine code

E—8.0l V-10 450 hp

Options and retail prices

SRDS27 2 dr Roadster	$66,000.00
SRDS29 2 dr GTS Coupe	66,000.00
EWB 8.0l V-10	Std
DEC Manual 6 speed transmission	Std
HAA Air conditioning delete (RT/10)	(1,000.00)
VKR* hardtop, delete (RT/10)	(2,500.00)
Cast aluminum polished wheels	300.00
*VKR-red, VKB-blue	

Exterior color codes

Viper Red	PRN
Viper Blue w/dual white stripes	6SB

Interior trim codes

Black/Black leather	MLX9
Black/Tan leather	CLXK

Facts

All the changes that were made on the 1996 GTS coupe were carried over and applied to the 1997 RT/10 as well.

Both Viper models were available in either Viper Red or Viper Blue with white painted stripes. The GTS was only available with a black leather interior while the RT/10 could be equipped with

1997 Dodge Viper GTS Coupe

either black or black/tan leather. There were 114 RT/10s built with the black interior and three with the tan.

There were several colored wheel combinations available in 1997. The blue RT/10 and blue or red GTSs could be equipped with the standard Sparkle Silver (unpainted) wheels or with the optional polished wheels.

Red RT/10s had standard Sparkle Gold wheels with gold exterior decals. The gold wheels were also available on the red GTS. Sparkle Silver and polished wheels were also available on the red RT/10. Both red RT/10s and GTSs were also available with yellow painted wheels and yellow decals.

In actuality, 114 RT/10s were equipped with the polished wheels and only 3 with the Gold Sparkle wheels. There were 1,657 GTSs that came with polished wheels and 14 red GTSs came with the yellow painted wheels.

Blue RT/10s were equipped with blue interior accents: blue steering wheel rim, shifter and handbrake lever. Red RT/10s with the black interior came with similar, but red accents, while red RT/10s with the tan interior came with the same accents in tan.

Although not a street production model, the GTS-R became available for racers. This was an all-out racing version of the GTS coupe. Most of the body panels are made of carbon fiber or carbon fiber/kevlar composite materials. A large rear wing was situated at the rear and in the interior, and a roll cage, racing harness and racing steering wheel were added.

Wheels were BBS units measuring 26.5x12 in. front and 26.5x 14 in. rear shod with Pilot SX radials. The 8.0l V-10 was modified to produce 525 hp and a fully race-prepped version putting out 700 hp was available at extra cost.

Chapter 24

1998 Dodge Viper

Production

RT/10 Roadster	379
GTS Coupe	837
Total	1,216

Serial numbers

1B3ER65EWV100001
1—country, U.S.A.
B—make, Dodge
3—vehicle type, passenger car
E—restraint system, driver & passenger air bags, manual seatbelts
R—vehicle line, Viper
6—series, Special/Sport
5—body style (5-convertible, open body, 9-coupe)
E—engine, EWB, 8.0l 10 cyl
X—check digit, 0 thru 9 or X
W—model year, 1998
V—assembly plant (Conner Ave.)
100001—consecutive sequence number

Engine code

E—8.0l V-10 450/460 hp

Options and retail prices

SRDS27 2 dr Roadster	$64,000.00
SRDS29 2 dr GTS Coupe	66,500.00
SRDS29 2 dr GT2	84,500.00
EWB 8.0l V-10	Std
DEC Manual 6 speed transmission	Std
HCD Air conditioning delete (RT/10)	(1,000.00)
VKR Body-colored hardtop	2,500.00
CSD Tonneau cover	250.00
WFL Cast aluminum polished wheels	500.00

Exterior color codes

Viper Red	PRN
Viper Bright Silver Metallic	PA9
Stone White	6SW

Extra cost two-tone paint:

Viper Bright Silver Metallic/Viper Blue Pearl Coat secondary	6SB
Viper Red/Viper Bright Silver Metallic Clear Coat secondary	6RS

Interior trim codes

Black/Black leather	CLX9
Black/Tan leather	CLXK

1998 Dodge Viper GT2

Facts

Changes to the 1998 models were minimal. New tubular exhaust manifolds reduced emission and weight, and a passenger side air bag cut-off switch was added. A new color was added, Viper Bright Silver Metallic. The only other color available was Viper Red.

There were 102 GT2 Championship Edition Viper GTS coupes built to commemorate Chrysler's FIA GT2 World Championship. Emulating the race GTS-R models, the GT2s were painted white with blue stripes and had a distinctive front fascia, black ground effects, side sills, a front air-splitter and a carbon fiber rear wing. Special exterior badging and graphics were also included.

The GT2 also used the Team ORECA five-point restraint system and a K&N air cleaner with smooth air cleaner hoses. Eighteen-inch forged aluminum BBS wheels with chrome Viper Head center caps shod with Michelin Pilot SX-MXX3 tires were also part of the package. The blue leather interior included a numbered GT2 owners portfolio specific to each car with signed and numbered photos of Team ORECA and Driver Champion Justin Bell, special collectible items, a numbered camera with photos of each car in actual production, and a unique fitted car cover embroidered with each car's VIN.

The GT2's engine was the recipient of a mild power boost. The engine was rated at 460 hp at 5200 rpm and 500 ft.-lbs. torque at 3700 rpm.

There were 252 RT/10s finished in Viper Red and 127 in Viper Bright Silver Metallic. Of the GTSs, 447 were painted Viper Red (of which 11 had silver stripes), 288 in Silver (21 of which had blue stripes), and there were also the 102 GT2s in white with blue leather interior.

Of the 379 RT/10s built, 341 were for the U.S. market and 38 for Canada. There were no export versions. Of the 837 GTSs built, 731 were for the U.S. market, 32 for Canada and 74 were exported to other countries.

Chapter 25

1999 Dodge Viper

Production*
RT/10 Roadster	679
GTS Coupe	707
Total	1,386

*projected as of 9/99

Serial numbers
1B3ER65EXV100001
1—country, U.S.A.
B—make, Dodge
3—vehicle type, passenger car
E—restraint system, driver & passenger air bags, manual seatbelts
R—vehicle line, Viper
6—series, Special/Sport
5—body style (5-convertible, open body, 9-coupe)
E—engine, EWB, 8.0l 10 cyl
X—check digit, 0 thru 9 or X
X—model year, 1999
V—assembly plant (Conner Ave.)
100001—consecutive sequence number

Engine code
E—8.0l V-10 450/460 hp

Options and retail prices
SRDS27 2 dr Roadster	$65,725.00
SRDS29 2 dr GTS Coupe	68,225.00
EWB 8.0l V-10	Std
DEC Manual 6 speed transmission	Std
VK7 Body-colored hardtop (RT/10)	2,500.00
CSD Tonneau cover (RT/10)	250.00
AGF Comfort Group (GTS)	910.00
ACR Competition Group	10,000.00
APV Dual painted stripes (GTS)	2,000.00
MLXU Connolly Package	500.00

Exterior color codes
Viper Red	PRN
Viper Bright Silver Metallic	PA9
Viper Black	PX3

Interior trim codes
Black/Black leather	CLX9
Cognac	MLXU

Stripes codes
Viper Bright Silver Metallic (w/PX3 or PRN)	QA9
Viper GTS Blue Pearl coat (w/PA9)	QBE

Facts

The 1999 Viper came with power exterior mirrors, a new shift knob and a remote release for the GTS's glass hatch. Aluminum was used to accent the interior, and new 18-in. aluminum wheels were used on all models. Besides the standard black leather interior, an optional Connolly leather in Cognac was available.

The only major addition to the option list was the ACR Edition. ACR stands for American Club Racer—a street-legal package that is race-worthy enough to compete in certain street-legal classes. The ACR was available only on the GTS coupe model and in any standard color combination.

The ACR package includes special ACR badging and graphics including a commemorative dash plate. The engine received the same 10 hp improvement as the 1998 GT2, and the ACR also used the BBS 18-in. wheels with Michelin Pilot Sport tires. Vents replaced the front lamps, and the standard Viper A/C system and audio system were deleted. Koni racing shock absorbers and special Merritor springs were also part of the package.

Although the air conditioning and audio system were deleted with the ACR package, the ACR could be equipped with them if the AGF Comfort Group was ordered.

1999 Dodge Viper ACR

Chapter 26

2000 Dodge Viper

Serial numbers

1B3ER65EZV100001
1—country, U.S.A.
B—make, Dodge
3—vehicle type, passenger car
E—restraint system, driver & passenger air bags, manual seatbelts
R—vehicle line, Viper
6—series, Special/Sport
5—body style (5-convertible, open body, 9-coupe)
E—engine, EWB, 8.0l 10 cyl
X—check digit, 0 thru 9 or X
Y—model year, 2000
V—assembly plant (Conner Ave.)
100001—consecutive sequence number

Engine code

E—8.0l V-10 450/460 hp

Options and retail price

SRDS27 2 dr Roadster	$67,225.00
SRDS29 2 dr GTS Coupe	69,725.00
EWB 8.0l V-10	Std
DEC Manual 6 speed transmission	Std
VK7 Body-colored hardtop (RT/10)	2,500.00
CSD Tonneau cover (RT/10)	250.00
AGF Comfort Group (GTS)	910.00
ACR Competition Group	10,000.00
APV Dual painted stripes (GTS)	2,000.00
MLXU Connolly Leather Package	750.00

Exterior color codes

Viper Red	PRN
Viper Steel Gray	PS6
Viper Black	PX3

Stripes code

Viper Bright Silver Metallic w/PRN, PS6 or PX3	QA9

Hardtop color codes

Viper Red w/PRN	VKR	**Interior trim codes**	
Viper Black w/PX3	VKX	Black/Black leather	CLX9
Viper Steel Gray w/PS6	VKH	Connolly Package	MLXU

Facts

The 2000 Viper was essentially a carryover from 1999. A new color, Viper Steel Gray, replaced the previous Viper Bright Silver.

Chapter 27

1972 Dodge Challenger

Production

2 dr hardtop 6 cyl	842	2 dr hardtop Rallye 8 cyl	6,902
2 dr hardtop 8 cyl	15.175	Total	22,919

Serial numbers

JH23B2B100001

J — car line, Dodge Challenger

H — price class (H-high, S-special)

23 — body type (23-2 dr hardtop)

B — engine code

2 — last digit of model year

B — assembly plant code (B-Hamtramck)

100001 — consecutive sequence number

Serial number located on plate attached to left side of dash panel, visible through windshield.

Engine codes

C — 225 ci 1V 6 cyl 110 hp

G — 318 ci 2V V-8 150 hp

H — 340 ci 4V V-8 240 hp

Head casting numbers

318 ci — 2843675

340 ci — 3418915

Carburetors

318 ci 2V V-8 — Carter BBD6149S/manual, BBD6151A/manual w/NOx, BBD6150S/automatic, BBD6152S/automatic w/NOx

340 ci 4V V-8 — Carter TQ6138S/manual, TQ6139S/automatic

Option order codes and retail prices

JH23 2 dr hardtop 6 cyl	$2,778.00
JH23 2 dr hardtop V-8	2,904.00
JS23 2 dr hardtop Rallye	3,056.00
A01 Light Package	35.00
A06 Basic Group, NA w/340 engine	294.30
A36 Performance Axle Package (w/340 ci only)	59.90
B41 Front power disc brakes	62.30
C16 Console	51.60
D21 Manual 4 speed transmission (w/340 ci only)	192.85
D34 TorqueFlite transmission	203.35
(w/340 ci)	223.30
D51 2.76 axle ratio (w/340 ci & D34; NC w/D91)	12.20
D53 3.23 axle ratio (w/225 ci & 318 ci w/D34)	12.20
D91 Sure-Grip differential (std w/A36, NA 6 cyl)	40.65
E55 340 ci 4V engine (Challenger)	245.85
(Rallye)	179.00
F28 70 amp battery	13.30
G11 Tinted glass — all windows	35.85
G15 Tinted windshield	24.35

G35 Chrome outside left racing mirror	14.60
G36 Body-color remote left, manual right dual	
racing mirrors (w/A06)	10.50
(wo/A06)	25.10
G37 Chrome remote outside left & manual right	
racing mirrors (w/A06)	10.50
(wo/A06)	25.10
H31 Rear window defogger	28.15
H51 Air conditioning (NA 6 cyl, NA w/3 speed manual)	364.80
J21 Electric clock (std w/J97)	15.70
J25 Variable-speed wipers w/electric washers	
(std w/J97)	10.35
J52 Inside hood release	9.50
J55 Undercoating w/hood insulator pad	20.25
J97 Rallye instrument panel (w/8 cyl engines w/A06)	74.70
(w/8 cyl engines wo/A06)	85.00
M05 Door edge protectors	5.80
M25 Sill molding	12.70
M51 Power-operated sunroof w/vinyl roof	434.00
M85 Bumper guards, front & rear rubber inserts	26.65
N95 Emission control system & testing (required Calif)	25.55
R11 Solid-state AM radio (wo/A06)	59.40
R26 Solid-state AM radio w/stereo tape player (wo/A06)	196.25
AM radio w/stereo tape (w/A06)	136.85
R31 Rear seat speakers, single (requires R11)	13.45
R32 Rear seat speakers, dual (w/R35 or R36)	24.35
R35 AM/FM stereo radio (wo/A06)	191.40
(w/A06)	132.00
S13 Suspension, Rallye (std w/340 ci)	13.95
S77 Power steering (std w/A06)	104.10
W11 Deluxe wheel covers, std w/A06	24.50
W21 Set of 4 Rallye road wheels w/std spare wo/A06	52.80
W21 Set of 4 Rallye road wheels w/std spare w/A06	28.35
W23 Set of 4 chrome styled road wheels w/std spare	
wo/A06	81.10
W23 Set of 4 chrome styled road wheels w/std spare	
w/A06	56.65
High-impact paint colors	13.45
Vinyl roof	80.20
Vinyl side molding	13.90
Tires	
(without A06, replaces 7.35x14 BSW tires)	
T22 7.35x14 WSW	26.10
T34 F78x14 WSW	67.15
T86 F70x14 WSW (requires S13)	85.75
T87 F70x14 RWL (requires S13)	96.95
Tires	
(without A06 replaces F70x14 WSW tires)	
T34 F78x14 BSW	NC
T87 F70x14 RWL	11.25
Tires with A06 replaces 7.35x14 WSW	
T34 F78x14 WSW	41.05

Exterior color codes

Light Blue	HB1
Bright Blue Metallic	HB5
Bright Red	FE5
Light Green Metallic	GF3
Dark Green Metallic	GF7
Eggshell White	GW1
Black	TX9
Light Gold	GY5
Gold Metallic	GY8
Dark Gold Metallic	GY9
Dark Tan Metallic	GT8
Light Gunmetal Metallic	GA4
Medium Tan Metallic	GT6
Super Blue	GB3
Hemi Orange	EV2
Top Banana	FY1

Interior trim codes

Blue	B6B5
Green	B6F6
Black	B6X9
White	B6XW
Gold	B6Y3

Vinyl roof color codes

Black	V1X
White	V1W
Gold	V1Y
Green	V1F

Side stripes codes

Black	V6X
White	V6W

Facts

The Challenger got a new front grille opening and a restyled taillight panel with four taillight pods, two on each side.

All the big-block engines and the 198 ci six-cylinder were eliminated from the option list. No convertibles were offered either. Two models were offered—the Challenger and the Challenger Rallye, which replaced the R/T as the performance model.

All 1972 Challengers were hardtops, as the rear side windows were functional and not fixed. The regular Challenger could be had with the 225 ci six-cylinder or the 318 ci V-8. All 1972 Challenger engines came with electronic ignition.

The Rallye came with strobe side stripes, a performance hood, Rallye wheels, heavy-duty suspension and only one engine, the 340 ci small-block. Standard transmission was a three-speed manual. Dual exhaust with bright tips still gave that performance look from the rear. No 15 in. wheels — and, accordingly, no 60 Series tires— were available.

1972 Dodge Challenger

Chapter 28

1973 Dodge Challenger

Production
2 dr hardtop 8 cyl   27,930

Serial numbers
JH23G3B100001
J — car line, Dodge Challenger
H — price class (H-High)
23 — body type (23-2 dr hardtop)
G — engine code
3 — last digit of model year
B — assembly plant code (B-Hamtramck)
100001 — consecutive sequence number
  Serial number located on plate attached to left side of dash panel, visible through windshield.

Engine codes
G — 318 ci 2V V-8 150 hp
H — 340 ci 4V V-8 240 hp

Head casting numbers
318 ci — 2843675
340 ci — 3671587

Carburetors
318 ci 2V V-8 — Carter BBD6316S/manual, BBD6343S/manual Calif, BBD6317S/automatic, BBD6344S/automatic Calif
340 ci 4V V-8 — Carter TQ6318S/manual, TQ341S/ manual Calif, TQ6319S/automatic, TQ6340S/automatic Calif

Option order codes and retail prices
JH23 2 dr hardtop V-8	$3,011.00
A01 Light Package	35.35
A04 Basic Group	297.85
A36 Performance Axle Package (w/340 ci only)	60.50
A57 Rallye Package (w/A04)	145.45
(wo/A04)	182.25
B41 Front power disc brakes (required w/340 ci)	40.95
C16 Console	52.20
D21 Manual 4 speed transmission (w/340 ci only)	195.25
D34 TorqueFlite transmission (w/318 ci)	206.00
(w/340 ci)	226.05
D53 3.23 axle ratio (w/318 ci w/D34)	12.30
D91 Sure-Grip differential (std w/A36)	41.10
E55 340 ci 4V engine w/A57	181.25
(wo/A57)	248.90
F23 375 amp battery	13.40
G11 Tinted glass — all windows	36.30
G35 Chrome outside left racing mirror	14.80

G36 Body-color remote left, manual right dual racing	
mirrors (w/A04)	10.65
(wo/A04)	25.40
G37 Chrome remote outside left & manual right racing	
mirrors (w/A04)	10.65
(wo/A04)	25.40
H31 Rear window defogger	28.45
H51 Air conditioning (NA w/3 speed manual, required	
B41)	369.30
J21 Electric clock (std w/J97)	15.85
J25 3 speed windshield wipers w/electric washers	10.45
J52 Inside hood release	9.55
J54 Sport hood (std w/A57 & w/340 ci)	19.95
J55 Undercoating w/hood insulator pad	20.50
J97 Rallye instrument panel (w/A04)	75.65
(wo/A04)	86.05
M25 Sill molding	12.80
N95 Emission control system & testing (required Calif)	25.85
R11 Solid-state AM radio (wo/A04)	60.15
R26 Solid-state AM radio w/stereo tape cassette player	
(wo/A04)	198.65
AM radio w/stereo tape (w/A04)	138.50
R31 Rear seat speakers, single (requires R11)	13.60
R32 Rear seat speakers, dual (w/R26 or R35)	24.65
R35 AM/FM stereo radio (wo/A04)	193.75
(w/A04)	133.65
S13 HD suspension (std w/340 ci)	14.05
S77 Power steering (std w/A04)	105.40
W11 Deluxe wheel covers (std w/A04)	24.80
W21 Rallye road wheels (w/A04)	28.65
W21 Rallye road wheels (wo/A04)	53.40
W23 Chrome styled road wheels (w/A04)	57.30
W23 Chrome styled road wheels (wo/A04)	82.05
High-impact paint colors	13.60
Vinyl roof	81.15
Vinyl side molding (std w/A57)	14.00
Tires	
(replaces 5 7.35x14 tires — extra charge)	
T22 7.35x14 WSW (std w/318 ci)	26.40
T34 F78x14 WSW	67.85
T86 F70x14 WSW (requires S13)	86.65
T87 F70x14 RWL (requires S13)	98.00
Tires	
(w/A57 or 340 ci)	
(replaces 5 F70x14 WSW tires — extra charge)	
T34 F78x14 BSW	NC
T87 F70x14 RWL	11.35
Tires w/A04 replaces 7.35x14 WSW	
T34 F78x14 WSW	41.45

Exterior color codes

Black	TX9
Dark Silver Metallic	JA5
Eggshell White	EW1
Parchment	HL4
Light Gold	JY3
Dark Gold Metallic	JY9
Gold Metallic	JY6
Bronze Metallic	GK6
Pale Green	JF1
Dark Green Metallic	JF8
Light Blue	HB1
Super Blue	TB3
Bright Blue Metallic	GB5
Bright Red	FE5
Top Banana	FY1
Light Green Metallic	GF3

Interior trim codes

Blue	A6B5
Green	A6F6
Black	A6X9
Black/White	A6XW

Vinyl roof color codes

Black	V1X
White	V1W
Gold	V1Y
Green	V1F

Side stripes codes

Black	V7X
White	V7W
Blue	V7B
Green	V7F
Gold	V7Y

Facts

The most significant change from 1972 was the deletion of the 225 ci six-cylinder engine. Standard and only engine on the Challenger was the 318 ci V-8; the Rallye model came with the 340 ci V-8.

Suspension and driveline components remained unchanged. You could tell 1972s from 1973s by the size of the bumper pads: 1973s came with larger pads.

1973 Dodge Challenger

Chapter 29

1974 Dodge Challenger

Production
2 dr hardtop 8 cyl   11,354

Serial numbers
JH23G4B100001

J — car line, Dodge Challenger
H — price class (H-high, S-Special)
23 — body type (23-2 dr hardtop)
G — engine code
4 — last digit of model year
B — assembly plant code (B-Hamtramck)
100001 — consecutive sequence number
    Serial number located on place attached to left side of dash
panel, visible through windshield.

Engine codes
G — 318 ci 2V V-8 150 hp
J — 360 ci 4V V-8 245 hp

Head casting numbers
318 ci — 2843675
340 ci — 3671587

Carburetors
318 ci 2V V-8 — Carter BBD6464S/manual, BBD6465S, BBD8028S/
    automatic, BBD6467S, BBD8018S/automatic Calif
360 ci 4V V-8 — Carter TQ6452S/manual, TQ6454S/manual Calif,
    TQ6453S/automatic, TQ6455S/automatic Calif

Option order codes and retail prices
JH23 2 dr hardtop V-8	$3,109.00
A01 Light Package	36.60
A04 Basic Group, NA w/360 ci engine	307.10
A36 Performance Axle Package (w/360 ci only)	62.85
A57 Sport Decor Package (w/A04)	151.35
(wo/A04)	189.55
B41 Front power disc brakes (required w/360 ci)	42.55
C16 Console	54.25
D21 Manual 4 speed transmission (w/360 ci only)	203.05
D34 TorqueFlite transmission (w/318 ci)	214.20
(w/360 ci)	235.05
D53 3.23 axle ratio (w/318 ci w/D34)	12.75
D91 Sure-Grip differential (std w/A36)	42.70
E58 360 ci 4V engine (w/A57)	188.50
(wo/A57)	258.85
F23 375 amp battery	13.90
G11 Tinted glass — all windows	37.35
G54 Chrome remote control left racing mirror (w/A04)	15.35

G74 Chrome remote outside left & manual right racing mirrors (w/A04)		11.05
(wo/A04)		26.40
G75 Body-color remote left, manual right dual racing mirrors (w/A04)		11.05
(wo/A04)		26.40
H31 Rear window defogger		29.55
H51 Air conditioning (NA w/3 speed manual, required B41)		384.05
J21 Electric clock (std w/J97)		17.35
J25 3 speed windshield wipers w/electric washers		10.85
J52 Inside hood release		9.90
J55 Undercoating w/hood silencer pad		21.30
J97 Rallye 1 (w/A04)		78.65
(wo/A04)		89.45
M25 Sill molding (std w/A51)		13.30
N95 Emission control system & testing (required Calif)		26.85
R11 Solid-state AM radio (std w/A04)		62.55
R31 Rear seat speakers, single (requires R11)		14.10
R32 Rear seat speakers, dual, (w/R35)		25.60
R35 AM/FM stereo radio (wo/A04)		201.50
(w/A04)		138.95
S13 HD suspension (std w/360 ci)		14.60
S42 Front sway bar (required w/radial tires, std w/S13)		9.40
S77 Power steering (std w/A04)		107.25
W11 Deluxe wheel covers		25.75
W21 Rallye road wheels		55.50
W23 Chrome styled road wheels		85.30
Vinyl roof		84.35
Vinyl side molding (NA w/body tape stripes)		14.55

Tires

(replaces 5 7.35x14 tires — extra charge)

T22 7.35x14 WSW (std w/Challenger 318)		27.45
T34 F78x14 WSW		70.50
T36 FR78x14 WSW (requires S13 or S42)		180.25
T86 F70x14 WSW (requires S13)		88.90
T87 F70x14 RWL (requires S13)		100.65

Tires

(w/A57 or 360 ci engine)

(replaces 5 F70x14 WSW tires — extra charge)

T34 F78x14 BSW		NC
T36 FR78x14 WSW (requires S13 or S42)		91.40
T87 F70x14 RWL		11.75

Tires

(w/A04 replaces 7.35x14 WSW)

T34 F78x14 WSW		43.10

Exterior color codes

Gold Metallic	JY6	Frost Green Metallic	KG2
Dark Gold Metallic	JY9	Avocado Gold Metallic	KJ6
Sienna Metallic	KT5	Deep Sherwood Metallic	KG8
Dark Moonstone Metallic	KL8	Lucerne Blue Metallic	GE7
Burnished Red Metallic	GE7	Powder Blue	KB1

Exterior color codes

Yellow Blaze	KY5
Golden Fawn	KY4
Parchment	HL4
Bright Red	FE5
Eggshell White	EW1
Black	TX9

Interior trim codes

Blue	A6B6
Green	A6G8
Black	A6X9
White	A6XW

Vinyl roof color codes

Black	V1X
White	V1W
Gold	V1Y
Green	V1G

Side tape stripes codes

Black	V6X
White	V6W

Facts

The year 1974 was the last for the Challenger. During its abbreviated model run, the most significant change from 1973 was the substitution of the 360 ci V-8 in place of the 340 engine.

A three-speed manual was standard, with the four-speed manual and TorqueFlite optional.

Although radial tires were not standard equipment, they were available.

Front and rear bumpers, complying with federal requirements, now could withstand a 5 mph impact.

1974 Dodge Challenger

Chapter 30

1967 Dodge Coronet R/T

Production
2 dr hardtop 8 cyl	9,553
Convertible 8 cyl	628
Total	10,181

Serial numbers
WS23L71100001

W — car line, Dodge Coronet

S — price class, special

23 — body type (23-2 dr hardtop, 27-convertible)

L — engine code

7 — last digit of model year

1 — assembly plant code (1-Lynch Road, 5-Los Angeles, 7-St Louis)

100001 — consecutive sequence number

Serial number located on plate attached to left front door hinge post.

Engine codes
J — 426 ci 2x4V V-8 425 hp

L — 440 ci 4V V-8 375 hp

Head casting numbers
426 ci — 2780559

440 ci — 2780915

V-8 carburetors
426 ci — Carter AFB4139S/front, AFB4140S/rear, AFB4343S/rear, AFB4324S/automatic w/CAP, AFB4325S/automatic w/CAP

440 ci — Carter AFB4326S/manual, AFB4328S/manual w/CAP, AFB4327S/automatic, AFB4329S/automatic w/CAP

Distributors
426 ci — 2642482 IBS-4006P, 2642832 IBS-4006W/w/CAP

440 ci — 2642899 IBS-4006Z/manual, 2642911 IBS-4006Y/manual w/CAP, 2642748/automatic, 2642811/automatic w/CAP

Option order codes and retail prices
R/T V-8
WS23 2 dr hardtop	$3,199.00
WS27 Convertible	3,438.00
73 426 2x4V engine	564.00
292 Two-tone paint (NA convertible)	21.55
294 Paint — Sport stripe	30.65
306-7 Vinyl roof	75.10
351 Basic Group	173.25
355 Light Package (hardtop)	21.70
(convertible)	17.90

393 Manual 4 speed transmission (408 required)	NC
408 Sure-Grip differential	37.60
HD (required w/393)	138.90
411 Air conditioning w/heater	338.45
416 Heater (delete)	(70.30)
418 Rear window defogger (NA convertible)	20.20
421 Transaudio AM radio	57.35
426 Rear seat speaker (NA convertible)	14.05
451 Power brakes	41.75
456 Power steering	89.65
458 Power windows	100.25
471 Cleaner Air Package (mandatory Calif)	25.00
479 Disc brakes (requires 451)	69.50
481 Front bumper guards	16.80
482 Rear bumper guards	14.05
483 Front & rear bumper guards	30.85
484 Electric clock	15.30
486 Console	52.85
521 Tinted glass — all windows (exc convertible backglass)	39.50
522 Tinted glass — windshield only	21.20
531 Left headrests (w/bucket seats only)	20.95
532 Right headrests (w/bucket seats only)	20.95
533 Left & right headrests (w/bucket seats only)	41.90
536 Remote control outside left mirror	5.45
537 Manual outside right mirrors	6.35
556 Center passenger front lap belt (485 required R/T)	9.10
557 Center passenger rear lap belt	9.10
568 2 front shoulder belts	26.45
571 Full-horn-ring steering wheel	5.25
573 Deluxe wood-grain steering wheel	25.95
577 Tachometer (486 required)	48.70
579 Undercoating w/underhood pad	15.40
580 Set of 4 road wheels	97.30
581 Deluxe wheel covers	21.30
583 Sport wheel covers	38.95
589 Variable-speed windshield wipers	4.95
591 46 amp alternator	10.50
708 Special buffed paint	20.95
Vinyl trim	24.20
Tires — set of 5	
(replaces 7.75x14 Red Streak tires)	
43 7.75x14 WSW	NC

Exterior color codes*

Buffed Silver Metallic	AA1	Dark Copper Metallic	HH1
Black	BB1	Light Turquoise Metallic	KK1
Medium Blue Metallic	CC1	Dark Turquoise Metallic	LL1
Light Blue Metallic	DD1	Turbine Bronze Metallic	MM1
Dark Blue Metallic	EE1	Bright Red	PP1
Bright Blue Metallic	881	Dark Red Metallic	QQ1
Dark Green Metallic	GG1	Yellow	RR1

Exterior color codes*

Soft Yellow	SS1
Copper Metallic	TT1
White	WW1
Light Tan	XX1
Light Medium Tan Metallic	YY1
Gold Metallic	ZZ1
Mauve Metallic	661

Interior trim codes

	Vinyl bucket seats
Color	
Blue	P6B
Black/Gold	P6E
Copper	P6K
Black	P6X
Red	P6R
White/Black	P6W

Vinyl roof color codes

Black	306
White	307
Green	304

Convertible top color codes

Green	300
Black	301
White	302

Stripe color codes

White	31W
Black	31B
Dark Red Metallic	31H
Dark Blue Metallic	31C
Light Tan Metallic	31Y
Medium Copper Metallic	31S

Facts

The Dodge Coronet R/T was equivalent to Plymouth's GTX. R/T stood for Road and Track. The R/T differed from other Coronets, as it used a grille that looked similar to the one used by the Dodge Charger—without the retractable headlights. In the center of the hood, in front of the cowl, were simulated scoops. R/T badges appeared on the grille and on each rear quarter panel. Deletable side stripes were also part of the R/T.

The R/T was available as either a hardtop or a convertible. Standard engine was the 375 hp 440 Magnum, with the 426 Hemi optional. The suspension included heavy-duty torsion bars, springs, shocks and front sway bar. Brakes were four-wheel drums, but front discs were optional.

The 440 4V engine was in its second year of production in 1967, but this was the first year of the 440 hp cylinder heads. They were closed-chamber heads with 2.08 in. intake and 1.74 in. exhaust valves. Because both the intake and exhaust ports were reshaped, they provided considerably more flow than they had on the previous 440 cylinder head.

Hemi-powered R/Ts were few. Only 59 hardtops were built (27 with TorqueFlite and 28 with four-speed), and just two convertibles were built (one with TorqueFlite and one with four-speed).

Chapter 31

1968 Dodge Coronet R/T and Super Bee

Production

R/T
		Super Bee	
2 dr hardtop 8 cyl	9,989	2 dr coupe 8 cyl	7,842
Convertible 8 cyl	569		
Total	10,558		

Serial numbers

WS21L8A100001

W — car line, Dodge Coronet

S — price class (S-special, M-medium)

21 — body type (21-2 dr coupe, 23-2 dr hardtop, 27 - convertible)

L — engine code

8 — last digit of model year

A — assembly plant code (A-Lynch Road, E-Los Angeles, G-St Louis)

100001 — consecutive sequence number.

Serial number located on plate attached to left side of dash panel, visible through windshield.

Engine codes

H — 383 ci 4V V-8 335 hp

J — 426 ci 2x4V V-8 425 hp

L — 440 ci 4V V-8 375 hp

Head casting numbers

383 ci — 2843906

426 ci — 2780559

440 ci — 2843906

Carburetors

383 ci 4V V-8 — Carter AVS4426S/manual, AVS4401S/automatic, AVS46358/automatic w/AC

426 ci 2x4V — Carter AFB4430S/front, AFB4431/rear, AFB4432/rear automatic

440 ci 4V V-8 — Carter AVS4428S/manual, AVS4429S/automatic, AVS4637S/automatic w/AC

Distributors

383 ci — 2875356/manual, 2875358/automatic

426 ci — 2875140 IBS-4014A

440 ci — 2875102 IBS-4014/manual, 2875209/automatic

Option order codes and retail prices

Super Bee V-8
WM21 2 dr coupe	$3,027.00

R/T V-8
WS23 2 dr hardtop	3,353.00
WS27 Convertible	3,613.00
73 426 ci engine (Super Bee)	714.30
(R/T)	604.75

292 Two-tone paint		22.65
304 Vinyl roof		81.60
306 Vinyl roof		81.60
307 Vinyl roof		81.60
351 Basic Group (NA w/426 ci)		192.30
355 Light Package		16.05
358 High-performance axle (w/383 ci only; NA w/359)		87.50
359 Trailer Towing Package (wo/411)		24.50
(w/411)		14.35
395 TorqueFlite (w/Super Bee)		38.95
408 Sure-Grip differential		42.35
(w/HD performance axle)		138.90
411 Air conditioner (NA w/426 ci)		342.85
418 Rear window defogger (NA convertible)		21.30
420 Solid-state AM radio w/stereo tape player		196.25
421 Solid-state AM radio		61.55
426 Rear seat speaker (NA convertible)		14.05
451 Power brakes		41.75
456 Power steering		94.85
458 Power windows (R/T)		100.25
473 Automatic speed control (NA 426 ci, 451 required)		52.50
481 Front bumper guards		14.55
482 Rear bumper guards		15.55
483 Front & rear bumper guards		31.10
484 Clock (NA w/tachometer)		16.05
485 Center seat cusion & folding armrest (R/T)		52.85
486 Console (R/T)		52.85
495 Front disc brakes (451 requiredj)		72.95
508 Performance hood paint treatment		17.55
521 Tinted glass — all windows (exc convertible		
backglass)		39.50
522 Tinted glass — windshield only		22.35
529 Custom sill molding		20.45
531 Left head restraints		21.95
532 Right head restraints		21.95
533 Left & right head restraints		43.90
536 Remote outside left mirrors		9.40
537 Manual outside right mirrors		6.65
540 Belt molding (std w/vinyl roof)		13.20
547 Center pillar molding (2dr coupe, Super Bee)		4.10
551 Foam front seat cushion (w/bench seat)		8.30
565 Armrest w/ashtrays (Super Bee)		8.10
566 2 rear shoulder belts (NA convertible)		26.45
568 2 front shoulder belts (convertible)		26.45
571 Full-horn-ring steering wheel (Super Bee)		14.90
(R/T)		9.35
573 Sport simulated-wood-grain steering wheel (coupe)		31.20
(all others)		25.95
577 Tachometer (8 cyl only, NA w/clock)		48.70
579 Undercoating w/underhood pad		16.10
580 Styled road wheels, 14 in. (NA w/426 ci)		97.30

581 Deluxe wheel covers, 14 in.		21.30
15 in. (w/426 ci)		24.60
583 Sport wheel covers (NA w/426 ci)		36.25
589 3 speed windshield wipers		5.20
591 46 amp alternator		11.00
626 70 amp battery (std R/T)		8.10
708 Special buffed paint		21.95
Accent stripes		14.70
Paint — Sport stripe		20.40

Tires
(replaces F'70x14 Red Streak tires)

46 F'70x14 White Streak		NC

Exterior color codes

Silver Metallic	AA1	Bright Blue Metallic	QQ1
Black	BB1	Burgundy Metallic	RR1
Dark Blue Metallic	EE1	Yellow	SS1
Light Green Metallic	FF1	Medium Green Metallic	TT1
Medium Gold Metallic	JJ1	Light Blue Metallic	UU1
Dark Turquoise Metallic	LL1	White	WW1
Racing Green Metallic	GG1	Beige	XX1
Bronze Metallic	MM1	Medium Tan Metallic	YY1
Red	PP1		

Interior trim codes

Color	R/T vinyl bucket seats	Super Bee vinyl bench seats
Blue	S6B	H4B
White/Blue	S6C	H4C
White/Green	S6D	H4D
White/Black	S6W	H4W
White/Red	S6V	H4V
Green	S6F	H4F
Red	S6R	H4R
Black	S6X	H4X
Gold/Black	S6N*	—

*Two-door hardtop only.

Vinyl roof color codes

Green	304
Black	306
White	307

Convertible top color codes

Green	300
Black	301
White	302

Bodyside stripes codes*

Black	31B
Red	31H
White	31W
Blue	31C
Green	31P

*Standard R/T.

Bumblebee stripes codes*

Black	310
Red	314
White	317

*Standard Super Bee, optional R/T.

Facts

The R/T got a minor restyle in 1968. Most noticeable were the Power Bulge hood and the optional rear bumblebee stripes. Body-side stripes were standard with the R/T. R/T identification could be found on the front grille, on each front fender and on the taillight panel.

The standard Magnum 440 engine was still rated at 375 hp, but the cylinder heads featured an open-combustion-chamber design. In addition, the 440 received a higher-performance intake manifold and the Carter AVS (Air Valve Secondary) carburetor. The 426 Hemi was the only available engine option.

Complementing Plymouth's Road Runner was the Super Bee. Based on the Coronet two-door coupe, with pop-out rear windows, the Super Bee, too, was an economy racer. Its engine availability was identical with that of the Road Runner: the 335 hp 383 ci was standard and the 426 Hemi optional. The driveline and suspension, too, were identical.

The 335 hp version of the 383 engine was the strongest to date. It used the same cylinder heads as the 440 Magnum and, in the process, got a better-flowing intake manifold.

The Super Bee was set off by the same Power Bulge hood that came on the R/T and the distinctive Super Bee stripes and bee logo that wrapped around the tail end of the car. In the interior, bench seats were standard equipment.

R/T convertibles were assembled at the St Louis plant.

Hemi production for R/Ts was 220 in hardtops and nine in convertibles (eight with TorqueFlite and one with four-speed). Only 125 Super Bees were equipped with the Hemi (94 with TorqueFlite and 31 with four-speed).

1968 Dodge Coronet Super Bee

Chapter 32

1969 Dodge Coronet R/T and Super Bee

Production

Super Bee		R/T	
2 dr hardtop 8 cyl	18,475	2 dr coupe 8 cyl	6,518
2 dr coupe 8 cyl	7,650	Convertible 8 cyl	437
Total	26,125	Total	6,955

Serial numbers

WM23L9A100001

W — car line, Dodge Coronet

M — price class (M-medium, S-special)

23 — body type (21-2 dr coupe, 23-2 dr hardtop, 27 - convertible)

L — engine code

9 — last digit of model year

A — assembly plant code (A-Lynch Road, E-Los Angeles, G-St Louis)

100001 — consecutive sequence number.

    Serial number located on plate attached to left side of dash panel, visible through windshield.

Engine codes

H — 383 ci 4V V-8 335 hp

J — 426 ci 2x4V V-8 425 hp

L — 440 ci 4V V-8 375 hp

M — 440 ci 3x2V V-8 390 hp

Head casting numbers

383 ci — 2843906

426 ci — 2780559

440 ci — 2843906

Carburetors

383 ci 4V V-8 — Carter AVS46150S/manual, AVS4616S, AVS4638S & 4682S, 4638S/automatic

426 ci 2x4V V-8 — Carter AFB4619S/front, 4620S/rear manual, 4621S/rear automatic

440 ci 4V V-8 — Carter AVS4617S/manual, AVS4618S & 4640S/automatic

440 ci 3x2V V-8 — Holley R4393A/front, R4391/center manual, R4392/center automatic, R4394/rear

Distributors

383 ci — 2875750/manual, 2875731/automatic

426 ci — 2875140 IBS-4014A

440 ci — 2875772 IBS-4014B/manual, 2875758/automatic

440 ci 3x2V — 2875981 IBS-4017/manual, 2875982 IBS-4017A/automatic

Option order codes and retail prices

Super Bee

WM21 2 dr coupe	$3,059.00
WM23 2 dr hardtop	3,121.00

R/T

WS23 2 dr hardtop	3,425.00
WS27 Convertible	3,643.00
A01 Light Group (Super Bee)	25.95
(R/T)	17.80
A04 Coronet Radio Group	
(deluxe Super Bee w/bench seats)	207.00
(Super Bee w/buckets, R/T)	198.70
A12 440 Cid 6 Bbl Engine Package	468.80
A31 High Performance Axle Package	
(NA w/H51; w/383 ci 4V)	102.15
A32 Super Performance Axle Package	
(NA w/H51; w/440 ci & D34)	271.50
(NA w/H51; w/426 ci & D34)	242.15
A33 Track Pak (required w/440 ci 4V & 426 ci 8V w/D21)	142.85
A34 Super Track Pak (w/440 ci 4V & 426 ci 8V w/D21)	256.45
A35 Trailer Towing Package (w/D34, wo/H51)	25.30
(w/D34, w/H51)	14.75
A36 Performance Axle Package (w/383 ci 4V)	102.15
(w/440 ci 4V & D34)	92.25
(w/426 ci 8V & D34)	64.40
A48 Decor Group (coupe)	17.85
A62 Rallye instrument panel cluster (R/T)	90.30
B41 Front disc brakes (B51 required)	50.15
B51 Power brakes	42.95
C13 Front shoulder belts (convertible)	26.45
C14 Rear shoulder belts (NA convertible)	26.45
C16 Console (bucket seats required)	54.45
C21 Center front seat w/armrest (w/bucket seats only)	54.45
C62 Manual 6 way seat adjuster (left bucket only)	33.30
C65 Air foam front bench seat	8.30
C92 Protective rubber floor mats	13.60
D34 TorqueFlite (Super Bee)	39.30
D91 Sure-Grip differential	42.35
E74 426 ci engine (Super Bee)	830.65
(R/T)	717.90
F11 46 amp alternator	11.00
F25 70 amp battery (std w/426 ci & R/T)	8.40
G11 Tinted glass — all windows	
(exc convertible backglass)	40.70
G15 Tinted glass — windshield only	25.90
G31 Manual outside right mirrors	6.85
G33 Remote control outside left mirrors	10.45
H31 Rear window defogger	21.90
H51 Air conditioner w/heater (D34 required on R/T)	357.65
J25 3 speed windshield wipers	5.40
J41 Dress-up pedals (Super Bee)	5.45
J55 Undercoating w/underhood pad	16.60
L31 Fender-mounted turn signals (NA w/N96)	10.80
M05 Door edge protectors	4.65
M07 B-pillar moldings	4.25

M25 Custom sill moldings (Super Bee)   21.15
M31 Bodyside belt moldings   13.60
M46 Simulated air scoop quarter panel   35.80
M81 Front bumper guards   16.00
M83 Rear bumper guards   16.00
M85 Front & rear bumper guards   32.00
N88 Automatic speed control (D34 & B51 required)   57.95
N96 Air scoop Ramcharger hood (std w/426 ci)   73.30
P31 Power windows (hardtops & convertible)   105.20
R11 Music Master radio   61.55
R21 Solid-state AM/FM radio   134.95
R22 Solid-state AM radio w/stereo tape   196.25
R31 Rear seat speaker (NA convertible)   14.05
S77 Power steering   100.00
S78 Deluxe full-horn-ring steering wheel   5.45
S81 Sports-type wood-grain steering wheel   26.75
W11 Deluxe wheel covers, 14 in.   21.30
W15 Deep-dish wheel covers, 14 in.   36.25
W21 Chrome styled road wheels, 14 in. (NA w/426 ci)   86.15
Bucket seats   100.85
Two-tone paint   23.30
Vinyl roof   89.20
Tires
(383 & 440 engines, replaces F70x14 Red Streak tires)
T82 F70x14 WSW   NC
T85 F70x14 Red Streak fiberglass-belted   26.45
U64 F70x15 WSW fiberglass-belted   34.10
U65 F70x15 Red Streak fiberglass-belted   34.10
Tires
(426 engine, replaces F70x15 Red Streak fiberglass-belted
  tires)
U64 F70x15 WSW fiberglass-belted   NC

Exterior color codes

Silver Metallic	A4	Red	R6
Light Blue Metallic	B3	Light Bronze Metallic	T3
Bright Blue Metallic	B5	Copper Metallic	T5
Light Green Metallic	F3	Dark Bronze Metallic	T7
Medium Green Metallic	F5	White	W1
Dark Green Metallic	F8	Black	X9
Beige	L1	Yellow	Y2
Bright Turquoise Metallic	Q5	Cream	Y3
Bright Red	R4	Gold Metallic	Y4

Interior trim codes
Super Bee

Color	Coupe bench seats	Hardtop & opt Decor Group for coupe bench seats	Hardtop & opt Decor Group for coupe bucket seats
Blue	H2B	H2B	M6B
Green	—	H2G	M6G

Interior trim codes

Super Bee Color	Coupe bench seats	Hardtop & opt Decor Group for coupe bench seats	Hardtop & opt Decor Group for coupe bucket seats
Tan	H2T	H2T	M6T
Black	H2X	H2X	M6X
White/Blue	—	H2C	M6C
White/Green	—	H2F	M6F
White/Black	—	H2W	M6W

R/T Color	Hardtop bucket seats	Convertible bucket seats
Blue	P6D	P6D
Green	P6G	—
Tan	P6T	P6T
Red	P6R	—
Pewter/Black	P6S	—
Black	P6X	P6X
White/Blue	P6C	P6C
White/Green	P6F	—
White/Tan	P6H	P6H
White/Red	P6V	—
White/Black	P6W	P6W

Vinyl roof color codes

Antique Green	V1F
Saddle Bronze	V1T
Pearlescent White	V1W
Black	V1X

Bumblebee stripes codes

Black	V9X
Red	V9R
White	V9W

Convertible top color codes

Black	V3X
White	V3W

Facts

The R/T got some styling refinements for 1969. The standard hood was the same as in 1968 but a two-scoop hood was fitted when the optional Ramcharger fresh air system was ordered. The functional system was standard with the Hemi. As on the GTX, the side marker lights were rectangular, the rear bumblebee stripe was changed to a wide stripe flanked by thin pinstripes on each side and the taillights were similar to those on the Dodge Charger, except that a third light unit appeared in the center of the blacked-out taillight panel. Also optional were two simulated rear quarter panel scoops, located just in front of the rear wheelwells.

A pillarless Super Bee hardtop became available and outsold the Super Bee coupe. No convertible was available.

The Super Bee shared the same front grille with the R/T, with Super Bee identification. The Super Bee did not come with the simulated side scoops and the taillight panel housed only two taillight assemblies. The R/T hood scoops were used on the Super Bee.

All 1969 R/Ts and Super Bees with the 426 Hemi engine came with 15 in. wheels as standard.

Early production Hemi-equipped cars (those built before August 28, 1968) may have gotten the W23 option cast center road wheels, made by Kelsey-Hayes. These were deleted from the option list because of a manufacturing defect. Dealers were instructed to swap with other wheels—in the case of the Hemi, 14 in. steel Magnum road wheels.

Identical to Plymouth's Air Grabber fresh air system was the Ramcharger system on R/Ts and Super Bees. The Track Pak high-performance axle packages were also identical for 1969 Plymouths and Dodges.

When the Road Runner got the 440 6V (Six-Pack) engine as a midyear option, so did the Super Bee. Specifications for the Super Bee were identical with those for the Road Runner. Even though the Road Runner always outsold the Super Bee, more Six-Pack Super Bees were built—1,487 coupes and 420 hardtops.

The 440 Six-Pack Package consisted of 3x2V Holley carburetors on an aluminum Edelbrock manifold, selected rocker arms, low-taper camshaft and flat-faced tappets for improved durability, a dual-point distributor, special valve springs and chrome-plated valve stems, molybdenum-filled top piston rings, a viscous-drive and heavy-duty cooling. Other features were a fiberglass lift-off hood with functional air scoop secured by four tie-down pins, G70x15 Red Streak tires on plain steel wheels with chrome lug nuts, the Dana 9¾ in. rear with 4.10:1 axle ratio and Sure-Grip differential, and four-speed manual transmission with Hurst shifter (TorqueFlite was optional).

Color choice on the Six-Pack Super Bee was limited to four Hi-Impact colors: Bright Red (R4), Bright Green (F6), Bright Yellow (color was written on order form) and Hemi Orange (V2). Hemi Orange was available with mid-March production. Later in April, Bahama Yellow (96) paint was made available.

On April 7, 1969, a Scat Pack special package (A39 with vinyl roof and A40 without vinyl roof) was made available. It included the air scoop Ramcharger hood, chrome hood pins, special hood paint treatment, three-speed windshield wipers and F70x14 RWL or Red Streak tires.

The Scat Pack Package was not available with the Radio Group, floral roof, air conditioning, speed control, 426 Hemi engine, trailer towing, fender-mounted turn signals and 440 6V engine.

Total 426 Hemi production for R/Ts was 97 hardtops (39 with TorqueFlite and 58 with four-speed) and ten convertibles (six with TorqueFlite and four with a four-speed). For Super Bees, it was 92 hardtops (54 with TorqueFlite and 38 with four-speed) and 166 coupes (74 with TorqueFlite and 79 with four-speed).

Chapter 33

1970 Dodge R/T and Super Bee

Production

Super Bee		R/T	
2 dr hardtop 8 cyl	10,614	2 dr hardtop 8 cyl	2,172
2 dr coupe 8 cyl	3,640	Convertible 8 cyl	236
Total	14,254	Total	2,408

Serial numbers

WS23U0B100001

W — car line, Dodge Coronet
S — price class (M-medium, S-special)
23 — body type (21-2 dr coupe, 23-2 dr hardtop, 27-convertible)
U — engine code
0 — last digit of model year
B — assembly plant code (A-Lynch Road, E-Los Angeles,
  G-St Louis)
100001 — consecutive sequence number
    Serial number located on plate attached to left side of dash
panel, visible through windshield.

Engine codes

N — 383 ci 4V V-8 335 hp
R — 426 ci 2x4V V-8 425 hp
U — 440 ci 4V V-8 375 hp
V — 440 ci 3x2V V-8 390 hp

Head casting numbers

383 ci — 2843906
426 ci — 2780559
440 ci — 2843906

V-8 carburetors

383 ci 4V V-8 — Holley R4736A/manual w/Ram Air,
  R4738A/manual w/Ram Air w/ECS, R4367A/manual,
  R4217A/manual w/ECS, R4737A/automatic w/Ram Air,
  R4739A/automatic w/Ram Air w/ECS, R4218A/automatic
  w/ECS, R4368SA/automatic, R4369A/automatic w/AC
426 ci 2x4 V — Carter AFB4742S/front,
  AFB4745S/rear manual, AFB4746S/rear automatic
440 ci 4V — Carter AVS4737S/manual, AVS4739A/manual
  w/ECS, AVS4738S/automatic, AVS4741S/automatic w/AC,
  AVS4740S/automatic w/ECS
440 ci 3x2 V — Holley R4382A/front, R4175A/front w/ECS,
  R4374A/center manual, R4375A/center manual w/ECS,
  R4144A/center automatic, R4376A/center automatic w/ECS,
  R4365A/rear, R4383A/rear w/ECS

Distributors

383 ci — 3438231
426 ci — 2875987/manual, 2875989 IBS-4014F/automatic
440 ci — 3438222

440 ci 3x2V — 3438314/manual up to approx 01/01/70,
3438348/manual after approx 01/01/70, 2875982/automatic
up to approx 01/01/70, 3438349/automatic after approx
01/01/70

Option order codes and retail prices
Super Bee

WM21 2 dr coupe V-8	$3,012.00
WM23 2 dr hardtop V-8	3,074.00
R/T	
WS23 2 dr hardtop V-8	3,569.00
WS27 Convertible V-8	3,785.00
A01 Light Group (Super Bee)	34.70
(R/T)	26.55
A04 Coronet Radio Group	198.50
A31 High Performance Axle Package	
(NA w/H51 or A35—383 ci)	102.15
A32 Super Performance Axle Package (NA w/H51 or A35)	
(w/440 ci & D34)	250.65
(w/426 ci & D34)	221.40
A33 Track Package	
(NA w/H51 w/440 ci 4V, 440 ci 6V, 426 ci w/D21)	142.85
A34 Super Track Pak	
(NA H51 w/440 ci 4V, 440 ci 6V, 426 ci w/D21)	235.65
A35 Trailer Towing Package	
(D34 required, NA 440 ci 6V & 426 ci)	14.05
A36 Performance Axle Package (NA w/A35)	
(w/383 ci 4V w/D21 or D34)	102.15
(w/440 ci 4V or 440 ci 6V w/D34)	92.25
(w/426 ci & D34)	64.40
A62 Rallye instrument panel cluster (R/T)	90.30
B41 Disc brakes (requires B51)	27.90
B51 Power brakes	42.95
C13 Front shoulder belts (convertible)	26.45
C14 Rear shoulder belts (NA convertible)	26.45
C15 Seatbelt Group	13.75
C16 Console (w/bucket seats only)	54.45
C21 Center seat cushion & folding armrest	
(w/bucket seats, NA w/C16)	54.45
C62 Manual 6 way seat adjuster (left bucket only)	33.30
C92 Protective rubber floor mats	13.60
D21 Manual 4 speed transmission (Super Bee)	197.25
D34 TorqueFlite (Super Bee)	227.05
D91 Sure-Grip differential	
(std w/performance axle packages)	42.35
E74 426 ci engine (Super Bee)	848.45
(R/T)	718.05
E87 440 ci 3x2V engine (Super Bee)	249.55
(R/T)	119.05
F11 50 amp alternator	11.00
F25 70 amp battery	12.95

G11 Tinted glass—all windows (exc convertible backglass)	40.70
G15 Tinted glass—windshield only	25.90
G31 Manual outside right mirror	6.85
G33 Remote control outside left mirror	10.45
H31 Rear window defogger	26.25
H51 Air conditioning w/heater (D34 required)	357.65
J45 Hood hold-down pins	15.40
J55 Undercoating w/underhood pad	16.60
L42 Headlight time delay & warning signal (w/A01)	13.00
(wo/A01)	18.20
M05 Door edge protectors	4.65
M83 Rear bumper guards	16.00
N42 Bright exhaust tips (NA Calif)	20.80
N85 Tachometer w/clock (Super Bee)	68.45
N88 Automatic speed control	
(8 cyl only, NA 440 ci 6V & 426 ci)	57.95
N95 Evaporative emission control (Calif)	37.85
N96 Air scoop Ramcharger hood (std w/426 ci)	73.30
N97 Noise Reduction Package	
(required Calif w/383 ci & 440 ci)	NC
P31 Power windows (hardtops & convertible)	105.20
R11 Music Master AM radio (wo/A04)	61.50
R21 Solid-state AM/FM radio (wo/A04)	134.95
(w/A04)	73.50
R22 Solid-state AM radio w/stereo tape player (wo/A04)	196.25
(w/A04)	134.75
R31 Rear seat speaker (NA convertible)	15.15
S77 Power steering	105.20
S81 Sports-type wood-grain steering wheel	26.75
S83 Rim Blow steering wheel	26.75
High-impact paint colors	14.05
Two-tone paint (NA convertible)	28.30
Vinyl bucket seats (Super Bee)	100.85
Vinyl roof	95.70
Wheels & wheel covers	
W11 Deluxe wheel covers, 14 in. (wo/A04)	21.30
W13 Deep-dish, 14 in. (wo/A04)	36.25
(w/A04)	15.00
W15 Wire wheel covers, 14 in. (wo/A04)	64.10
(w/A04)	42.85
W21 Rallye road wheels, 14 or 15 in. (wo/A04)	43.10
(w/A04)	21.95
W23 Chrome styled road wheels w/trim ring, 14 in.	
(wo/A04)	86.15
(w/A04)	64.95
Tires—set of 5	
(replaces F70x14 WSW tires—all engines)	
T87 F70x14 RWL	NC
U84 F60x15 RWL	63.25

Exterior color codes

Light Blue Metallic	EB3	Beige	BL1
Bright Blue Metallic	EB5*	Dark Tan Metallic	FT6
Dark Blue Metallic	EB7	Hemi Orange	EV2*
Bright Red	FE5	White	EW1
Light Green Metallic	FF4	Black	TX9
Dark Green Metallic	EF8*	Top Banana	FY1*
Sublime	FJ5*	Cream	DY3*
Go-Mango	EK2*	Gold Metallic	FY4*
Dark Burnt Orange		Plum Crazy	FC7*
Metallic	FK5*	*Dual colored mirrors available.	

Interior trim codes

Color	Std bench seats	Opt bucket seats	R/T bucket seats
Blue	H2B7	M6B7	D6B7
Green	H2F8	M6F8	D6F8
Tan	H2T5	M6T5	D6T5
Burnt Orange	H2K4	M6K4	D6K4
Black/White	H2XW	M6XW	D6XW
Black	H2X9	M6X9	D6X9
Gold/Black	—	M6XY	D6XY*

*Hardtop only.

Vinyl roof color codes

Green	V1F
White	V1W
Black	V1X
Gater Grain	V1G

Convertible top color codes

White	V3W
Black	V3X

Bumblebee stripes codes*

Black	V8X
Red	V8R
White	V8W
Green	V8F
Blue	V8B

*R/T and Super Bee.

Longitudinal tape stripe codes*

Black	V6X
White	V6W
Red	V6R
Green	V6F
Blue	V6B

*Optional Super Bee.

Facts

The year 1970 was the last for the Coronet R/T and the Coronet Super Bee. The Super Bee continued for another year, but it was then a Charger Super Bee. The regular Coronet remained available only as a four-door sedan or wagon.

Like the GTX and Road Runner, the R/T and Super Bee were restyled. Whereas the GTX and Road Runner resembled the previous offerings, the R/T and Super Bee came with distinctive, dual-loop front bumpers. The R/T came with rear quarter panel fender scoops and a blacked-out taillight panel that incorporated three taillights on each side. The R/T hood featured two bulge-type hood scoops. A bumblebee stripe was standard. R/T identification could be found on the area separating the two front grille loops, on the taillight panel and on the side scoops.

The R/T was available as either a hardtop or a convertible.

Engines available on the R/T were the 440 4V as standard and the 440 6V and 426 Stage III Hemi as optional. For better emission control, the Hemi got a hydraulic lifter camshaft. The TorqueFlite automatic was standard equipment.

The Super Bee shared the same body style as the R/T, but it came as a coupe and a hardtop. No convertible was available. The Super Bee could be identified by the dual simulated hood scoops, which were functional with the Ramcharger option; Super Bee emblems on the taillight panel and in between the front bumpers; and the usual Super Bee wraparound rear stripes. Optional was an alternate C-stripe arrangement. The Super Bee did not have the rear quarter panel side scoops.

The Super Bee's standard 383 engine now came with a three-speed manual, rather than the previous four-speed. Optional engines were the 440 6V and 426 Hemi.

The 440 6V received some improvements to combat high-rpm failure: the connecting rods were changed to increase the beam cross section, the camshaft was faced with Lubrite to prevent scuffing and the oil control rings had increased tension.

The 440 and 426 engines got solenoid throttle stops for emission reasons.

A rear spoiler (J81) painted dull black was made optional at the end of October 1969.

Dual color-keyed mirrors were made available for early March 1970 production.

The Tuff steering was released for mid-March production.

Green Go (FJ6) and Panther Pink (FM3) paints were midyear introductions.

1970 Dodge Coronet R/T

Chapter 34

1967 Plymouth Belvedere GTX

Production
2 dr hardtop 8 cyl	11,429
Convertible 8 cyl	686
Total	12,115

Serial numbers
RS23L77100001

R — car line, Plymouth Belvedere

S — price class, special

23 — body type (23-2 dr hardtop, 27-convertible)

L — engine code

7 — last digit of model year

7 — assembly plant code (1-Lynch Road, 5-Los Angeles, 7-St Louis)

100001 — consecutive sequence number

Serial number located on plate attached to left front door hinge post.

Engine codes
J — 426 ci 2x4V V-8 425 hp

L — 440 ci 4V V-8 375 hp

Head casting numbers
426 ci — 2780559

440 ci — 2780915

V-8 carburetors
426 ci — Carter AFB4139S/front, AFB4140S/rear, AFB4343S/rear, AFB4324S/front automatic w/CAP, AFB4325S/rear automatic w/CAP, AFB4402S/rear automatic w/CAP

440 ci — Carter AFB4326S/manual, AFB4328S/manual w/CAP, AFB4327S/automatic, AFB4329S/automatic w/CAP

Distributors
426 ci — 2642482 IBS-4006P, 2642832 IBS-4006W/w/CAP

440 ci — 2642899 IBS-4006Z/manual, 2642911 IBS-4006Y/manual w/CAP, 2642748/automatic, 2642822/automatic w/CAP

Option order codes and retail prices
GTX V-8
RS23 2 dr hardtop	$3,178.00
RS27 Convertible	3,418.00
73 426 2x4V engine	564.00
292 Two-tone paint (NA convertible)	21.55
294 Paint—Sport stripe	30.65
306 Vinyl roof	75.10
307 Vinyl roof	75.10
351 Basic Group	173.25

355 Light Package (hardtop)	21.70
(convertible)	17.90
393 Manual 4 speed transmission (408 required)	NC
408 Sure-Grip differential	37.60
HD (required w/393)	138.90
411 Air conditioning w/heater	338.45
416 Heater (delete)	(70.30)
418 Rear window defogger (NA convertible)	20.20
421 Transaudio AM Radio	57.35
426 Rear seat speaker (NA convertible)	14.05
451 Power brakes	41.75
456 Power steering	89.65
458 Power windows	100.25
471 Cleaner Air Package (mandatory Calif)	25.00
479 Disc brakes (requires 451)	69.50
481 Front bumper guards	16.80
482 Rear bumper guards	14.05
483 Front & rear bumper guards	30.85
484 Electric clock	15.30
485 Center front seat w/folding armrest	52.85
486 Console	52.85
521 Tinted glass — all windows	39.50
522 Tinted glass — windshield only	21.20
531 Left headrests (w/bucket seats only)	20.95
532 Right headrests (w/bucket seats only)	20.95
533 Left & right headrests (w/bucket seats only)	41.90
536 Remote control outside left mirror	5.45
537 Manual outside right mirrors	6.35
556 Center passenger front lap belt (485 required GTX)	9.10
557 Center passenger rear lap belt	9.10
568 2 front shoulder belts	26.45
571 Full-horn-ring steering wheel	5.25
573 Deluxe wood-grain steering wheel	25.95
577 Tachometer (486 required)	48.70
579 Undercoating w/underhood pad	15.40
580 Set of 4 road wheels	97.30
581 Deluxe wheel covers	21.30
583 Sport wheel covers	38.95
589 Variable-speed windshield wipers	4.95
591 46 amp alternator	10.50
708 Special buffed paint	20.95
Tires—set of 5	
(replaces 7.75x14 Red Streak tires)	
43 7.75x14 WSW	NC

Exterior color codes

Buffed Silver Metallic	AA1	Dark Copper Metallic	HH1
Black	BB1	Light Turquoise Metallic	KK1
Light Blue Metallic	DD1	Dark Turquoise Metallic	LL1
Dark Blue Metallic	EE1	Turbine Bronze Metallic	MM1
Bright Blue Metallic	881	Bright Red	PP1
Dark Green Metallic	GG1	Dark Red Metallic	QQ1

Yellow	RR1
Ivory	SS1
Medium Copper Metallic	TT1
White	WW1
Beige	XX1
Light Tan Metallic	YY1
Gold Metallic	ZZ1

Interior trim codes

Color	Vinyl bucket seats
Blue	H6B
Red	H6R
Black	H6X
Copper	H6K
White & Blue	H6C
White & Red	H6V
White & Black	H6W

Vinyl roof color codes

Black	306
White	307
Green	304

Convertible top color codes

Green	300
Black	301
White	302

Stripe color codes

White	31W
Black	31B
Dark Red Metallic	31H
Dark Blue Metallic	31C
Light Tan Metallic	31Y
Medium Copper Metallic	31S

Facts

The Belvedere GTX was Plymouth's first separate performance intermediate. Using the Belvedere two-door hardtop, the GTX came with two nonfunctional hood scoops, a pit stop gas cap on the left rear fender, chrome dual exhaust tips and Red Streak tires. Hood and deck stripes were optional. Vinyl bucket seats were standard equipment.

Standard engine was the 440 ci 4V Super Commando rated at 375 hp. It came with a Dual Snorkel air cleaner and chrome valve covers.

Optional was the 426 ci Hemi engine. As in years to come, Hemi production was always small. For 1967, it amounted to 108 in GTX hardtops (63 with TorqueFlite and 45 with four-speed) and 17 in GTX convertibles (ten with TorqueFlite and seven with four-speed).

1967 Plymouth Belvedere GTX

Chapter 35

1968 Plymouth Belvedere GTX and Road Runner

Production

GTX		Road Runner	
2 dr hardtop 8 cyl	17,246	2 dr coupe 8 cyl	29,240
Convertible 8 cyl	1,026	2 dr hardtop 8 cyl	15,358
Total	18,272	Total	44,598

Serial numbers

RS21L8A100001

R — car line, Plymouth Belvedere

S — price class (S-special, M-medium)

21 — body type (21-2 dr coupe, 23-2 dr hardtop, 27-convertible)

L — engine code

8 — last digit of model year

A — assembly plant code (A-Lynch Road, E-Los Angeles, G-St Louis)

100001 — consecutive sequence number

Serial number located on plate attached to left side of dash panel, visible through windshield.

Engine codes

H — 383 ci 4V V-8 335 hp

J — 426 ci 2x4V V-8 425 hp

L — 440 ci 4V V-8 375 hp

Head casting numbers

383 ci — 2843906

426 ci — 2780559

440 ci — 2843906

Carburetors

383 ci 4V — Carter AVS4426S/manual, AVS4401S/automatic, AVS46358/automatic w/AC

426 ci 2x4V — Carter AFB4430S/front, AFB4431S/rear manual, AFB4432S/rear automatic

440 ci 4V — Carter AVS4428S/manual, AVS4429S/automatic, AVS4637S/automatic w/AC

Distributors

383 ci — 2875356/manual, 2875358/automatic

426 ci — 2875140 IBS-4014A

440 ci — 2875102 IBS-4014/manual, 2875209/automatic

Option order codes and retail prices

Road Runner V-8

RM21 2 dr coupe	$2,896.00
RM23 2 dr hardtop	3,034.00

GTX V-8

RS23 2 dr hardtop	3,355.00
RS27 Convertible	3,590.00

73 426 ci engine (Road Runner)		714.30
(GTX)		604.75
292 Two-tone paint		22.65
304 Vinyl roof		81.60
306 Vinyl roof		81.60
307 Vinyl roof		81.60
351 Basic Group (NA w/426 ci)		192.30
355 Light Package		26.45
358 High-performance axle (w/383 ci only; NA w/359)		87.50
359 Trailer Towing Package (wo/411)		24.50
(w/411)		14.35
360 Road Runner Decor Group		79.20
395 TorqueFlite (w/Road Runner)		38.95
408 Sure-Grip differential		42.35
(w/HD performance axle)		138.90
411 Air conditioning (NA w/426 ci, GTX)		342.85
418 Rear window defogger (NA convertible)		21.30
420 Solid-state AM radio w/stereo tape player		196.25
421 Solid-state AM radio		61.55
426 Rear seat speaker (NA convertible)		14.05
451 Power brakes		41.75
456 Power steering		94.85
458 Power windows (GTX)		100.25
473 Automatic speed control (NA 426 ci, 451 required)		52.50
479 Front disc brakes (451 required)		72.95
481 Front bumper guards		14.55
482 Rear bumper guards		15.55
483 Front & rear bumper guards		31.10
484 Clock (NA w/tachometer)		16.05
485 Center seat cushion & folding armrest (GTX)		52.85
486 Console (GTX)		52.85
508 Performance hood paint treatment		17.55
521 Tinted glass — all windows		39.50
522 Tinted glass — windshield only		22.35
529 Custom sill molding		20.45
531 Left head restraints		21.95
532 Right head restraints		21.95
533 Left & right head restraints		43.90
536 Remote outside left mirrors		9.40
537 Manual outside right mirrors		6.65
540 Belt molding (std w/vinyl roof)		13.20
547 Center pillar molding (2 dr coupe, Road Runner)		4.10
551 Foam front seat cushion (w/bench seat)		8.30
565 Armrest w/ashtrays (Road Runner coupe)		8.10
566 2 rear shoulder belts (NA convertible)		26.45
568 2 front shoulder belts (convertible)		26.45
571 Full-horn-ring steering wheel (Road Runner coupe)		14.90
(all others)		9.35
573 Sport simulated-wood-grain steering wheel (coupe)		31.20
(all others)		25.95
577 Tachometer (8 cyl only, NA w/clock)		48.70
579 Undercoating w/underhood pad		16.10

580 Styled road wheels, 14 in. (NA w/426 ci)	97.30
581 Deluxe wheel covers, 14 in.	21.30
15 in. (w/426 ci)	24.60
583 Sport wheel covers (NA w/426 ci)	36.25
583 3 speed windshield wipers	5.20
591 46 amp alternator	.11.00
626 70 amp battery (std w/426 ci)	8.10
708 Special buffed paint	21.95
Accent stripes	14.70
Paint—Sport stripe	20.40
Tires	
(replaces F70x14 Red Streak tires)	
46 F70x14 White Streak	NC

Exterior colors codes

Silver Metallic	AA1	Medium Bronze Metallic	MM1
Black	BB1	Red	PP1
Medium Blue Metallic	CC1	Bright Blue Metallic	QQ1
Pale Blue Metallic	DD1	Maroon Metallic	RR1
Dark Blue Metallic	EE1	Yellow	SS1
Light Green Metallic	FF1	Medium Green Metallic	TT1
Dark Green Metallic	GG1	Light Blue Metallic	UU1
Light Gold	HH1	White	WW1
Medium Gold Metallic	JJ1	Beige	XX1
Light Turquoise Metallic	LL1	Medium Tan Metallic	YY1

Interior trim codes

Color	GTX vinyl bucket seats	Road Runner coupe vinyl bench seats	Road Runner hardtop vinyl bench seats
Blue	S6B	D4B	H4B
Parchment	—	D4L	—
Silver/Black	—	D4S	—
White/Blue	S6C	—	H4C
White/Green	S6D	—	H4D
Green	S6F	—	H4F
Gold/Black	S6N*	—	H4N
Red	S6R	—	H4R
White/Red	S6V	—	H4V
Black	S6X	—	H4X

*Two-door hardtop only.

Vinyl roof color codes

Green	304
Black	306
White	307

Convertible top color codes

Green	300
Black	301
White	302

Body accent stripes codes

Color	GTX	Road Runner
White	313	31W
Black	311	31B
Red	312	31H
Blue	315	31C
Green	316	31P

Facts

The 1968 GTX received a minor restyle. A new front grille and a rear taillight treatment provided a cleaner look. Lower door and rear quarter panel stripes terminated in GTX lettering. Government-mandated side marker lights, amber front and red rear, were used on all Chrysler cars. All GTXs came with bright rocker panel strips.

The GTX came with side-facing nonfunctional hood scoops. During the year, a functional system, the Air Grabber, became an option on both the GTX and Road Runner.

Mechanically, no change was made from 1967. The 440 engine was standard and the 426 Hemi engine optional. The 440 cylinder head now came with an open-chamber design and an improved intake manifold.

Convertibles were built at the St Louis plant.

A total 410 hardtop GTXs got the Hemi engine, and 36 convertibles were equipped with it.

A popular Plymouth performance car was introduced along with the GTX in 1968. This was the Road Runner, and it was designed to appeal to the low end of the performance market. It used either the two door hardtop or the two door coupe, with the coupe having a center side window divider and using pop-out rear windows. This no-frills package provided a stark "taxicab" interior, minimal ornamentation and a special version of the 383 B engine as standard equipment. This 383 ci engine used 440 cylinder heads, a high-rise-type intake manifold, the 440 hp camshaft and dual exhausts to boost horsepower to 335. A four-speed manual transmission was standard and the TorqueFlite automatic was optional.

The suspension was similar to that on the GTX: heavy-duty all around, with front disc brakes optional.

Bench seats were used in the interior. The Road Runner Decor Group spiffed things up a bit with expanded interior color selection, a steering wheel with partial horn ring, center pillar moldings and a rear deck lid applique.

The Road Runner got the same hood as that on the GTX.

The only optional Road Runner engine was the 426 Hemi.

1968 Plymouth Belvedere GTX Hemi 426

Chapter 36

1969 Plymouth GTX and Road Runner

Production

GTX

2 dr hardtop 8 cyl	14,385
Convertible 8 cyl	625
Total	15,010

Road Runner

2 dr coupe 8 cyl	32,717
2 dr hardtop 8 cyl	47,365
Convertible 8 cyl	2,027
Total	82,109

Serial numbers

RM23L9A100001

R — car line, Plymouth Belvedere
M — price class (M-medium, S-special)
23 — body type (21-2 dr coupe, 23-2 dr hardtop, 27-convertible)
L — engine code
9 — last digit of model year
A — assembly plant code (A-Lynch Road, E-Los Angeles, G-St Louis)
100001 — consecutive sequence number
Serial number located on plate attached to left side of dash panel, visible through windshield.

Engine codes

H — 383 ci 4V V-8 335 hp
J — 426 ci 2x4V V-8 425 hp
L — 440 ci 4V V-8 375 hp
M — 440 ci 3x2V V-8 390 hp

Head casting numbers

383 ci — 2843906
426 ci — 2780559
440 ci — 2843906

Carburetors

383 ci 4V V-8 — Carter AVS4615S/manual, AVS4616S & 4711S, 4682S, 4638S/automatic
426 ci 2x4 V V-8 — Carter AFB4619S/front all, AFB4620S/rear manual, AFB4621S/rear automatic
440 ci 4V V-8 — Carter AVS4617S/manual, AVS4618S & 4640S/automatic
440 ci 3x2V V-8 — Holley R4393A/front all, R4391A/center manual, R4392A/center automatic, R4394A/rear all

Distributors

383 ci — 2875750/manual, 2875731/automatic
440 ci — 2875772 IBS-4014B/manual, 2875758/automatic
440 ci 6V — 2875981 IBS-4017/manual, 2875982 IBS-4017A/automatic

Option order codes and retail prices

Road Runner

RM21 2 dr coupe	$2,599.00
RM23 2 dr hardtop	3,083.00

RM27 Convertible	3,313.00
GTX	
RS23 2 dr hardtop	3,416.00
RS27 Convertible	3,635.00
A01 Light Group	29.60
A04 Basic Group (w/solid-state AM radio)	177.40
(w/solid-state AM/FM radio)	250.80
(w/solid-state AM radio/tape player)	312.10
A12 440 ci 6 Bbl Engine Package (replaces std 383 ci)	462.80
A31 High Performance Axle Package	
(NA w/H51; w/383 ci 4V)	102.15
A32 Super Performance Axle Package	
(NA w/H51; w/440 ci & D34)	271.50
(NA w/H51; w/426 & D34)	242.15
A33 Track Pak (required w/440 ci 4V & 426 ci 8V w/D21)	142.85
A34 Super Track Pak (w/440 ci 4V & 426 ci 8V w/D21)	256.45
A35 Trailer Towing Package (w/D34, wo/H51)	25.30
(w/D34, w/H51)	14.75
A36 Performance Axle Package (w/383 ci 4V)	102.15
(w/440 ci 4V & D34)	92.25
(w/426 ci 8V & D34)	64.40
A87 Decor Package (Road Runner)	81.50
B41 Front disc brakes (B51 required)	48.70
B51 Power brakes	42.95
C13 Front shoulder belts (convertible)	26.45
C14 Rear shoulder belts (NA convertible)	26.45
C16 Console (w/bucket seats only)	54.45
C21 Center seat cushion & folding armrest	
(w/bucket seats)	4.60
C23 Rear armrests w/ashtrays (Road Runner coupe)	8.40
C62 Comfort Position manual 6 way seat adjuster	
(left bucket)	33.30
C65 Foam front seat cushions (w/bench seat)	8.30
C92 Color-keyed carpet protection mats	13.60
D21 Manual 4 speed transmission (GTX)	NC
D34 TorqueFlite (Road Runner)	39.30
D91 Sure-Grip differential	42.35
E74 426 ci engine (Road Runner)	813.45
(GTX)	700.90
F11 46 amp alternator	11.00
F25 70 amp battery (std w/426 ci)	8.40
G11 Tinted glass — all windows (exc convertible backglass)	40.70
G15 Tinted glass — windshield only	25.90
G31 Manual outside right mirrors	6.85
G33 Remote control outside left mirrors	10.45
H31 Rear window defogger	21.90
H51 Air conditioner w/heater (D34 required on GTX)	357.65
J21 Clock (NA w/tachometer)	16.50
J25 3 speed windshield wipers	5.40
J55 Undercoating w/underhood pad	16.60
L72 Headlights-on warning signal	7.25

M05 Door edge protectors	4.65
M07 B-pillar moldings	4.25
M25 Custom sill moldings (Road Runner)	21.15
M31 Bodyside belt moldings	13.60
M81 Front bumper guards	16.00
M83 Rear bumper guards	16.00
M85 Front & rear bumper guards	32.00
N85 Tachometer (8 cyl only)	50.15
N88 Automatic speed control (D34 & B51 required)	57.95
N96 Air Grabber (J25 required)	55.30
P31 Power windows (hardtops & convertible)	105.20
R11 Solid-state AM radio	61.55
R21 Solid-state AM/FM radio	134.95
R22 Solid-state AM radio w/stereo tape	196.25
R31 Rear seat speaker (NA convertible)	14.05
S77 Power steering	100.00
S78 Deluxe Full-horn-ring steering wheel	
(NA hardtop, convertible)	15.40
(NA coupe)	5.45
S81 Sport simulated-wood-grain steering wheel (NA coupe)	26.75
V21 Performance hood paint	18.05
W11 Deluxe wheel covers, 14 in.	21.30
15 in. (w/426 ci)	24.60
W15 Deep-dish wheel covers, 14 in.	44.90
W21 Chrome styled road wheels, 14 in. (NA w/426 ci)	86.15
Accent stripes	15.15
Bucket seats	100.85
Sport stripe	25.25
Two-tone paint	23.30
Vinyl roof	89.20
Tires	
(383 & 440 engines, replaces F70x14 Red Streak tires)	
T82 F70x14 WSW	NC
T85 F70x14 Red Streak fiberglass-belted	26.45
U64 F70x15 WSW fiberglass-belted	34.10
U65 F70x15 Red Streak fiberglass-belted	34.10
Tires	
(426 engine, replaces F70x15 Red Streak fiberglass-belted tires)	
U64 F70x15 WSW fiberglass-belted	NC

Exterior color codes

Silver Metallic	A4	Scorch Red	R6
Ice Blue Metallic	B3	Honey Bronze Metallic	T3
Blue Fire Metallic	B5	Bronze Fire Metallic	T5
Jamaica Blue Metallic	B7	Saddle Bronze Metallic	T7
Frost Green Metallic	F3	Alpine White	W1
Limelight Metallic	F5	Black Velvet	X9
Ivy Green Metallic	F8	Sunfire Yellow	Y2
Sandpebble Beige	L1	Yellow Gold	Y3
Seafoam Turquoise Metallic	Q5	Spanish Gold Metallic	Y4
Performance Red	R4		

Interior trim codes
Road Runner — bench seats

Color	Coupe	Hardtop & opt Decor Group for coupe	Convertible
Blue	M2B	H2B	H2B
Green	—	H2G	—
Tan	M2T	H2T	H2T
Pewter/Black	—	H2S	—
Black	M2X	H2X	H2X
White/Blue	—	H2C	H2C
White/Green	—	H2F	—
White/Tan	—	H2H	H2H
White/Black	—	H2W	H2W

Road Runner — bucket seats

Color	Hardtop & opt Decor Group for coupe	Convertible
Blue	M6B	M6B
Green	M6G	—
Tan	M6T	M6T
Pewter/Black	M6S	—
Black	M6X	M6X
White/Blue	M6C	M6C
White/Green	M6F	—
White/Tan	M6H	M6H
White/Black	M6W	M6W

GTX — bucket seats

Color	Hardtop	Convertible
Blue	P2D	P6D
Green	P6G	—
Tan	P6T	P6T
Red	P6R	—
Pewter/Black	P6S	—
Black	P6X	P6X
White/Blue	P6C	P6C
White/Green	P6F	—
White/Tan	P6H	P6H
White/Red	P6V	—
White/Black	P6W	P6W

Vinyl roof color codes

Antique Green	V1F
Saddle Bronze	V1T
Pearlescent White	V1W
Black	V1X

Convertible top color codes

Black	V3X
White	V3W

Sport stripes color codes

White	V6W
Red	V6R

Accent stripe color codes

Blue	V7B
Green	V7F
Red	V7R
White	V7W
Black	V7X

Facts

Sharing the same bodyshell as the 1968s, the 1969 GTX was the recipient of a restyled front grille, with the hood and fender tops getting an optional blacked-out treatment. Hood scoops were similar to those of 1968 and had top openings. These were painted red with the performance hood treatment. The rear was restyled, with recessed square taillights. The lower body area was painted flat-black and the side marker lights were rectangular rather than round.

Engine choice was the same as in 1968. New performance options were the availability of the various packages. The Air Grabber fresh air system, optional with the 440 engine, was standard with the 426 Hemi engine.

An additional body style was added to the Road Runner line-up—a convertible. Engine availability was unchanged for 1969.

All convertibles were built at the St Louis plant.

A midyear introduction was the 440 six-barrel (Six-pack) Road Runner. This was a complete package that included a flat-black fiberglass hood held in place by four hood pins, a four-speed manual transmission, a 4.10:1 rear axle ratio in a Dana 9¾ in. rear with Sure-Grip, 15x6 flat-black painted wheels and a special version of the 440 ci V-8. Rated at 390 hp, the six-barrel 440 engine came with three two-barrel carburetors mounted on an aluminum Edelbrock intake manifold.

Hemi production for the GTX was 198 hardtops (99 with TorqueFlite and 99 with four-speed) and 11 convertibles (six with TorqueFlite and five with four-speed).

Hemi production for the Road Runner was 356 coupes (162 with TorqueFlite and 194 with four-speed), 422 hardtops (188 with TorqueFlite and 234 with four-speed) and ten convertibles (six with TorqueFlite and four with four-speed).

1969 Plymouth Road Runner

Chapter 37

1970 Plymouth GTX and Road Runner

Production

Road Runner

2 dr hardtop 8 cyl	20,899
2 dr coupe 8 cyl	14,744
Convertible 8 cyl	684
Superbird 8 cyl	2,783*
Total	39,110

GTX

2 dr hardtop 8 cyl   7,202

*Other quoted production figures are 1,920, 1,935 and 1,971.

Serial numbers

RS23U0B100001

R — car line, Plymouth Belvedere

S — price class (M-medium, S-special)

23 — body type (21-2 dr coupe, 23-2 dr hardtop, 27-convertible)

U — engine code

0 — last digit of model year

B — assembly plant code (A-Lynch Road, E-Los Angeles, G-St Louis)

100001 — consecutive sequence number

Serial number located on plate attached to left side of dash panel, visible through windshield.

Engine codes

N — 383 ci 4V V-8 335 hp

R — 426 ci 2x4V V-8 425 hp

U — 440 ci 4V V-8 375 hp

V — 440 ci 3x2V V-8 390 hp

Head casting numbers

383 ci — 2843906

426 ci — 2780559

440 ci — 2843906

Carburetors

383 ci 4V V-8 — Holley R4376A/manual w/Ram Air, R4738A/manual w/Ram Air & ECS, R4737A/automatic w/Ram Air, R4739A/automatic w/Ram Air & ECS, R4367A/manual, R4217A/manual w/ECS, R4368A/automatic, R4218A/automatic w/ECS, R4369A/automatic w/AC

426 ci 2x4V V-8 — Carter AFB4742S/front, AFB4745S/rear manual, AFB4646/rear automatic

440 ci 4V V-8 — Carter AVS4737S, AVS4739A/manual w/ECS, AVS4738S/automatic, AVS4741S/automatic w/AC, AVS4740S/automatic w/ECS

440 ci 3x2V V-8 — Holley R4382A/front, R4175A/front w/ECS, R4374A/center manual, R4375A/center manual w/ECS, R4144A/center automatic, R4376/center automatic w/ECS, R4365A/rear, R4383A/rear w/ECS

Distributors

383 ci — 3438233 (interchanges w/3438433)

426 ci — 2875987/manual, 2875989 IBS-4014F/automatic

440 ci — 3438222
440 ci 3x2V — 3438312/manual up to approx 01/01/70,
    3438348/manual after approx 01/01/70, 2875982/automatic
    up to approx 01/01/70, 3438349/automatic after approx
    01/01/70

Option order codes and retail prices
Road Runner

RM21 2 dr coupe	$2,896.00
RM23 2 dr hardtop	3,034.00
RM27 Convertible	3,289.00
Superbird	
RM23 2 dr hardtop	4,298.00
GTX	
RS23 2 dr hardtop	3,535.00
A01 Light Package	26.55
A04 Basic Group	198.50
A31 High Performance Axle Package (NA w/H51 or A35 — 383 ci)	102.15
A32 Super Performance Axle Package (NA w/H51 or A35)	
(w/440 ci & D34)	250.65
(w/426 ci & D34)	221.40
A33 Track Package (NA w/H51 w/440 ci 4V, 440 ci 6V, 426 ci w/D21)	142.85
A34 Super Track Pak (NA w/H51 w/440 ci 4V, 440 ci 6V, 426 ci w/D21)	235.65
A35 Trailer Towing Package (D34 required, NA 440 ci 6V & 426 ci)	14.05
A36 Performance Axle Package (NA w/A35)	
(w/383 ci 4V w/D21 or D34)	102.15
(w/440 ci 4V or 440 ci 6V w/D34)	92.25
(w/426 ci & D34)	64.40
A87 Road Runner Decor Group	
B41 Disc brakes (requires B51)	27.90
B51 Power brakes	42.95
C13 Front shoulder belts (convertible)	26.45
C14 Rear shoulder belts (NA convertible)	26.45
C15 Deluxe seatbelts	13.75
C16 Console (w/bucket seats only)	54.45
C21 Center seat cushion & folding armrest (w/bucket seats, NA w/C16)	54.45
C62 Comfort Position 6 way seat adjuster (left bucket only)	33.30
C92 Color-keyed accessory floor mats	13.60
D21 Manual 4 speed transmission (Road Runner)	197.25
D34 TorqueFlite (Road Runner)	227.05
D91 Sure-Grip differential (std w/performance axle packages)	42.35
E74 426 ci 8V engine (Road Runner)	841.05
(GTX)	710.60

E87 440 ci 6V engine (Road Runner)	249.55
(GTX)	119.05
F11 50 amp alternator	11.00
F25 70 amp battery	12.95
G11 Tinted glass — all windows (exc convertible backglass)	40.70
G15 Tinted glass — windshield only	25.90
G31 Manual outside right mirror	6.85
G33 Remote control outside left mirror	10.45
H31 Rear window defogger	26.25
H51 Air conditioning w/heater (D34 required)	357.65
J21 Electric clock	18.45
J41 Pedal dress-up	5.45
J45 Hood hold-down pins	15.40
J55 Undercoating w/underhood pad	16.60
L42 Headlight time delay & warning signal	18.20
M05 Door edge protectors	4.65
M07 B-pillar molding (Road Runner)	4.25
M25 Custom sill molding (Road Runner)	21.15
M31 Belt molding	13.60
M83 Rear bumper guards	16.00
N42 Bright exhaust trumpets (NA Calif, std w/426 ci)	20.80
N85 Tachometer, incl clock	68.45
N88 Automatic speed control (8 cyl only, NA 440 ci 6V & 426 ci)	57.95
N95 Evaporative emission control (Calif)	37.85
N96 Air Grabber (std w/426 ci)	65.55
N97 Noise Reduction Package (required in Calif w/383 ci & 440 ci)	NC
P31 Power windows (hardtops & convertibles)	105.20
R11 Solid-state AM radio (wo/A04)	61.55
R21 Solid-state AM/FM radio (wo/A04)	134.95
(w/A04)	73.50
R22 Solid-state AM radio w/stereo tape player (wo/A04)	196.25
(w/A04)	134.75
R31 Rear seat speaker (NA convertibles)	14.05
S77 Power steering	105.20
S81 3 spoke wood-grain steering wheel	
(wo/A87, Road Runner coupe)	32.10
(wo/A87, all others)	26.75
(w/A87, Road Runner coupe)	26.75
S83 2 spoke Rim Blow steering wheel	
(wo/A87, Road Runner coupe)	29.00
(wo/A87, all others)	19.15
(w/A87, Road Runner coupe)	16.05
V21 Performance hood paint	18.05
Dust Trail tape stripe (Road Runner)	15.55
High-impact paint colors	14.05
Two-tone paint (NA convertible)	28.30
Vinyl bucket seats (Road Runner)	100.85
Vinyl roof	95.70

Wheels & wheel covers

W11 Deluxe wheel covers	21.30
W15 Wire wheel covers	64.10
W21 Rallye road wheels, 14 or 15 in.	43.10
W23 Chrome styled road wheels, 14 in. only	86.15

Tires — set of 5

(replaces F70x14 WSW tires — all engines)

T87 F70x14 RWL	NC
U84 F60x15 RWL	63.25

Exterior color codes

Ice Blue Metallic	EB3	Deep Burnt Orange Metallic	FK5
Blue Fire Metallic	EB5	Sandpebble Beige	BL1
Jamaica Blue Metallic	EB7	Burnt Tan Metallic	FT6
In Violet Metallic	FC7	Tor-Red	EV2
Rallye Red	FE5	Alpine White	EW1
Lime Green Metallic	FF4	Black Velvet	TX9
Ivy Green Metallic	EF8	Lemon Twist	FY1
Lime Light	FJ5	Yellow Gold	DY3
Vitamin C Orange	EK2	Citron Mist Metallic	FY4

Interior trim codes

Road Runner — bench seats

Color	Coupe	Coupe w/A87 & hardtop	Convertible
Black	M2X9	H2X9	H2X9
Blue	M2B5	H2B5	H2B5
Green	—	H2F8	—
Tan	M2T5	H2T5	—
Burnt Orange	—	H2K4	H2KW
White/Blue	—	H2BW	H2BW
White/Burnt Orange	—	H2KW	H2KW
White/Black	—	H2XW	H2XW

Road Runner — bucket seats

Color	Coupe w/A87 & hardtop	Convertible
Blue	P6B5	P6B5
Green	P6F8	—
Burnt Orange	P6K4	P6K4
Tan	P6T5	—
White/Blue	P6BW	P6BW
White/Burnt Orange	P6KW	P6KW
Charcoal/Black	P6XA	P6XA
White/Black	P6XW	P6XW
Gold/Black	P6XY	—

GTX

Color	Cloth and vinyl bench seats	Vinyl bucket seats
Blue	P3B5	P6B5
Burnt Orange	P3K4	P6K4
Black	P3X9	—
Green	—	P6F8

GTX Color	Cloth and vinyl bench seats	Vinyl bucket seats
Tan	—	P6T5
White/Blue	—	P6BW
White/Burnt Orange	—	P6KW
Charcoal/Black	—	P6XA
White/Black	—	P6XW
Gold/Black	—	P6XY

Vinyl roof color codes

Green	V1F
White	V1W
Black	V1X
Gator Grain	V1G

Convertible top color codes

White	V3W
Black	V3X

Sport stripes color codes*

Black	V6X
White	V6W
Gold	V6Y

*GTX.

Transverse tape stripes codes*

White	V8W
Black	V8X
Gold	V8Y

*Road Runner, coupe with A87, standard others.

Dust Trail tape stripes code

Gold	V6Y

*Road Runner.

Facts

The midsize Plymouths were restyled for 1970. Although still resembling the 1969s, the 1970 GTX and Super Bee came with a restyled nose and rear. The sides featured a cleaner treatment and a single rear brake scoop. The hood had a built-in power bulge. The GTX was available only in a hardtop; the Road Runner was still available in three configurations—hardtop, coupe and convertible.

Engine line-up for the GTX expanded to three choices—the 375 hp 440 ci, the 390 hp 440 ci 6V and the 426 ci Hemi, which was still rated at 425 hp. Unlike the 426s of 1969, the 1970 version came with a hydraulic lifter camshaft, for improved emissions.

The fresh air intake system was changed for 1970. Still called the Air Grabber, the scoop was barely noticeable when it was in the closed position, as its top was flush with the hood. When it was opened, the front of the scoop lifted up, thereby letting air into the air cleaner and also exposing the Air Grabber decals affixed on both sides of the scoop. As before, the Air Grabber was standard with the 426 Hemi and optional with either 440 engine.

A welcome addition to the option list was the attractive Rallye wheels. Of particular interest was the 15x7 size. The only tires that could be had with these wheels were F60x15 Goodyear Polyglas GTs.

The drivelines on both the GTX and the Road Runner were unchanged: heavy-duty all around. Heavy-duty drum brakes were still standard equipment, with front discs optional.

The Road Runner came with the 383 ci as standard, but the standard transmission was downgraded to a three-speed manual. The four-speed manual and TorqueFlite automatic were optional. Optional engines were the 440 6V and 426 Hemi.

The 440 3x2V got some engine improvements. The connecting rods were changed to increase the beam cross section, the camshaft was faced with Lubrite to prevent scuffing and the oil control rings came with increased tension. As a cost-saving measure, the Edelbrock aluminum intake manifold was replaced with a cast-iron unit.

Both the Road Runner and the GTX could be had with the optional hood paint treatment, a broad band of black paint bordered by a stripe on each side. The GTX came with standard side stripes. The Road Runner Dust Trail stripes showed the Road Runner cartoon character leaving a dust trail from the side scoops to the front of the car.

The ultimate 1970 Road Runner was the Superbird. Modeled after the 1969 Daytona Charger, the Superbird looked similar, yet used no interchangeable body parts. The nose cone was unique and the rear wing pedestals were racked farther back. The area around the retractable headlights was painted black and Superbird Road Runner decals appeared on each wing pedestal and on the left headlight panel. On each fender were large Plymouth emblems.

All Superbirds came with a front spoiler, a black vinyl roof, power steering, power disc brakes, a black or white interior (bench seats standard, buckets optional), hood pins, simulated rear-facing fender scoops, aerodynamic windshield moldings, the A36 Performance Axle Package with an automatic or A33 Track Pak with the four-speed manual, and 14 in. wheels standard. The 15x7 in. Rallye wheels and F60x15 tires were optional. Color availability was limited to Alpine White, Vitamin C Orange, Lemon Twist, Lime Light, Blue Fire Metallic, Tor-Red and Corporation Blue.

Superbird engine availability was the same as the GTXs. Standard was the 375 hp 440, with the Six-Pack 440 and 426 Hemi optional. Air conditioning and the Air Grabber were not available with the Superbird.

A total 135 Superbirds were built with the 426 Hemi engine. Another 716 got the 440 Six-Pack.

A total 678 GTXs came with the 440 Six-Pack and 72 came with the 426 Hemi.

The 440 Six-Pack Road Runner production was 651 coupes, 1,846 hardtops and 34 convertibles.

The 426 Hemi Road Runner production was 74 coupes (30 w/TorqueFlite and 44 w/four-speed), 135 hardtops and three convertibles (two with TorqueFlite and one with four-speed).

Total 426 Hemi Road Runner hardtop production, including the Superbird, was 210 (93 with TorqueFlight and 117 with four-speed).

1970 Plymouth Road Runner 440 Six-Pack convertible

1970 Plymouth GTX 440 Six-Pack

1970 Plymouth Road Runner Superbird

Chapter 38

1971 Plymouth GTX and Road Runner

Production

Road Runner		GTX	
2 dr hardtop 8 cyl	13,046	2 dr hardtop 8 cyl	2,626

Serial numbers

RS23U1A100001

R — car line, Plymouth Satellite

S — price class (M-medium, S-special)

23 — body type (23-2 dr hardtop)

U — engine code

1 — last digit of model year

A — assembly plant code (A-Lynch Road, G-St Louis, R-Windsor)

100001 — consecutive sequence number

Serial number located on plate attached to left side of dash panel, visible through windshield.

Engine codes

N — 383 ci 4V V-8 300 hp (250 hp net)

R — 425 ci 2x4V V-8 425 hp (350 hp net)

U — 440 ci 4V V-8 370 hp (305 hp net)

V — 440 ci 3x2V V-8 390 hp (330 hp net)

Head casting numbers

383 ci — 3462346

426 ci — 2780559

440 ci — 3462346

V-8 carburetors

383 ci 4V — Holley R4667A/manual, R4734A/manual w/fresh air, R4668A/automatic, R4735A/automatic w/fresh air

426 ci 2x4V — Carter AFB4971S/front, AFB4969S/rear manual, AFB4970S/rear automatic

440 ci 4V — Carter AVS4967S/manual, AVS4968S/automatic

440 ci 3x2V — Holley R4671A/front, R4669A/center manual, R4670A/center automatic, R4672A/rear

Distributors

383 ci — 3438690

426 ci — 2875987/manual, 3438579/automatic, 3438891/manual w/electronic ignition, 3438893/automatic w/electronic ignition

440 ci — 3438694

440 ci 3x2V — 3438577

Option order codes and retail prices*
Road Runner V-8

RM23 2 dr hardtop $3,120.00

GTX V-8

RS23 2 dr hardtop	3,707.00
A01 Light Package	31.95
A02 Driver Aid Group (w/A01 only)	14.20
A04 Basic Group (Road Runner)	199.90
A28 Noise Reduction Package (required in Calif w/440 ci 6V)	36.50
A31 High Performance Axle Package (NA w/AC or trailer towing available w/340 & 383 4V engines w/D21 & D34)	81.80
A33 Track Package (NA w/H51, w/440 ci 6V, 426 ci w/D21)	149.80
A34 Super Track Pak (NA w/AC, w/440 ci 6V, 426 ci w/D21)	219.30
A35 Trailer Towing Package (NA w/440 ci 6V & 426 ci, B41 required)	26.30
A36 Performance Axle Package	
(w/340 ci & 383 ci, w/D21 or D34)	81.80
(w/440 ci 6V & D34)	81.80
(w/426 ci & D34)	45.35
A45 Aerodynamic Spoiler Package (NA w/M91)	59.40
A87 Decor Package (Road Runner)	85.60
B41 Disc brakes (requires B51)	22.50
B51 Power brakes	41.55
C16 Console (w/bucket seats only)	57.65
C21 Center seat cushion & folding armrest (buckets only)	57.65
C62 Comfort Position manual 6 way seat adjuster (left bucket)	35.00
C92 Color-keyed accessory floor mats	14.25
D21 Manual 4 speed transmission (required w/440 ci & 426 ci, Road Runner)	206.40
D34 TorqueFlite (Road Runner)	237.50
E55 340 ci 4V engine (Road Runner only)	45.90
E74 426 ci 8V engine (Road Runner)	883.55
(GTX)	746.50
E87 440 ci 6V engine (Road Runner)	262.15
(GTX)	125.00
F11 50 amp alternator	11.80
F25 70 amp-hr battery	14.80
G11 Tinted glass — all windows	43.40
G15 Tinted windshield	29.80
G31 Chrome outside right mirror (requires G33)	11.75
G33 Chrome outside left mirror	16.25
G36 Color-keyed remote outside left & manual right racing mirrors (wo/A04)	28.00
(w/A04)	11.75
H31 Rear window defogger	31.34
H41 Strato ventilation	18.20
H51 Air conditioning (NA w/440 ci 4V & D21, 440 ci 6V & 426 ci)	383.25

·

J21 Electric clock (NA w/tachometer)	18.45
J25 Variable-speed wipers w/electric washers	5.85
J41 Pedal dress-up	5.85
J45 Hood pins	16.55
J52 Inside hood release	10.55
J55 Undercoating w/hood insulator pad	22.60
J68 Backlight louvers	68.45
L42 Nightwatch time delay & headlight-on warning light	19.45
M05 Door edge protectors	6.50
M26 Wheel lip molding (Road Runner)	14.05
M31 Belt molding (Road Runner)	14.60
M51 Power sunroof (w/canopy vinyl roof)	455.95
(w/full vinyl roof)	484.65
M73 Painted bumpers	37.85
M75 Rear bumper tape treatment	16.35
M81 Front bumper guards	16.85
M83 Rear bumper guards	16.85
M85 Front & rear bumper guards	33.70
M91 Deck lid luggage rack	35.00
N25 Engine block heater	15.55
N42 Decorative exhaust tips (std w/426 ci, NA Calif)	21.90
N85 Tachometer (NA w/clock)	52.70
N88 Automatic speed control (D34 required)	60.90
N95 NOx emission control (required Calif)	12.95
N96 Air Grabber (NA w/H51 & D34)	68.90
N97 Noise Reduction Package (required Calif)	NC
P31 Power windows	101.30
R11 Solid-state AM radio	66.40
R26 Solid-state AM radio w/stereo tape player (wo/A04)	219.15
AM radio w/stereo tape (w/A04)	147.40
R31 Rear seat speakers, single (requires R11)	15.05
R33 Tape recorder microphone (w/R26 or R36)	11.70
R35 AM/FM stereo radio (wo/A04)	213.70
(w/A04)	135.60
R36 AM/FM stereo radio w/stereo tape player (wo/A04)	366.40
(w/A04)	300.10
S15 Extra-HD suspension	
(w/340 ci or 383 ci 4V, Road Runner)	NC
S62 Tilt steering wheel w/Rim Blow	
(NA w/C16, S77 & D34 required)	55.70
S77 Power steering	96.55
S83 Wood-grain Rim Blow steering wheel	
(Road Runner wo/A87)	30.50
(Road Runner w/A87)	20.10
(GTX)	20.10
S84 Tuff Rallye steering wheel	
(S77 required, Road Runner wo/A87	30.50
(S77 required, Road Runner w/A87)	20.10
(S77 required, GTX)	20.10
W11 Deluxe wheel covers, 14 in.	27.35
W12 Wheel trim rings, 14 or 15 in. (w/hubcaps only)	27.35

W15 Wire wheel covers, 14 in.	70.15
W21 Rallye road wheels, 14 or 15 in., w/std spare	58.95
W23 Chrome styled road wheels, 14 in. only w/std spare	90.55
W34 Collapsible spare tire (NA w/A35, 440 ci or 426 ci)	13.60
Canopy vinyl roof (Road Runner)	67.05
Cloth & vinyl bench seat (GTX)	NC
Cloth & vinyl bucket seat (w/A87, Road Runner)	105.95
C-pillar strobe stripe (Road Runner)	34.00
Full vinyl roof	95.75
High-impact paint colors	15.05
Hood & fender transverse stripe	
(GTX, NA w/426 ci or N96)	22.50
Two-tone paint	31.10
Vinyl bucket seat (w/87, Road Runner)	105.95
Tires — Road Runner	
(replaces F70x14 WSW tires w/340 ci or 383 ci 4V)	
T34 F78x14 WSW	NC
T46 G78x14 WSW	18.75
T87 F70x14 RWL	12.50
T93 G70x14 RWL	31.25
U86 G60x15 RWL (requires S15)	94.30
Tires — Road Runner & GTX	
(RWL, w/440 & 426 engines, replaces G70x14 tires)	
T46 G78x14 WSW (NA w/426 ci)	NC
U86 E60x15 RWL	63.10
*As of April 1, 1971.	

Exterior color codes

Winchester Gray Metallic	GA4	Gold Leaf Metallic	GY8
Glacial Blue Metallic	GB2	Tawny Gold Metallic	GY9
True Blue Metallic	GB5	Meadow Green	GJ3
Evening Blue Metallic	GB7	Green Go	FJ6
Amber Sherwood Metallic	GF3	Lemon Twist	FY1
Sherwood Green Metallic	GF7	Tor-Red	EV2
Autumn Bronze Metallic	GK6	Plum Crazy	FC7
Tunisian Tan Metallic	GT2	Butterscotch	EL5
Snow White	GW3	Citron Yella	GY3
Formal Black	TX9		

Buckets-standard GTX, optional Road Runner

Blue	D6B5	Gunmetal	D6XA
Green	D6F7	Orange/Black*	D5XV
Tan	D6T7	Black*	D5X9
Gold	D6Y3	Green*	D5F7
		*cloth/vinyl	

Road Runner	Standard bench	Optional bench
Blue	C2B5	M2B5
Green	C2F7	M2F7
Tan	C2T7	M2T7
Gold	—	M2Y3
Black	—	M2X9
Gunmetal	—	M2X6

Vinyl roof color codes

Black	V1X
White	V1W
Green	V1F
Gold	V1Y

Facts

As the Belvedere name was no longer used, the GTX and Road Runner were now based on the Satellite two-door hardtop. No coupes or convertibles were available. Styling was totally different from that in 1970, as Chrysler applied the big-car fuselage styling on the intermediates. Rounded fender and quarter panels gave the car a more muscular look. The front of the car was dominated by a large chrome loop bumper.

Both GTX and Road Runner came with a performance hood that incorporated side-facing scoops, which were also inscribed with numbers indicating engine size.

Optional on both cars were color-keyed elastomeric front bumpers. Optional too were a black rear valance tape treatment, rear window louvers and spoilers, all of which enhanced the super-car image.

A strobe over the roof stripe was optional on the Road Runner, and the GTX got a unique hood and fender transverse stripe arrangement. A new partial canopy vinyl roof treatment was available only on the Road Runner.

Engine availability was unchanged for the 1971 GTX. The Road Runner still got the 383 ci four-barrel engine standard, but the 275 hp 340 ci four-barrel was added to the option list. The smaller engine enabled the Road Runner to qualify for a lower insurance premium. A total of 1,681 Road Runners came with the small-block 340.

Hemi production was even lower, with 55 Road Runners (27 with TorqueFlite and 28 with a four-speed) and 30 GTXs (19 with TorqueFlite and 11 with four-speed).

1971 Plymouth Road Runner 440 Six-Pack

Chapter 39

1972 Plymouth Road Runner

Production
2 dr hardtop 8 cyl   6,831

Serial numbers
RM23P2A100001

R — car line, Plymouth Satellite
M — price class (M-medium)
23 — body type (23-2 dr hardtop)
P — engine code
2 — last digit of model year
A — assembly plant code (A-Lynch Road, G-St Louis, R-Windsor)
100001 — consecutive sequence number
    Serial number located on plate attached to left side of dash panel, visible through windshield.

Engine codes
H — 340 ci 4V V-8 240 hp
P — 400 ci 4V V-8 255 hp
U — 440 ci 4V V-8 280 hp

Head casting numbers
340 ci — 3418915
400 ci — 3462346
440 ci — 3462346

Carburetors
340 ci 4V V-8 — Carter TQ6138S/manual, TQ6139S/automatic
400 ci 4V V-8 — Carter TQ6140S/manual, TQ6165S/manual w/air pump, TQ6090S/automatic, TQ6166S/automatic w/air pump
440 ci 4V V-8 — Holley R6252A/manual, R6252A/manual, R6256A/manual w/air pump, R6255A/automatic, R6253A/automatic, R6257A/automatic w/air pump

Option order codes and retail prices
RM23 2 dr hardtop V-8	$3,239.00
A01 Light Package	33.15
A33 Track Pak Package (required w/440 ci 4V & D21, NA w/H51)	168.55
A36 Performance Axle Package (NA 440 ci w/D21)	98.65
A87 Decor Package (w/vinyl bench seat)	88.25
(w/vinyl bucket seats)	197.35
B41 Front power disc brakes	71.70
C16 Console	59.35
C21 Center seat cushion & folding armrest	59.35
C92 Color-keyed accessory floor mats	13.85
D21 Manual 4 speed transmission	212.60
D34 TorqueFlite transmission	244.65
D51 2.76 axle ratio (w/340 or 400 engines)	14.05
D91 Sure-Grip differential	46.75
E55 340 ci 4V engine	67.35

E86 440 ci 4V engine	161.30
F25 70 amp battery	15.30
G11 Tinted glass — all windows	44.75
G15 Tinted windshield	30.65
G35 Chrome outside left racing mirror	16.80
G36 Body-color remote left, manual right dual racing	
mirrors (w/A06)	12.20
(wo/A06)	28.95
G37 Chrome remote outside left & manual right	
racing mirrors (w/A06)	12.20
(wo/A06)	28.95
H31 Rear window defogger	32.40
H51 Air conditioning (NA 6 cyl, NA w/3 speed manual)	399.65
J21 Electric clock (NA w/tachometer)	19.05
J25 Variable-speed wipers w/electric washers	6.10
J45 Hood pins	17.10
J52 Inside hood release	10.90
J55 Undercoating w/hood insulator pad	21.45
M05 Door edge protectors	6.70
M25 Custom sill molding	23.00
M26 Wheel opening moldings	14.50
M31 Belt molding	15.10
M51 Power-operated sunroof w/vinyl roof	469.65
M85 Front & rear bumper guards	34.65
N23 Electronic ignition system (w/400 ci 4V)	35.40
N42 Decorative exhaust tips (D34 required w/440 ci 4V)	22.55
N95 Emission control system & testing (required Calif)	29.40
N96 Air Grabber (NA w/H51 or 400 ci 4V, 440 ci 4V in	
Calif)	71.00
P31 Power windows	125.45
R11 Solid-state AM radio	68.40
R26 Solid-state AM radio w/stereo tape player (wo/A06)	225.70
R31 Rear seat speakers, single (requires R11)	15.50
R35 AM/FM stereo radio (wo/A06)	220.20
R36 AM/FM stereo radio w/stereo tape player (wo/A06)	377.40
S62 Tilt steering wheel w/Rim Blow (S77 & D34 required)	57.40
S77 Power steering (std w/A04)	119.75
S84 Tuff Rallye steering wheel (wo/A87)	31.50
(w/A87)	20.70
V21 Black hood tape treatment	22.70
V25 Black deck tape treatment	22.70
W11 Deluxe wheel covers, 14 in.	28.20
W15 Wire wheel covers	72.35
(wo/A06)	44.20
W21 Set of 4 Rallye road wheels w/std spare	60.75
(w/A07)	32.60
W23 Set of 4 chrome style road wheels w/std spare	93.35
(w/A07)	65.15
Canopy vinyl roof	69.10
C-pillar & roof strobe stripes	
(NA w/hood & fender stripes)	35.05

Full vinyl roof		98.65
High-impact paint colors		15.50
Hood & fender tape stripes (NA w/C-stripe)		23.20

Tires — Road Runner

(replaces F70x14 WSW tires — all engines)

T87 F70x14 RWL	12.95
T93 G70x14 RWL	32.25
U86 G60x15 RWL	97.30

Exterior color codes

Winchester Gray Metallic	GA4	Spinnaker White	EW1
Basin Street Blue	TB3	Honeydew	GY4
True Blue Metallic	GB5	Gold Leaf Metallic	GY8
Rallye Red	FE5	Tawny Gold Metallic	GY9
Amber Sherwood Metallic	GF3	Formal Black	TX9
Mojave Tan Metallic	HT6	Tor-Red	EV2
Chestnut Metallic	HT8	Lemon Twist	FY1

Interior trim codes

Color	Vinyl bench seats	Vinyl bench seats w/Decor Group	Vinyl bucket seats w/Decor Group
Blue	B2B5	C2B5	D6B5
Green	B2F6	C2F6	D6F6
Gold	—	—	D6Y3
Black	B2X9	C2X9	D6X9
White	—	C2XW	D6XW
Tan	—	C2T5	—

Vinyl roof color codes

Color	Full	Canopy
Black	V1X	V4X
White	V1W	V4W
Gold	V1Y	V4Y
Green	V1F	V4F
Tan	V1T	V4T

Hood and fender stripes codes

Black	V9X
White	V9W

Facts

The most noticeable change in 1972 was the redesigned rear bumper and taillight treatment. The front loop bumper was unchanged.

The GTX was no longer available, leaving the Road Runner as Plymouth's premier muscle car offering. However, if a Road Runner was ordered with the 440 engine, it became a Road Runner GTX and featured GTX emblems on the front fenders and trunk lid, in addition to the Road Runner emblems. A performance hood that had side-facing simulated scoop openings was standard equipment. Two stripe treatments were available, a hood strobe tape stripe and a hood and rear deck tape treatment that was also available on other two-door Satellites.

A 400 ci version of the B engine replaced the 383 ci as standard equipment. Sharing the same stroke, 3.38 in., the 400 came with a larger bore, measuring 4.34 in. Intake port configuration was slightly revised from that of the 383, and the 400 came with a cast crankshaft. The 400 also came with a Carter Thermoquad carburetor. Optional was the 340 or the 440—both with a single four-barrel carburetor. The 440 was also modified, using the redesigned heads but still used a premium forged crankshaft. Although factory literature and Chrysler's parts books show that the 440 Six-Pack was available, no production figures have surfaced. By 1990, Galen Govier had located one car with the Six-Pack motor.

A total 2,168 Road Runners came with the 340 engine, and only 672 came with the 440 4V.

All Road Runner engines got electronic ignitions in 1972.

Following the themes set in 1968, the Road Runner came with a bench seat interior, with buckets available.

Although the Track Pak axle packages were no longer available, the Road Runner could still be equipped with wide, 60 Series tires.

Road Runner suspension now included a rear sway bar and manual front disc brakes.

Chapter 40

1973 Plymouth Road Runner

Production
2 dr coupe 8 cyl   17,443

Serial numbers
RM21G3A100001
R — car line, Plymouth Satellite
M — price class (M-medium)
21 — body type (21-2 dr coupe)
G — engine code
3 — last digit of model year
A — assembly plant code (A-Lynch Road, G-St Louis, R-Windsor)
100001 — consecutive sequence number
    Serial number located on plate attached to left side of dash panel, visible through windshield.

Engine codes
G — 318 ci 2V V-8 170 hp
H — 340 ci 4V V-8 240 hp
P — 400 ci 4V V-8 260 hp
U — 440 ci 4V V-8 280 hp

Head casting numbers
318 ci — 2843675
340 ci — 3671587
400 ci — 3462346
440 ci — 3462346

Carburetors
318 ci 2V V-8 — Carter BBD6316S/manual, BBD6343S/manual Calif, BBD6317S/automatic, BBD6344S/automatic Calif
340 ci 4V V-8 — Carter TQ6318S/manual, TQ6339S/manual Calif, TQ6319S/automatic, TQ6340S/automatic Calif
400 ci 4V V-8 — Carter TQ6320S/manual, TQ6341S/manual Calif, TQ6321S/automatic, TQ6342S/automatic Calif
440 ci 4V V-8 — Carter TQ6324S/automatic, TQ6322S/automatic, TQ6410S/automatic Calif, TQ6411S/automatic Calif

Option order codes and retail prices
RM21 2 dr coupe V-8	$2,987.00
A01 Light Package	31.45
A34 Trailer Towing Wiring Package	39.50
A36 Performance Axle Package	93.65
A87 Exterior Decor Package	80.55
A88 Interior Decor Package (w/vinyl bench seat)	58.60
(w/vinyl bucket seats)	162.05
B41 Front power disc brakes (required w/340 ci)	40.45
C16 Console	56.35
C21 Center cushion w/folding armrest	56.35
C92 Color-keyed accessory floor mats	13.95
D21 Manual 4 speed transmission (318, 340, 400 engines)	201.85

D34 TorqueFlite transmission (w/318 ci)	211.10
(w/340 ci, 400 ci, 440 ci)	231.65
D51 2.71 or 2.76 axle ratio	13.30
D52 2.94 axle ratio	13.30
D91 Sure-Grip differential (std w/A36)	44.35
E55 340 ci 4V engine	153.00
E68 400 ci 4V engine	121.15
E86 440 ci 4V engine	241.90
F25 440 amp battery (std w/440 ci)	14.50
G11 Tinted glass — all windows	42.45
G15 Tinted glass — windshield	29.10
G35 Chrome outside left racing mirror	15.95
G36 Body-color remote left, manual right dual	
racing mirrors	27.45
G37 Chrome remote outside left & manual right	
racing mirrors	27.45
H31 Rear window defogger	30.75
H41 Strato ventilation (NA w/H51)	17.80
H51 Air conditioning (NA w/3 speed manual, required	
B41)	378.45
J15 Cigar lighter	3.20
J21 Electric clock (NA w/N85)	18.05
J25 3 speed windshield wipers w/electric washers	5.75
J52 Inside hood release	10.35
J55 Undercoating w/hood insulator pad	22.15
M25 Sill molding	21.80
M52 Manually operated sunroof	168.45
M85 Bright front & rear bumper guards	15.80
N85 Tachometer	51.55
N95 Emission control system & testing (required Calif)	25.55
P31 Power windows	119.10
R11 AM radio	64.90
R21 AM/FM radio	136.00
R31 Rear seat speakers, single	14.70
R35 AM/FM stereo radio	209.05
R36 AM/FM stereo radio w/stereo cassette	358.30
S77 Power steering	113.70
S84 Tuff steering wheel (wo/A88)	29.90
(w/A88)	19.65
W23 Chrome styled road wheels	57.65
Full vinyl roof	99.65
High-impact paint colors	14.70
Hood performance tape stripe treatment	21.55
Tires	
(replaces 5 F70x14 RWL tires — extra charge)	
T93 G70x14 RWL	18.40
U86 G60x15 RWL	80.10

Exterior color codes

Silver Frost Metallic	JA5	True Blue Metallic	GB5
Sky Blue	HB1	Rallye Red	FE5
Basin Street Blue	TB3	Mist Green	GY3

Exterior color codes

Autumn Bronze Metallic	GK6	Tahitian Gold Metallic	JY9
Sahara Beige	HL4	Spinnaker White	EW1
Honey Gold	JY3	Formal Black	TX9
Golden Haze Metallic	JY6	Lemon Twist	FY1
		Amber Sherwood Metallic	GF3

Interior trim codes

Color	Std Bench seats	Bench seats w/Decor Group	Bucket seats w/Decor Group
Blue	B2B5	C2B5	D6B5
Green	B2F6	C2F6	D6F6
Parchment	—	C2L3	D6L3
Black	B2X9	C2X9	D6X9
Gold	—	C2Y4	D6Y4
White	—	—	D6YW

Vinyl roof color codes

Black	V1X
White	V1W
Gold	V1Y
Parchment	V1L

Bodyside stripes codes

Black	V8X
White	V8W
Red	V8R

Hood stripes codes

Black	V9X
White	V9W
Red	V9R

Facts

Although the same bodyshell was used, the 1973 Road Runner got a slightly redesigned rear bumper and taillight configuration, and the front grille was redesigned. The loop bumper lost favor and was replaced by a conventional design running underneath the headlights and grille. The Road Runner came with a special bodyside and over-the-roof tape stripe treatment, and a performance hood. The interior got some cosmetic change and the optional bucket seats were redesigned.

Standard engine was downgraded to a 318 ci small-block with dual exhausts. Optional were the 340, 400 and 440 ci engines. The 318 came with the three-speed manual transmission. A four-speed manual was available only with the 340 and 400. The 440 was available only with the TorqueFlite automatic (117 built) and once again became a Road Runner GTX.

Suspension was unchanged in design from that used in 1972 but used different bushings to give a smoother ride.

Chapter 41

1974 Plymouth Road Runner

Production
2 dr hardtop 8 cyl   9,656

Serial numbers
RM21G4G100001

R — car line, Plymouth Satellite

M — price class (M-medium)

21 — body type (21-2 dr coupe)

G — engine code

4 — last digit of model year

G — assembly plant code (A-Lynch Road, G-St Louis, R-Windsor)

100001 — consecutive sequence number

    Serial number located on plate attached to left side of dash panel, visible through windshield.

Engine codes
G — 318 ci 4V V-8 170 hp

L — 360 ci 4V V-8 245 hp

P — 400 ci 4V V-8 250 hp

U — 440 ci 4V V-8 275 hp

Head casting numbers
318 ci — 2843675

360 ci — 3671587

400 ci — 3769902

440 ci — 3769902

Carburetors
318 ci 2V V-8 — Carter BBD8010S/manual, BBD8028S/automatic, BBD6465S/automatic, BBD6467S/automatic Calif

360 ci 4V V-8 — Carter TQ6452S/manual, TQ6454S/manual Calif, TQ6453S/automatic, TQ6455S/automatic Calif

400 ci 4V V-8 — Carter TQ6457S/manual, TQ6456S/automatic Calif

440 ci 4V V-8 — Carter TQ9015S/automatic, TQ6463S, TQ9049S, TQ9016S/automatic Calif

Option order codes and retail prices
RM21 2 dr coupe V-8	$3,305.00
A01 Light Package	38.60
A34 Light Trailer Towing Package (D34 required)	68.00
A36 Performance Axle Package	84.10
A56 Handling Package	60.70
A87 Exterior Decor Package	84.55
A88 Interior Decor Package (w/vinyl bench seat)	61.40
(cloth & vinyl bench seat)	98.30
(w/bucket seats)	170.40
(w/cloth & vinyl bucket seats)	266.55
B41 Front disc brakes	46.45
C16 Console	59.25
C21 Center cushion w/folding armrest	59.25

C92 Color-keyed accessory floor mats	14.65
D21 Manual 4 speed transmission (NA w/440 ci 4V)	212.50
D34 TorqueFlite transmission	243.85
D51 2.71 axle ratio (w/318 ci, 360 ci 4V, w/D34)	13.95
D52 2.94 axle ratio (w/318 ci & manual transmission)	13.95
D53 3.21 or 3.23 axle ratio (360 ci 4V, 400 ci 4V & D34)	13.95
D91 Sure-grip differential (std w/A36)	46.65
E58 360 ci 4V engine	161.10
E68 400 ci 4V engine	127.40
E86 440 ci 4V engine	254.65
F25 440 amp battery (std w/440 ci)	15.20
G01 Electric rear window defogger	64.30
G11 Tinted glass — all windows	44.70
G15 Tinted glass — windshield	30.60
G35 Chrome outside left racing mirror	15.95
G54 Chrome remote control left racing-type mirror	16.75
G74 Dual chrome remote control left racing mirrors	28.90
G75 Dual painted remote control left racing mirrors	28.90
H31 Forced air rear window defogger	32.30
H41 Strato ventilation (NA w/H51)	18.70
H51 Air conditioning (NA w/3 speed manual,	
required B41)	398.45
J15 Cigar lighter	4.40
J21 Electric clock (NA w/N85)	18.95
J25 3 speed windshield wipers w/electric washer	6.00
J45 Hood tie-down pins	17.05
J46 Locking gas cap	4.40
J52 Inside hood release	10.80
J55 Undercoating w/hood insulator pad	23.25
M25 Sill molding	22.90
M52 Manually operated sunroof	177.35
M85 Front & rear bumper guards, bright bases	16.55
N85 Tachometer (NA w/J21)	54.20
N88 Automatic speed control (B41 & D34 required)	66.80
N95 Emission control system & testing (required Calif)	29.35
P31 Power windows	125.35
R11 AM radio	68.30
R21 AM/FM radio	143.15
R31 Rear speaker, single	15.40
R35 AM/FM stereo radio	220.05
R36 AM/FM stereo radio w/stereo cassette	358.30
S25 HD shock absorbers	5.30
S76 Deluxe steering wheel w/partial horn ring (wo/A88)	20.60
(w/A88)	9.80
S77 Power steering	119.70
S84 Tuff steering wheel (wo/A88)	31.40
(w/A88)	20.60
W23 Chrome styled road wheels (wo/A87)	60.70
(w/A87)	32.60
Canopy vinyl roof	69.05
Full vinyl roof	104.80
Hood performance tape stripe treatment	22.65

Tires

(replaces 5 G70x14 RWL tires — extra charge)
U26 GR70x15 WSW   114.90

Exterior color codes

Silver Frost Metallic	JA5	Sahara Beige	HL4
Lucerne Blue Metallic	KB5	Golden Haze Metallic	JY6
Frosty Green Metallic	KG2	Tahitian Gold Metallic	JY9
Avocado Gold Metallic	KJ6	Spinnaker White	EW1
Dark Moonstone Metallic	KL8	Formal Black	TX9
Powder Blue	KB1	Sienna Metallic	KT5
True Blue Metallic	GB5	Yellow Blaze	KY5
Rallye Red	FE5	Aztec Gold	JL6

Interior trim codes

Color	Std bench seats	Vinyl bench seats w/Decor Group	Vinyl bucket seats w/Decor Group	Cloth & vinyl bucket seats
Blue	B2B6	C2B6	D6B6	—
Green	B2G6	C2G6	D6G6	—
Gold	—	C243	D643	—
Black	B2X9	C2X9	D6X9	—
White	—	—	D6XW	—
Parchment	—	C2L3	—	—
Wimbledon	—	—	—	W5EW

Vinyl roof color codes

Color	Full	Canopy
Black	V1X	V4X
White	V1W	V4W
Gold	V1Y	V4Y
Parchment	V1L	—
Green	V1G	—

Hood & bodyside stripes codes

Black	V8X
White	V8W
Red	V8R

Hood stripes codes

Black	V9X
White	V9W
Red	V9R

Facts

A slight grille change differentiated the 1974 Road Runner. In the interior, cloth and vinyl bucket seats were optional.

Mechanically, the only change was the substitution of the 340 engine with the 360 4V. The 440 was still available (79 built) albeit with an automatic transmission and again, such cars were Road Runner GTXs. No 60 Series tires were available, but a GR70 radial was optional.

The Road Runner continued in 1975, but it was based on the Fury, with emphasis on luxury rather than performance.

From 1976 to 1980, the Road Runner Package or option group was part of Plymouth's Volare offering.

1974 Plymouth Road Runner

Chapter 42

1968 Dodge Charger

Production
2 dr hardtop 6 cyl	906
2 dr hardtop 8 cyl	74,019
2 dr hardtop R/T 8 cyl	17,665
Total	92,590

Serial numbers
XS29L8B100001

X — car line, Dodge Charger

S — price class (S-special, P-premium)

29 — body type (29-2 dr sports hardtop)

L — engine code

8 — last digit of model year

B — assembly plant code (B-Hamtramck, G-St Louis)

100001 — consecutive sequence number

Serial number located on plate attached to left side of dash panel, visible through windshield.

Engine codes
B — 225 ci 1V 6 cyl 145 hp

F — 318 ci 2V V-8 230 hp

G — 383 ci 2V V-8 290 hp

H — 383 ci 4V V-8 330 hp

J — 426 ci 2x4V V-8 425 hp

L — 440 ci 4V V-8 375 hp

Head casting numbers
318 ci — 2843675

383 ci — 2843906

426 ci — 2780559

440 ci — 2843906

Carburetors
318 ci 2V V-8 — Carter BBD4420S/manual, BBD4421S/automatic

383 ci 2V V-8 — Carter BBD4422S/manual, BBD4423S, BBD4578S/ automatic

383 ci 4V V-8 — Carter AVS4426S/manual, AVS4401S/automatic, AVS4635S/automatic w/AC

426 ci 2x4V — Carter AFB4430S/front, AFB4431/rear manual, AFB4432/rear automatic

440 ci 4V V-8 — Carter AFB4428S/manual, AFB4429S/automatic, AFB4637A/automatic w/AC

Distributors
383 ci 2V — 2875354

383 ci 4v — 2875356/manual, 2875358/automatic

426 ci — 2875140 IBS-4014A

440 ci — 2875102 IBS-4014/manual, 2875209/automatic

Option order codes and retail prices
Charger V-8

XP29 2 dr sports hardtop	$3,014.00

Charger R/T V-8

XS29 2 dr sports hardtop	3,480.00

292 Two-tone paint	22.65
351 Charger Radio Group (NA w/426 ci)	250.75
355 Light Package	16.05
358 High-performance axle (w/383 ci only; NA w/359)	87.50
359 Trailer Towing Package (wo/411; NA R/T)	46.35
(wo/411, R/T)	24.50
(w/411; NA R/T)	36.25
(w/411, R/T)	14.35
393 Manual 4 speed transmission (NA w/318 ci)	188.05
395 TorqueFlite (w/318 ci)	206.30
(w/383 ci 2V)	216.20
(w/383 ci 4V)	227.05
408 Sure-Grip differential	42.35
(w/HD performance axle)	138.90
411 Air conditioner (NA w/383 ci 2V, 426 ci, 440 ci w/393)	342.85
418 Rear window defogger	21.30
420 AM radio w/stereo tape player	196.25
421 Music Master radio	61.55
422 Astrophonic radio	92.70
426 Rear seat speaker	14.70
451 Power brakes	41.75
456 Power steering	94.85
458 Power windows	100.25
473 Automatic speed control (NA 426 ci, 451 required)	52.50
478 HD drum brakes (std w/359, R/T, NA w/495)	21.95
485 Center front seat w/armrest	52.85
486 Console	52.85
495 Front disc brakes (451 required)	72.95
517 Hood-mounted turn signals	10.50
521 Tinted glass — all windows	39.50
522 Tinted glass — windshield only	22.35
531 Left head restraints	21.95
532 Right head restraints	21.95
533 Left & right head restraints	43.90
536 Remote outside left mirrors	9.40
537 Manual outside right mirrors	6.65
538 Locking gas cap	4.25
550 2 front, 2 rear deluxe seatbelts	10.50
556 Center passenger front seatbelts	6.50
557 Center passenger rear seatbelts	6.50
566 2 rear shoulder belts	26.45
568 2 front shoulder belts	26.45
571 Full-horn-ring steering wheel	9.35
573 Sports-type wood-grain steering wheel	25.95
577 Tachometer w/clock	48.70
579 Undercoating w/underhood pad	16.10
580 Chrome road wheels (NA w/426 ci)	97.30
581 Deluxe wheel covers, 14 in. (NA w/426 ci)	21.30
15 in. (w/426 ci)	24.60
584 Deep-dish, 14 in. (NA w/426 ci)	38.00
587 Simulated Mag, 14 in. (NA w/426 ci)	64.10

589 3 speed windshield wipers (std w/426 ci)		5.20
591 46 amp alternator (std w/411)		11.00
626 70 amp battery (std R/T)		8.10
638 Firm Ride shock absorbers (std R/T)		4.45
708 Special buffed Silver Metallic paint		21.95
Vinyl roof		85.90

Engines

61 383 ci 2V V-8 engine	69.75
62 383 ci 4V V-8 engine	137.55
73 426 ci 2x4V engine (R/T only)	604.75

Tires

(318, 383 engines)

33 7.35x14 WSW	32.70
41 7.75x14 BSW	14.05
43 7.75x14 WSW	46.55
44 F70x14 Red Streak (std w/440 ci, F70x15 w/426 ci)	70.70
46 F70x14 WSW (std w/440 ci, F70x15 w/426 ci)	70.70
51 8.25x14 BSW	27.90
53 8.25x14 WSW	63.75

Exterior color codes

Silver Metallic	AA1
Black	BB1
Dark Blue Metallic	EE1
Light Green Metallic	FF1
Medium Gold Metallic	JJ1
Medium Turquoise Metallic	LL1
Racing Green Metallic	GG1
Bronze Metallic	MM1
Red	PP1
Bright Blue Metallic	QQ1
Burgundy Metallic	RR1
Yellow	SS1
Medium Green Metallic	TT1
Light Blue Metallic	UU1
White	WW1
Beige	XX1
Medium Tan Metallic	YY1
Bright Red	33

Interior trim codes

Color	Vinyl
Blue	C6B
Red	C6R
Black	C6X
Green	C6F
Gold	C6Y
White/Black	C6W
White/Blue	C6C
White/Green	C6D
White/Red	C6V
White/Gold	C6E

Viny roof color codes

Green	304
Black	306
White	307

Bumblebee stripes codes

Black	310
Red	314
White	317

Facts

The 1968 Charger featured a complete restyle, in and out, from the previous 1967 model to what is generally considered the best-looking Chrysler product of the sixties. Showing no resemblance to any other Dodge, the beautiful Charger was pure B body. Two models were available, the Charger and the performance Charger R/T.

Standard engine was the 318 ci with a two-barrel carburetor. Optional were 383 ci engines in two- or four-barrel form.

More interesting was the Charger R/T. Standard engine was the 440 ci 375 hp, with the 426 Hemi optional. As with the Coronet R/T, the standard transmission was the three-speed TorqueFlite automatic. In fact, the Charger R/T shared the same suspension and driveline components as the Coronet R/T.

R/T identification included R/T medallions on the front grille and on the rear taillight panel. The R/T came with bumblebee stripes, which were a deletable option.

All Chargers came with bucket seats, concealed headlights and quick-fill gas cap.

The Performance Axle Package (358) consisted of a 3.55 axle ratio, Sure-Grip differential, high-capacity radiator and seven-blade slip-drive fan with shroud.

Late in the model year, the 225 ci six-cylinder engine became a no-cost option on the Charger.

Production figures indicated that a total 19,012 of the 383 ci powered Chargers were built. Total 440 ci production was 17,107, and 475 Charger R/Ts came with the Stage II 426 ci Hemi engine. The Stage II engine came with a more aggressive mechanical lifter camshaft.

After June 1, 1968, all Charger R/T models ordered with the Hemi engine and four-speed combination were built with exposed headlights, flush grille and chrome windshield reveal molding.

Of the 475 Hemi-equipped cars, 264 came with TorqueFlite automatic transmission and 211 with four-speed.

1968 Dodge Charger R/T Hemi 426

Chapter 43

1969 Dodge Charger

Production

2 dr sports hardtop
  6 cyl   542
2 dr sports hardtop
  8 cyl   65,840

2 dr sports hardtop
  R/T 8 cyl   19,298
  Total   85,680*
*Includes 503 Daytona and 500
  Charger 500 models.

Serial numbers

XS29L9A100001
X — car line, Dodge Charger
S — price class (P-premium, S-special, S-fasttop)
29 — body type (29-2 dr sports hardtop)
L — engine code
9 — last digit of model year
A — assembly plant code (A-Lynch Road, G-St Louis)
100001 — consecutive sequence number
    Serial number located on plate attached to left side of dash panel, visible through windshield.

Engine codes

B — 225 ci 1V I6 145 hp
F — 318 ci 2V V-8 230 hp
G — 383 ci 2V V-8 290 hp
H — 383 ci 4V V-8 330 hp
J — 426 ci 2x4V V-8 425 hp
L — 440 ci 4V V-8 375 hp

Head casting numbers

318 ci — 2843675
383 ci — 2843906
426 ci — 2780559
440 ci — 2843906

V-8 carburetors

318 ci 2V — Carter BBD4607S/manual, BBD4608S/automatic
383 ci 2V — Carter BBD4774S/manual, BBD4613S, BBD4614S/automatic
383 ci 4V — Carter AVS4615S, 4682S/manual, AVS4616S, 4711S, 4638S/automatic
426 ci 2x4V — Carter AFB4619/front, 4620S/rear manual, 4621S/rear automatic
440 ci 4V — Carter AVS4617S/manual, AVS4618S & 4640S/automatic

Distributors

383 ci — 2875750/manual, 2875731/automatic
426 ci — 2875140 IBS-4014A
440 ci — 2875772 IBS-4014B/manual, 2875758/automatic

Option order codes and retail prices
Charger

XP29 2 dr sports hardtop 6 cyl	$3,003.00
XP29 2 dr sports hardtop 8 cyl	3,109.00

R/T
XS29 2 dr sports hardtop 8 cyl	3,575.00

Charger 500
XX29 2 dr fasttop 8 cyl	3,843.00

Daytona Charger
XX29 2 dr fasttop 8 cyl	3,993.00
A01 Light Group	25.95
A04 Charger Radio Group (exc w/A47)	258.35
(w/A47)	220.35
A31 High Performance Axle Package (NA w/H51;	
w/383 ci 4V)	102.15
A32 Super Performance Axle Package (NA w/H51;	
w/440 ci & D34)	271.50
(NA w/H51; w/426 ci & D34)	242.15
A33 Track Pak (required w/440 ci 4V & 426 ci 8V w/D21)	142.85
A34 Super Track Pak (w/440 ci 4V & 426 ci 8V w/D21)	256.45
A35 Trailer Towing Package	
(w/D34, wo/H51; NA R/T, 500)	47.75
(w/D34, wo/H51; R/T, 500)	25.30
(w/D34, w/H51; NA R/T, 500)	37.30
(w/D34, w/H51; R/T, 500)	14.75
A36 Performance Axle Package (w/383 ci 4V)	102.15
(w/440 ci 4V & D34)	92.25
(w/426 ci 8V & D34)	64.40
A47 Charger Special Edition Package (NA w/426 ci)	161.85
B31 HD drum brakes (std w/A35, R/T, 500)	22.65
B41 Front disc brakes (B51 required)	50.15
B51 Power brakes	42.95
C14 Rear shoulder belts	26.45
C16 Console (w/bucket seats)	54.45
C21 Center front seat w/armrest (w/bucket seats only)	54.45
C25 Left head restraint	13.25
C28 Right head restraint	13.25
C31 Left & right head restraint	26.50
C62 Manual 6 way seat adjuster (left bucket only)	33.30
C92 Protective rubber floor mats	13.60
D21 Manual 4 speed transmission (w/383 ci 4V)	197.25
D34 TorqueFlite (w/225 ci)	189.05
(w/318 ci)	206.30
(w/383 ci 2V)	216.20
(w/383 ci 4V)	227.05
D91 Sure-Grip differential	42.35
E61 383 ci 2V engine (NA w/manual transmission)	69.75
E63 383 ci 4V engine	137.55
E74 426 ci engine	648.20
F11 46 amp alternator	11.00
F25 70 amp battery (std w/426 ci & R/T)	8.40
G11 Tinted glass — all windows	40.70
G15 Tinted glass — windshield only	25.90
G31 Manual outside right mirrors	6.85
G33 Remote control outside left mirrors	10.45
H31 Rear window defogger	21.90

H51 Air conditioner w/heater (D34 required on R/T)	357.65
J25 3 speed windshield wipers (std w/426 ci)	5.40
J46 Locking gas cap	4.40
J55 Undercoating w/underhood pad	16.60
L31 Hood-mounted turn signals	10.80
M05 Door edge protector moldings	4.65
M25 Sill moldings	21.15
M51 Power-operated sunroof, incl vinyl roof	461.45
M91 Luggage rack on rear deck lid (NA 500)	33.30
N85 Tachometer w/clock (8 cyl only)	50.15
N88 Automatic speed control (D34 & B51 required)	57.95
P31 Power windows	105.20
R11 Music Master radio	61.55
R13 Astrophonic radio	92.70
R21 Solid-state AM/FM radio	134.95
R22 Solid-state AM radio w/stereo tape	196.25
R31 Rear seat speaker	15.15
S25 Firm Ride shock absorbers (std R/T, 500)	4.60
S77 Power steering	100.00
S78 Deluxe steering wheel w/full horn ring	5.45
S81 Sports-type wood-grain steering wheel	26.75
W11 Deluxe wheel covers, 14 in. (NA w/426 ci)	21.30
W15 Deep-dish wheel covers, 14 in. (NA w/426 ci)	38.00
W18 Simulated Mag, 14 in. (NA w/426 ci)	64.10
(w/A47; NA w/426 ci)	26.15
W21 Chrome styled road wheels, 14 in. (NA w/426 ci)	86.15
(w/A47; NA w/426 ci)	48.25
Vinyl roof	93.55

Tires
(225 engine — replaces 7.35x14 BSW tires)

T22 7.35x14 WSW	32.70
T31 7.75x14 BSW	14.05
T32 7.75x14 WSW	46.55
T34 F78x14 WSW fiberglass-belted	72.95

Tires
(318 & 383 engines — replaces 7.75x14 BSW tires)

T32 7.75x14 WSW	32.70
T34 F78x14 WSW fiberglass-belted	59.05
T41 8.25x14 BSW	14.05
T42 8.25x14 WSW	49.85
T82 F70x14 White (requires B31 or B41)	57.00
T83 F70x14 Red (requires B31 or B41)	57.00
T85 F70x14 Red fiberglass-belted (requires B31 or B41)	83.35
U64 F70x15 White fiberglass-belted	90.95
U65 F70x15 Red fiberglass-belted	90.95

Tires
(440 engines — replaces F70x14 Red Streak tires)

T82 F70x14 WSW	NC
T85 F70x14 Red Streak fiberglass-belted	26.45
U64 F70x15 WSW fiberglass-belted	34.10
U65 F70x15 Red Streak fiberglass-belted	34.10

Tires

(426 engine, replaces F70x15 Red Streak fiberglass-belted
tires)

U64 F70x15 WSW fiberglass-belted   NC

Exterior color codes

Silver Metallic	A4	Red	R6
Light Blue Metallic	B3	Light Bronze Metallic	T3
Bright Blue Metallic	B5	Copper Metallic	T5
Medium Blue Metallic	B7	Dark Bronze Metallic	T7
Light Green Metallic	F3	White	W1
Medium Green Metallic	F5	Black	X9
Bright Green Metallic	F6	Yellow	Y2
Dark Green Metallic	F8	Cream	Y3
Bright Turquoise Metallic	Q5	Gold Metallic	Y4
Bright Red	R4		

Interior trim codes

Color	Vinyl bucket seats	Leather bucket seats	Cloth & vinyl bucket seats
Blue	C6D	CRD	—
Green	C6G	CRG	—
Red	C6R	—	—
Tan	C6T	CRT	—
White	C6W	—	—
Black	C6X	CRX	C5X
White/Black	C6W	—	—

Vinyl roof color codes

Green	V1F
Tan	V1T
White	V1W
Black	V1X

Bumblebee stripes codes

Black	V8X
Red	V8R
White	V8W

Facts

Styling changes for 1969 were as follows: all Chargers got a
grille divider, the rear taillights were changed from the previous
four round units to two longitudinal units and side marker lights
were changed to a rectangular design.

A new option group, the SE Package, included leather bucket
seats, simulated-wood-grain instrument panel appliqués, bright
pedal trim and a sports steering wheel. The SE Package was available on the Charger and the Charger R/T.

Engine line-up was unchanged from 1968 on both the regular
Charger and the Charger R/T. The 225 ci six-cylinder engine was
not officially listed on the option list. A slight change on the R/T was
the single-band bumblebee rear stripe available in three colors:
black, white and red.

A short-lived option was the W23 15 in. cast-center wheel.
These wheels were supposed to be replaced with the Magnum road
wheels by the selling dealer, as they contained manufacturing
defects.

A new Sure-Grip differential was used in 1969. Cone cluthes
replaced the previous disc-type clutches.

A transistorized voltage regulator replaced the previous conventional unit.

To promote Dodge's NASCAR racing activities, a special batch of 500 modified Chargers was built. These cars were known as Charger 500s. Powered by the 440 4V or 426 Hemi engine, with either a four-speed manual or a TorqueFlite automatic, the Charger 500 featured revised bodywork to make the car more aerodynamic. In the front, a 1968 Coronet grille was mounted flush in the Charger's grille cavity; in the rear, a flush-mounted rear window promoted improved airflow. The bodywork modifications were made by Creative Industries.

The Charger 500 did not prove to be the overwhelming winner it was intended to be. To gain supremacy on the NASCAR circuits, another batch of 503 Chargers was built. These were the Charger Daytonas. Featuring the same rear window treatment as the Charger 500, the Daytona went considerably further in the quest for better aerodynamics. An 18 in. nose cone was attached to the front of the car, and a high wing was mounted on the rear. Large Daytona lettering graced the rear quarter panels. Reverse-mounted front fender scoops, concealed headlights and special windshield pillar wind deflectors completed the aerodynamic package.

Engine availability on the Daytona was either the 375 hp 440 ci Magnum or the 426 ci Hemi, of which 70 were so equipped.

Bright Green (F6) paint was a December 1968 release. On February 4, 1969, performance hood paint (V21) was made available. The hood heat waste gate indentations were painted flat-black back to the cowl plenum.

Deluxe 15 in. wheel covers (W11) were released for Hemi-powered Chargers in February 1969.

Charger R/T production with the 426 ci Hemi totaled 432 units (225 with TorqueFlite and 207 with four-speed). These figures included the Daytona model.

1969 Dodge Charger Hemi 426

1969 Dodge Charger 500

1969 Dodge Charger Daytona

Chapter 44

1970 Dodge Charger

Production

Charger

2 dr sports hardtop 6 cyl	29	2 dr sports hardtop 8 cyl	27,432
2 dr sports hardtop 8 cyl	9,163	**R/T**	
		2 dr sports hardtop	9,509
Charger 500		Total	46,315
2 dr sports hardtop 6 cyl	182		

Serial numbers

XS29B0G100001

X — car line, Dodge Charger

S — price class (H-high, P-premium, S-special)

29 — body type (29-2 dr sports hardtop)

B — engine code

0 — last digit of model year

G — assembly plant code (G-St Louis)

100001 — consecutive sequence number

    Serial number located on plate attached to left side of dash panel, visible through windshield.

Engine codes

B — 225 ci 1V I6 145 hp

G — 318 ci 2V V-8 230 hp

L — 383 ci 2V V-8 290 hp

N — 383 ci 4V V-8 335 hp

R — 426 ci 2x4V V-8 425 hp

U — 440 ci 4V V-8 375 hp

V — 440 ci 3x2V V-8 390 hp

Head casting numbers

318 ci — 2843675

383 ci — 2843906

426 ci — 2780559

440 ci — 2843906

V-8 carburetors

318 ci 2V — Carter BBD4621S/manual, BBD4623S/manual w/ECS, BBD4722S/automatic, BBD4724S/automatic w/ECS, BBD4895S/automatic w/AC

383 ci 2V — Carter BBD4726S, 4725S/manual, 4372A, 4727S/manual w/ECS, 4894S/automatic w/AC, Holley R4371A/automatic w/AC

383 ci 4V — Holley R4736/manual, R4738/manual w/ECS, R4739/automatic w/ECS

426 ci 2x4V — Carter AFB4742S/front, AFB4745S/rear manual, AFB4746S/rear automatic

440 ci 4V — Carter AVS4737S/manual, AVS4739S/manual w/ECS, AVS4738/automatic, AVS4741S/automatic w/AC, AVS4740S/automatic w/ECS

440 ci 3x2V — Holley R4382A/front all, R4175A/front all w/ECS, R4374A/center manual, R4375A/center manual w/ECS, R4144A/center automatic, R4376A/center automatic w/ECS, R4365A/rear all, R4383A/rear all w/ECS

Distributors
383 ci — 3438231
383 ci 4V — 3438233 (interchanges w/3438433)
426 ci — 2875987/manual, 2875989 IBS-4014F/automatic
440 ci — 3438222
440 ci 3x2V — 3438314/manual up to approx 01/01/70, 3438348/ manual after approx 01/01/70, 2875982/automatic up to approx 01/01/70, 3438349/automatic after approx 01/01/70

Option order codes and retail prices
Charger

XH29 2 dr sports hardtop 6 cyl	$3,001.00
XH29 2 dr sports hardtop V-8	3,108.00
Charger 500	
XP29 2 dr sports hardtop 6 cyl	3,139.00
XP29 2 dr sports hardtop V-8	3,246.00
R/T	
XS29 2 dr sports hardtop V-8	3,711.00
A01 Light Group	34.70
A04 Charger Radio Group (wo/A47, wo/383 ci 4V)	261.80
(wo/A47, w/383 ci 4V)	256.40
(wo/A47, R/T)	256.40
(w/A47, wo/383 ci 4V)	225.55
(w/A47, w/383 ci 4V)	220.15
(w/A47, R/T)	220.15
A31 High Performance Axle Package (NA w/H51 or A35 — 383 ci)	102.15
A32 Super Performance Axle Package (NA w/H51 or A35)	
(w/440 ci & D34)	250.65
(w/426 ci & D34)	221.40
A33 Track Package (NA w/H51 w/440 ci 4V, 440 ci 6V, 426 ci w/D21)	142.85
A34 Super Track Pak (NA w/H51 w/440 ci 4V, 440 ci 6V, 426 ci w/D21)	235.65
A35 Trailer Towing Package (D34 required, NA 440 ci 6V & 426 ci)	41.75
(D34 required, NA 440 ci 6V & 426 ci, R/T)	14.05
A36 Performance Axle Package (NA w/A35)	
(w/383 ci 4V w/D21 or D34)	102.15
(w/440 ci 4V or 440 ci 6V w/D34)	92.25
(w/426 ci & D34)	64.40
B11 HD drum brakes (std w/A35)	22.65
B41 Disc brakes (requires B51)	27.90
B51 Power brakes	42.95
C14 Rear shoulder belts	26.45
C15 Seatbelt Group	13.75

C16 Console (w/bucket seats only)	54.45
C21 Center seat cushion & folding armrest (w/bucket seats, NA w/C16)	54.45
C62 Manual 6 way seat adjuster (left bucket only)	33.30
C92 Protective rubber floor mats	13.60
D13 Manual 3 speed floor shift transmission (w/383 ci 4V)	14.05
D21 Manual 4 speed transmission (w/383 ci 4V)	197.25
D34 TorqueFlite (w/225 ci)	190.25
(w/318 ci)	206.30
(w/383 ci 2V)	216.20
(w/383 ci 4V)	227.05
D91 Sure-Grip differential (std w/performance axle packages)	42.35
E61 383 ci 2V engine	69.75
E63 383 ci 4V engine	137.55
E74 426 ci 2x4V engine (R/T only)	648.25
E87 440 ci 3x2V engine	119.05
F11 50 amp alternator	11.00
F25 70 amp battery	12.95
G11 Tinted glass — all windows	40.70
G15 Tinted glass — windshield only	25.90
G31 Manual outside right mirror	6.85
G33 Remote control outside left mirror	10.45
H31 Rear window defogger	26.25
H51 Air conditioning w/heater (D34 required)	357.65
J25 3 speed windshield wipers (std w/383 ci 4V & R/T)	5.40
J45 Hood hold-down pins (R/T)	15.40
J55 Undercoating w/underhood pad	16.60
L42 Headlight time delay & warning signal (w/A01)	13.00
(wo/A01)	18.20
M05 Door edge protectors	4.65
M51 Power sunroof, incl vinyl roof	461.45
M81 Front bumper guards (rear std)	16.00
N42 Bright exhaust tips (R/T NA Calif)	20.80
N85 Tachometer, incl clock (8 cyl Charger & R/T)	68.45
(8 cyl Charger 500)	50.15
N88 Automatic speed control (8 cyl only, NA 440 ci 6V & 426 ci)	57.95
N95 Evaporative emission control (Calif)	37.85
N97 Noise Reduction Package (required Calif w/383 ci & 440 ci)	NC
P31 Power windows	105.20
R11 Music Master AM radio (wo/A04)	61.55
R13 Astrophonic AM radio (wo/A04)	92.70
(w/A04)	31.25
R21 Solid-state AM/FM radio (wo/A04)	134.95
(w/A04)	73.50
R22 Solid-state AM radio w/stereo tape player (wo/A04)	196.25
(w/A04)	134.75
R31 Rear seat speaker	15.15
S15 Rallye suspension (318 & 383 engines)	5.45

S17 Reduced-rate suspension (Charger & Charger 500)	NC
S25 HD shock absorbers (std R/T, std w/S15)	5.45
S77 Power steering	105.20
S81 Sports-type wood-grain steering wheel	26.75
S83 Rim Blow steering wheel (wo/A47)	19.15
V21 Hood performance paint treatment (R/T)	18.05
High-impact paint colors	14.05
Vinyl roof	100.00

Wheels & wheel covers

W11 Deluxe wheel covers, 14 in. (wo/A04 or A47)	21.30
W13 Deep-dish, 14 in. (wo/A04 or A47)	36.25
W15 Wire wheel covers, 14 in. (wo/A04 or A47)	64.10
(w/A04 or A47)	28.00
W21 Rallye road wheels, 14 or 15 in. (wo/A04 or A47)	43.10
(w/A04 or A47)	7.05
W23 Road wheels w/trim ring, 14 in. (wo/A04 or A47)	86.15
(w/A04 or A47)	50.10

Tires—set of 5

(replaces F78x14 BSW tires — 225 engine)

T34 F78x14 WSW	29.25
T45 G78x14 BSW	15.40
T46 G78x14 WSW	46.55

Tires

(replaces G78x14 BSW tires — 318 & 383 engines)

T46 G78x14 WSW	31.35
T86 F70x14 WSW (B11 or B41 required)	34.80
T87 F70x14 RWL (B11 or B41 required)	34.80
U84 F60x15 RWL (B11 or B41 & S15 required)	97.95

Tires

(replaces F70x14 WSW tires— R/T only)

T87 F70x14 RWL	NC
U84 F60x15 RWL	63.25

Exterior color codes

Light Blue Metallic	EB3	Dark Tan Metallic	FT6
Bright Blue Metallic	EB5*	Hemi Orange	EV2
Dark Blue Metallic	EB7	White	EW1
Bright Red	FE5	Black	TX9
Light Green Metallic	FF4	Top Banana	FY1*
Dark Green Metallic	EF8*	Cream	DY3
Sublime	FJ5*	Gold Metallic	FY4
Go-Mango	EK2*	Plum Crazy	FC7*
Dark Burnt Orange		*G36 color-keyed mirror avail-	
Metallic	FK5*	able.	
Beige	BL1		

Interior trim codes

Color	Std vinyl bench seats	Opt vinyl bucket seats	SE leather bucket seats	Opt cloth & vinyl bucket seats	R/T vinyl bucket seats
Blue	H2B5	P6B5	CRB5	—	C6B5
Green	H2F8	P6F8	CRF8	—	C6F8

Color	Std vinyl bench seats	Opt vinyl bucket seats	SE leather bucket seats		
Tan	H2T5	P6T5	CRT5	—	C6T5
Black	H2X9	P6X9	CRXA	C5XA	C6XA
Burnt Orange	H2K4	P6K4	—	—	C6K4
White/Black	H2XW	P6XW	—	—	C6XW

Vinyl roof color codes

Green	V1F
White	V1W
Black	V1X
Gator Grain	V1G

Longitudinal tape stripes codes*

Black	V6X
White	V6W
Red	V6R

Bumblebee stripes codes

Black	V8X
White	V8W
Red	V8R
Green	V8G
Blue	V8B
Green	V6G
Blue	V6B

*Optional.

Facts

Continuing on the same basic bodyshell, the 1970 Charger came with a chrome loop bumper that was popular with early seventies Chrysler products. Model line-up changed; the basic Charger was complemented by the Charger 500 and the Charger R/T.

The Charger 500 was not the same high-performance 500 of 1969. It was an upgraded basic Charger that included vinyl bucket seats (bench seats were standard), electric clock, wheel lip moldings and the 500 nameplate on the front and rear of the car.

The Special Edition Package was optional on the 500 and R/T. It included leather bucket seats, simulated-wood steering wheel and dash appliqué, pedal dress-up, Light Group, vinyl map pockets on the doors and deep-dish wheel covers.

The Charger R/T got a reverse-facing door-mounted scoop with R/T identification, a choice of longitudinal or bumblebee stripes, and the same suspension and brakes from 1969. An engine was added to the R/T option list, the 390 hp 440 Six-Pack that first appeared on the 1969½ Road Runner and Super Bee. The only difference was that the 1970 version of the Six-Pack engine came with a cast-iron intake manifold rather than the previous Edelbrock aluminum unit.

The 440 Six-Pack also came with stronger connecting rods to combat 1969½ high-rpm failures, a Lubrite-faced camshaft and oil control rings that had increased tension.

The 426 Hemi got a hydraulic lifter camshaft and a carburetor solenoid stop for emission reasons. It was still rated at 425 hp.

Midyear options included a rear spoiler (J81), a new performance hood treatment that had 440 or Hemi spelled out in block letters with silver reflective tape on either side (V24) and dual color-keyed mirrors (G36).

Chapter 45

1971 Dodge Charger R/T and Super Bee

Production

2 dr hardtop Super Bee		2 dr hardtop R/T 8 cyl	2,659
8 cyl	4,144	Total	6,803

Serial numbers

WS23R1A100001

W — car line, Dodge Charger

S — price class (M-medium, S-special)

23 — body type (23-2 dr hardtop)

R — engine code

1 — last digit of model year

A — assembly plant code (A-Lynch Road, E-Los Angeles, G-St Louis)

100001 — consecutive sequence number

Serial number located on plate attached to left side of dash panel, visible through windshield.

Engine codes

N — 383 ci 4V V-8 330 hp (250 hp net)

R — 426 ci 2x4V V-8 425 hp (350 hp net)

U — 440 ci 4V V-8 375 hp (305 hp net)

V — 440 ci 3x2V V-8 390 hp (330 hp net)

Head casting numbers

340 ci — 2531894

383 ci — 3462346

426 ci — 2780559

440 ci — 3462346

V-8 carburetors

340 ci 4V — Carter AVS4972S/manual, AVS4973S/automatic

383 ci 4V — Holley R4734A/manual w/fresh air, R4667A/manual wo/fresh air, R4735/automatic w/fresh air, R4668A/automatic wo/fresh air

426 ci 2x4V — Carter AFB4971S/front, AFB4969S/rear manual, AFB4970S/rear automatic

440 ci 4V — Carter AVS4967S/manual, AVS4966S, 4968S/automatic

440 ci 3x2V — Holley R4669A/center manual, R4670A/center automatic, R4671A/front, R4672A/rear

Distributors

340 ci — 3438522/manual, 3438517/automatic, 3656151/manual w/electronic ignition, 3438986/automatic w/electronic ignition

383 ci — 3438690

426 ci — 2875987/manual, 3438579/automatic, 3438891/manual w/electronic ignition, 3438893/automatic w/electronic ignition

440 ci — 3438693

440 ci — 3438577

Option order codes and retail prices*

Charger Super Bee

XM23 2 dr hardtop	$3,271.00
Charger R/T	
XS23 2 dr hardtop	3,223.00
A01 Light Package (Super Bee)	25.90
(R/T)	17.00
A02 Driver Aid Group (A01 required)	14.20
A04 Charger Radio Group	204.75
A09 Concealed headlamps (incl J52)	65.60
A28 Noise Reduction Package	
(440 ci 6V w/D34, required Calif)	33.55
A31 High Performance Axle Package	
(NA w/AC or trailer towing available w/340 ci	
& 383 ci 4V engines w/D21 & D34)	81.80
A33 Track Package	
(NA w/AC, w/440 ci 6V, 426 ci w/D21)	149.80
A34 Super Track Pac	
(NA w/AC, w/440 ci 6V, 426 ci w/D21)	219.30
A35 Trailer Towing Package	
(w/383 ci 4V, D34 & B41 required)	50.85
(w/440 ci 4V, D34 & B41 required)	26.30
A36 Performance Axle Package (w/340 ci & 383 ci)	81.80
(w/440 ci 6V & D34)	81.80
(w/426 ci & D34)	45.35
A45 Front & rear spoiler	59.40
A54 Colored Bumper Group	21.40
B41 Disc brakes (B51 required)	24.45
B51 Power brakes	45.15
C14 Rear shoulder belts	26.50
C16 Console (w/bucket seats only)	57.65
C62 Manual 6 way seat adjuster (left bucket only)	35.00
D21 Manual 4 speed transmission (Super Bee)	206.40
(R/T)	NC
D34 TorqueFlite (340 ci, 383 ci 4V, 426 ci, 440 ci)	237.50
D91 Sure-Grip differential (NA 6 cyl models)	45.35
E55 340 ci V-8 (Super Bee)	45.90
E74 426 ci 2x4V engine (Super Bee)	883.55
(R/T)	746.50
E87 440 ci 3x2V engine (Super Bee)	262.15
(R/T)	125.00
F25 70 amp-hr battery (std w/440 ci & 426 ci)	14.80
G11 Tinted glass — all windows	43.40
G15 Tinted glass — windshield only	29.80
G31 Chrome outside right racing mirror (requires G33)	11.75
G33 Chrome outside left racing mirror	16.25
G36 Color-keyed remote outside left & manual right	
racing mirrors	28.00
H31 Rear window defogger	31.45
H41 Forced upper air ventilation (NA w/H51)	18.20
H51 Air conditioning	388.00
J21 Electric clock (NA w/N85)	18.45

J24 Headlamp washer (w/concealed headlamps only)	29.30
J25 Variable-speed wipers w/electric washers	5.85
J41 Pedal dress-up (Super Bee)	5.40
J45 Hood pins	16.55
J52 Inside hood release	10.55
J55 Undercoating w/underhood pad	22.60
J81 Spoiler, rear only	37.30
L31 Fender-mounted turn signals	11.60
L42 Headlamp time delay (wo/A01)	19.45
(w/A01)	13.90
L72 Headlamp warning buzzer (incl in A01)	5.60
M05 Door edge protectors	6.50
M51 Power sunroof, incl full vinyl roof	484.65
M81 Front bumper guards (NA w/A54)	16.85
M83 Rear bumper guards (NA w/A54)	16.85
M85 Front & rear bumper guards (NA w/A54)	33.70
M91 Deck lid luggage rack	35.00
N25 Engine block heater	15.55
N95 NOx exhaust emission control (Calif)	11.95
P31 Power windows	121.75
R11 Music Master AM radio	66.40
R26 AM radio w/stereo cassette	219.15
R31 Rear seat speaker (w/R11 only, std all others)	15.05
R33 Microphone (w/cassette)	11.70
R35 Multiplex AM/FM stereo radio	213.70
R36 Multiplex AM/FM stereo radio w/stereo cassette	366.40
S13 Rallye suspension (Super Bee, std w/A35, NA R/T)	Std
S15 Extra-HD suspension (Super Bee w/340 ci & 383 ci 4V; std w/440 ci & 426 ci — w/383 ci or 340 ci)	NC
S62 Tilt steering wheel (S77 & D34 required incl Rim Blow)	55.70
S77 Power steering	116.25
S83 Wood-grain w/Rim Blow steering wheel	20.10
S84 Tuff steering wheel (D34 required)	20.10
W11 Deluxe wheel covers, 14 in.	27.35
W12 Wheel trim rings, 14 or 15 in. (w/hubcaps only)	27.35
W15 Wire wheel covers, 14 in.	70.15
W21 Rallye road wheels, 14 or 15 in. (15 in. requires W34)	58.95
W23 Chrome styled road wheels, 14 in. only w/std spare	90.55
W34 Collapsible spare tire (NA w/A35, E86, E87, E74)	13.60
Cloth & vinyl bucket seat (Super Bee)	105.95
High-impact paint colors	15.05
Two-tone paint	31.10
Vinyl bench seat (Super Bee)	105.95
Vinyl bodyside insert protection molding (Super Bee)	15.50
Vinyl roof	95.75
Tires — Super Bee	
(w/340 & 383 engines, replaces F70x14 WSW tires)	
T34 F78x14 WSW .	NC
T46 G78x14 WSW	18.75
T87 F70x14 RWL	12.50

T93 G70x14 RWL (required w/A35)		31.25
U86 G60x15 RWL		94.30

Tires — Super Bee, R/T
(w/426 & 440 engines, replaces G70x14 RWL tires)

T46 G78x14 WSW (NA w/426 ci)		NC
U86 G60x15 RWL		63.10

*April 1, 1971, revision.

Exterior color codes

Light Gunmetal Metallic	GA4	Bright Red	FE5
Light Blue Metallic	GB2	Bright White	GW3
Bright Blue Metallic	GB5*	Black	TX9
Dark Blue Metallic	GB7	Butterscotch	EL5
Dark Green Metallic	GF7	Citron Yella	GY3*
Light Green Metallic	GF3	Hemi Orange	EV2*
Gold Metallic	GY8	Green Go	FJ6*
Dark Gold Metallic	GY9	Plum Crazy	FC7*
Dark Bronze Metallic	GK6	Top Banana	FY1
Tan Metallic	GT5	*Colored bumper group (A54) availability	

Interior trim codes
Super Bee

Color	Vinyl bench seats	Opt vinyl bucket seats
Blue	C2B5	C6B5
Green	C2F7	C6F7
Tan	C2T7	C6T7
Black	C2X9	C6X9
Black/White	C2XW	C6XW
Gold	C2Y3	C6Y3
Black/Orange	—	—
Black/Gunmetal	—	C6XA

R/T

Color	Vinyl bucket seats	Opt cloth & vinyl bucket seats
Blue	D6B5	—
Green	D6F7	D5F7
Tan	D6T5	—
Black	D6X9	D5X9
Black/White	D6XW	—
Gold	D6Y3	—
Black/Orange	—	D5XV
Black/Gunmetal	D6XA	—

Vinyl roof color codes

Black	V1X
White	V1W
Green	V1F
Gold	V1Y

Vinyl bodyside moldings – Super Bee

Blue	V5B
Green	V5F
Gold	V5Y

Longitudinal accent stripes codes

Black	V7X
White	V7W
Red	V7R

Facts

The 1971 Charger got a totally new body, with ventless side windows, concealed windshield wipers and a semifastback roof design. Breaking with the past, the Charger now sported a split front bumper design.

As before, the performance Charger Model was the R/T, with its standard 440 ci engine and TorqueFlite automatic transmission. Optional engines were the 440 Six-Pack and 426 Hemi. The usual heavy-duty suspension, drum brakes and bucket seats were standard equipment. The R/T came with a blacked-out hood bulge, longitudinal side tape treatment and two unique vertical tape stripes on each door. The Ramcharger functional hood scoop was optional equipment, but standard with the 426 Hemi engine.

Because the Coronet line was consolidated, the Super Bee was no longer available as part of it. Instead, for its last year, the Super Bee became a separate Charger model. Similar in styling to the R/T, the Super Bee came with a blacked-out hood treatment that incorporated a large, round Super Bee decal. The Super Bee also got the same side stripes but without the two door stripes. Standard engine was the 383 ci 4V rated at 300 hp with a three-speed manual. Optional were the 340 ci, 440 Six-Pack and 426 Hemi engines. In the interior, the Super Bee came with a front bench seat but buckets were optional.

Color-keyed bumpers were optional on both the R/T and the Super Bee, as were front and rear spoilers.

Only 320 Super Bees got the 340 ci small-block.

Total 426 Hemi production was 22 in Super Bees (13 with TorqueFlite and nine with four-speed) and 63 in R/Ts (33 with TorqueFlite and 30 with four-speed).

1971 Dodge Charger Super Bee

Chapter 46

1970 Plymouth Sport Fury GT

Production

2 dr hardtop GT S/23 8 cyl	689
2 dr hardtop GT 8 cyl	666
Total	1,355

Serial numbers

PP23T0D100001
P—car line, Plymouth Fury
P—price class (P-premium, S-special)
23—body type (23-2 dr hardtop)
T—engine code
0—last digit of model year
D—assembly plant code (D-Belvedere)
100001—consecutive sequence number
Serial number located on plate attached to left side of dash panel, visible through the windshield.

Engine codes

G—318 ci 2V V-8	230 hp
L—383 ci 2V V-8	290 hp
L—383 ci 4V V-8	330 hp
T—440 ci 4V V-8	350 hp
V—440 ci 3x2V V-8	390 hp

Head casting numbers

318 ci—2843675
383 ci—2843906
440 ci—2843906

Carburetors

318 ci 2V V-8—Carter BBD4722S/automatic, 4724S/automatic w/ECS, 4895S w/o ECS, w/AC
383 ci 2V V-8—Carter BBDC4894S/automatic w/AC, Carter BBD4728S/automatic w/AC, Holley R4371A/automatic w/AC, Holley R4370A/automatic
383 ci 4V V-8—Carter 4736S/automatic, Holley R4368A/automatic, Carter 4732S/automatic w/AC, 4734A/automatic w/ECS, w/AC
440 ci 4V V-8—Holley R4366/automatic, R4360A/automatic w/ECS
440 ci 3x2V V-8—Holley R4382A front, R4175A front w/ECS, R4144A/center, R4376A/center w/ECS, R4365A/rear, R4383A/rear w/ECS

Distributors

318 ci—3438225
383 ci—3438231
383 ci 4V—3438233
440 ci—3438219

440 ci 3x2V—2875982/automatic up to approx. 01/01/70,
3438349/automatic after approx. 01/01/70

Option order codes and retail prices

PS23 2 dr hardtop S/23 GT	$3,379.00
PP23 2 dr hardtop	3,898.00
A01 Light Package	40.85
A04 Basic Group	225.55
A35 Trailer Towing Package (w/318 ci)	48.70
A35 Trailer Towing Package (w/383 ci 2V)	48.70
A35 Trailer Towing Package (w/383 ci 4V)	76.45
A35 Trailer Towing Package (w/440 ci 4V)	34.80
A76 Brougham Package	152.75
B41 Disc brakes	27.90
B51 Power brakes	42.95
C13 Rear shoulder belts	26.45
C15 Deluxe seatbelts	13.75
C92 Accessory floor mats	13.60
D34 TorqueFlite, 318 ci	206.30
D34 TorqueFlite, 383 ci 2V	216.20
D34 TorqueFlite, 383 4V & 440 engines (std on GT)	227.05
D51 2.73 ratio (w/383-4V, 440-4V & 440-3x2V engines)	10.35
D56 3.55 ratio (w/318 ci & manual trans.)	10.35
D91 Sure-Grip differential	48.70
E61 383 ci 2V engine, S/23	69.70
E63 383 ci 4V engine, S/23	137.60
E85 440 ci 4V engine, S/23	233.65
E87 440 ci 3x2V engine (GT only)	153.45
F11 50 amp alternator	11.00
F25 70 amp battery	12.95
G11 Tinted glass, all windows	42.00
G15 Tinted windshield	26.05
G31 Manual outside right mirror	6.85
G33 Manual remote control outside left mirror	10.45
H31 Rear window defogger	26.25
H51 Air conditioning	365.05
H53 Air conditioning with automatic temperature control	440.25
J21 Electric clock	16.50
J25 3 speed windshield wipers (std w/440-6V)	5.40
J41 Pedal dress-up	5.45
J55 Undercoating w/hood insulator pad	16.50
L42 Headlight time delay & warning signal	18.20
M05 Door edge protectors	4.65
M45 Wheel house opening skirt (NA w/W13, S13 req'd)	31.05
M81 Front bumper guards	16.80
M83 Rear bumper guards	16.80
M85 Front & rear bumper guards	33.60
N88 Automatic speed control (8 cyl only, NA w/440-6V)	60.85
N95 Evaporative control system (Calif)	37.85
P21 Power bench seat	100.35
P25 Power bucket or split bench seat	92.90

P31 Power windows	105.20
P41 Power door locks	45.00
P45 Power remote trunk release	14.55
R11 Solid-state AM radio (w/oA04)	61.55
R13 Solid-state deluxe radio (w/oA04)	90.45
R13 Solid-state deluxe radio (w/A04)	28.95
R22 Solid-state deluxe radio, w/stereo tape player (w/oA04)	196.25
R22 Solid-state deluxe radio, w/stereo tape player (w/A04)	134.75
R35 Multiplex AM/FM stereo radio (w/oA04)	213.60
R35 Multiplex AM/FM stereo radio (w/A04)	152.20
R31 Rear seat speaker, single (w/R11, R13)	14.05
R31 Rear seat speakers, dual (w/R22, R35)	25.90
S13 Heavy-duty suspension (w/318 ci)	23.25
S13 Heavy-duty suspension (w/383 ci & S23 model)	12.80
S25 Heavy-duty shock absorbers (std w/A35)	4.60
S62 Tilt steering wheel w/rim blow (D34 & S77 req'd)	52.95
S77 Power steering	105.20
S81 Wood-grain steering wheel	26.75
S83 2 spoke rim blow	19.30
W11 Deluxe wheel covers (w/oA04	21.30
W13 Sport wheel covers (w/oA04)	36.25
W13 Sport wheel covers (w/A04)	15.00
W23 Chrome styled road wheels (w/oA04)	44.55
W23 Chrome styled road wheels (w/A04)	44.55
Two-tone paint	23.30
Vinyl roof	105.50
Cloth & vinyl trim	NC
Vinyl bucket seats	100.25
Tires—set of 5 (replaces G78x15 WSW - 318 & 383 engines)	
U24 G78x15 WSW	31.35
U35 H78x15 BSW (minimum w/A35)	17.85
U36 H78x15 WSW	51.85
U75 H70x15 RWL (S13 req'd)	72.70

Exterior color codes

Silver Metallic	EA4
Ice Blue Metallic	EB3
Blue Fire Metallic	EB5
Jamaica Blue Metallic	EB7
Lime Green Metallic	FF4
Ivy Green Metallic	EF8
Burnt Orange Metallic	FK3
Deep Burnt Orange Metallic	FK5
Sandpebble Beige	BL1
Frosted Teal Metallic	FP6
Scorch Red	ER6
Sahara Tan Metallic	FT3
Burnt Tan Metallic	FT6
Alpine White	EW1
Black Velvet	TX9
Sunfire Yellow	DY2

| Citron Mist Metallic | FY4 |
| Citron Gold Metallic | FY6 |

Interior trim codes

Color	Bench Cloth & vinyl	Buckets Vinyl	Vinyl
Blue	H3B3	H4B3	H6B3
Green	H3F8	H4F8	H6F8
Charcoal/Black	H3XA	H4XA	H6XA
Burnt Orange	H3K4	H4K4	H6K4
Gold	H3Y4	—	—
Tan	—	H4T5	H6T5
White/Black	—	H4XW	—
Teal/Black	—	H4XP	—

Brougham Package

Color	Buckets Cloth	Buckets Vinyl	Split bench Cloth & vinyl	Split bench Vinyl
Blue	H5B3	—	H7B3	—
Green	H5F8	—	H7F8	—
Tan	—	D6T5	—	H8T5
Charcoal/Black	—	D6XA	—	H8XA

Vinyl roof color codes

Green	V1F
White	V1W
Black	V1X
Gator Grain	V1G
Champagne	V1L
Tortoise Grain	V1Y

Strobe stripes & sport hood treatment (std)

White	V6W
Black	V6X
Burnt Orange	V6K

Body side molding color codes (std)

Blue	V5B
Green	V5F
Tan	V5T
Black	V5X
Citron Gold	V5Y

Facts

The Plymouth Sport Fury GT combined luxury and performance in a big car. Two versions were produced, the S/23 GT and the GT.

Based on the two-door Fury hardtop, the standard engine

on the S/23 model was the 318 ci V-8 with optional engines ranging from the 383 ci 2V, 383 ci 4V and the Super Commando 440 ci 4V rated at 350 hp. Standard on the Fury GT was the 440 ci 4V with only one optional engine, the 440 ci 6-bbl engine rated at 390 hp. All Fury S/23s and GTs came with the TorqueFlite automatic transmission.

The S/23 designation appeared on the rear decklid and on the front fenders just in front of the side strobe stripes.

Both models had the same side strobe tape treatment and hood runner stripes. The hood incorporated two power bulges, but the GT also got chrome .exhaust tips. H70x15 tires on steel road wheels were standard with the 440 ci V-8 engines; however, the 318 and 383 ci V-8 engines could also be upgraded with these wheels.

The 440 ci 6-bbl engine was the same engine that first appeared on the 1969 Road Runner and Super Bee. Based on the 375 hp Magnum 440 ci V-8, the 390 hp rating was achieved through the use of a 3x2V carburetor setup. The only difference from the 1969 version was the substitution of a cast-iron intake manifold rather than the Edelbrock aluminum manifold.

1970 Plymouth Sport Fury S/23

Chapter 47

1971 Plymouth Sport Fury GT

Production
2 dr hardtop GT 8 cyl   333

Serial numbers
PP23T1D100001
P—car line, Plymouth Fury
P—price class (P-premium)
23—body type (23-2 dr hardtop)
T—engine code
1—last digit of model year
D—assembly plant code (D-Belvedere)
100001—consecutive sequence number
Serial number located on plate attached to left side of dash panel,
visible through the windshield.

Engine code
T—440 ci 4V V-8 370 hp (net rating 305 hp)

Head casting number
440 ci—2843906

Carburetor
Carter AVS4966S

Distributor
3438694

Option order codes and retail prices
PP23 2 dr hardtop	$3,975.00
A01 Light Package	43.70
A04 Basic Group	225.55
A35 Trailer Towing Package	26.30
A76 Brougham Package	162.05
C13 Rear shoulder belts	26.50
C92 Accessory floor mats	14.25
D51 2.73 axle ratio	13.60
D91 Sure-Grip differential	48.70
F11 50 amp alternator	11.80
G11 Tinted glass, all windows	47.15
G15 Tinted windshield	33.95
G31 Manual outside right mirror	7.40
G33 Manual remote control outside left mirror	12.95
H31 Rear window defogger	31.45
H41 Strato ventilation (NA w/H51)	18.20
H51 Air conditioning	391.15
J21 Electric clock	17.50

J24 Headlights washer & wiper (J25 req'd)	29.30
J25 3 speed windshield wipers (std w/440-6V)	5.85
J41 Pedal dress-up	5.85
J55 Undercoating w/hood insulator pad	2.60
L42 Headlight time delay & warning signal	19.45
M05 Door edge protectors	6.50
M51 Power sunroof with vinyl roof	484.65
M81 Front bumper guards	19.45
N25 Engine block heater	15.55
N88 Automatic speed control (8 cyl only)	64.85
N95 NOx exhaust emission control	STD
P21 Power bench seat	104.95
P25 Power bucket or split bench seat	92.95
P31 Power windows	120.45
P41 Power door locks	47.30
P45 Power remote trunk release	15.55
R11 Solid-state AM radio (w/oA04)	66.40
R13 Deluxe solid-state AM radio (w/oA04)	93.50
R13 Deluxe solid-state AM radio (w/A04)	27.20
R22 Solid-state AM radio w/stereo tape player (w/oA040	366.40
R22 Solid-state AM radio w/stereo tape player (w/A04)	300.10
R35 AM/FM stereo radio (w/oA04)	213.70
R35 AM/FM stereo radio (w/A04)	147.40
R31 Rear seat speaker, single (w/R11, R13)	15.05
R31 Rear seat speaker, dual (w/R26, R35, R36)	27.20
R33 Microphone (w/26 or R36)	11.70
S25 Heavy-duty shock absorbers (std w/A35)	5.20
S77 Power steering	111.40
S62 Tilt steering wheel w/rim blow (D34 & S77 req'd)	55.70
S83 2 spoke rim blow	26.90

Wheels & wheel covers

W15 Wire wheel covers (w/oA04)	11.20
W23 Chrome styled road wheels (w/oA04)	44.45
Two-tone paint	31.10
High-impact paint colors	15.05
Vinyl roof	105.65
Vinyl bucket seats	105.25

Exterior color codes

Slate Gray Metallic	A8
Glacial Blue Metallic	GB2
Evening Blue Metallic	GB7
Mood Indigo Metallic	C8
Burnished Red Metallic	E7
Amber Sherwood Metallic	GF3
Sherwood Green Metallic	GF7
April Green Metallic	J4
Autumn Bronze Metallic	GK6
Sandalwood Beige	L1
Coral Turquoise Metallic	Q5

Tahitian Walnut Metallic				FT3
Tor Red				EV2
Spinnaker White				GW3
Formal Black				TX9
Curious Yellow				GY3
Gold Leaf Metallic				GY8
Tawny Gold Metallic				GY9

Interior trim codes

Color	Bench Cloth & vinyl	Bench Vinyl	Buckets Vinyl	Opt. Brougham Cloth & vinyl buckets
Blue	H3B7	M4B7	H6B7	H5B7
Green	H3F8	M4F8	H6F8	H5F8
Charcoal/				
Black	H3XA	M4XA	H6XA	H5XA
Gold	H3Y4	M4Y4	—	H5Y4
Tan	H3T5	M4T5	—	—
White/				
Black	—	—	H6XW	—

Vinyl roof color codes

Green	V1F
White	V1W
Black	V1X
Blue	V1B
Gold	V1G

Facts

The Sport Fury GT continued for one more model year. Only one engine was available, the 440-4V Super Commando V-8 engine, rated at 370 hp (305 net) mated to the TorqueFlite automatic transmission. Power disc brakes, Rallye road wheels with H70x15 RWL letters, heavy-duty suspension, hood stripes and side strobe stripes were all standard equipment. Large GT letters were located at the back of the hood. The GT's front fender tops were also adorned with three small metal strips, just behind the hood-mounted turn signal indicators.

The GT also got the redesigned front grille and rear taillights common to the 1971 Fury line. Miniscule sales sealed the GT's fate for 1972.

Chapter 48

1997 Plymouth Prowler

Production
Prowler   120

Serial numbers
1P3EW65EXV100001
1—country, U.S.A.
P—make, Plymouth
3—vehicle type, passenger car
E—restraint system, driver & passenger air bags, manual seatbelts
W—vehicle line, Prowler
6—series, Special/Sport
5—body style, convertible, open body
F—engine (EGE) 3.5l V-6
X—check digit, 0 thru 9 or X
V—model year, 1999
V—assembly plant (Conner Ave.)
100001—consecutive sequence number

Engine code
F—214 hp SOHC V-6

Retail price
PRPS27 2 dr Roadster $38,300.00

Exterior color code
Prowler Purple   PH7

Interior trim code
Agate   LLAZ

Facts
The Prowler first appeared as a concept car at the 1993 North American International Auto Show in Detroit. Because of a favorable response, Chrysler went ahead with a production version which was introduced at the 1996 North American International Auto Show. Regular production began in July 1997 at the Conner Avenue assembly plant—the same plant where the Dodge Viper is built.

The Prowler was powered by the Chrysler 3.5l V-6 rated at 214 hp at 5850 rpm with 221 ft.-lbs. torque at 3100 rpm. The only transmission was a rear-mounted four-speed automatic with the "Autostick" feature. The final drive ratio is 3.89:1.

Other standard features included a four-wheel independent suspension, four-wheel disc brakes and power-assisted rack and pinion steering. The Prowler used Goodyear Eagle GS-D tires: P225/45HR17 front, P295/40HR20 rear, mounted on 17x7.5 in. front and 20x10 in. rear cast aluminum wheels.

The Prowler came as a complete package. All of the power accessories are included and there were no options.

Only one color was available—Prowler Purple with an Agate leather interior.

1999 Plymouth Prowler

Production

Prowler (1998 build)	1,594
Prowler (1999 build)	1,325*

*As of July, 1999

Serial numbers

1P3EW65XXV100001
1—country, U.S.A.
P—make, Plymouth
3—vehicle type, passenger car
E—restraint system, driver & passenger air bags, manual seatbelts
W—vehicle line, Prowler
6—series, Special/Sport
5—body style, convertible, open body
X—engine (EGG) 3.5l V-6
X—check digit, 0 thru 9 or X
V—model year, 1999
V—assembly plant (Conner Ave.)
100001—consecutive sequence number

Engine code

X—253 hp High Output V-6

Options and retail prices

PRPS27 2 dr Roadster	$39,300.00
EGG Engine, High Output 3.5l V-6	Std
DGB Automatic 4 speed transmission	Std
WFC Chrome wheels	1,000.00
PRD Prowler Red	1,000.00
PY3 Prowler Yellow	1,000.00
PXT Prowler Black	1,000.00

Exterior color codes

Prowler Purple	PH7
Prowler Red	PRD
Prowler Yellow	PY3
Prowler Black	PXT

Interior trim code

Agate	LLAZ

Facts

Because of a delay in getting the new High Output 3.5l V-6, production for the 1999 model actually began in early 1998. There wasn't a 1998 model, though the production figures listed above are broken up to show 1998 and 1999 build production figures.

The 3.5l gave the Prowler more power and the new, smoother running engine reduced vibration and harshness throughout the car. The engine was rated at 253 hp at 6400 rpm with 255 ft.-lbs. torque at 3950 rpm.

Changes from the 1997 model include depowered air bags, a key-operated passenger-side disable air bag switch, illuminated window switches with express-down on the driver side, a chrome wheel option and a revised trim on the Prowler's 3200-watt boom-box speakers.

In March of 1998, Prowler Yellow was made available, followed by Prowler Black in November of the same year. In December 1998, Prowler Red was added—all of these colors were optional at an extra cost. Prowler Purple was standard equipment.

Chapter 50

2000 Plymouth Prowler

Serial numbers
1P3EW65XZV100001
1—country, U.S.A.
P—make, Plymouth
3—vehicle type, passenger car
E—restraint system, driver & passenger air bags, manual seatbelts
W—vehicle line, Prowler
6—series, Special/Sport
5—body style, convertible, open body
X—engine (EGG) 3.5l V-6
X—check digit, 0 thru 9 or X
Y—model year, 2000
V—assembly plant, Conner Ave.
100001—consecutive sequence number

Engine code
X—253 hp High Output V-6

Options and retail prices
PRPS27 2 dr Roadster	$42,700.00
EGG 3.5l V-6	Std
DGB Automatic 4 speed transmission	Std
ACW Woodward Edition Group	1,500.00

Exterior color codes
Prowler Silver	PSA
Prowler Red	PRD
Prowler Black	PXT

Interior trim code
Agate	LLAZ

Facts
Changes for the 2000 model included black bumpers replacing the previous gray ones, a modified suspension that improved ride quality, a speed-sensitive volume system for the sound system, an electrochromatic mirror that includes a compass, and temperature indicator and a mini-trip computer.

Leather was used on the shift boot, and a new color was added, Prowler Silver. Prowler Purple and Prowler Yellow were deleted. The Woodward Edition Group consisted of a special two-tone red-and-black paint combination with a red pinstripe hand-painted around the upper beltline and bears the initials of the customer/artist, Dr. Ru.

Bought for $6,000
06/26/12 from Peter Banman
S'side PEI

1970 Plymouth Valiant Duster 340

P/U @ MacKay's Auto Body
? 21,799 ?
√24,817

Production
2 dr hardtop 8 cyl

207851

Serial numbers
VS29H0R~~100001~~
V—car line, Plymouth Valiant
S—price class (S-special)
29—body type (29-2 dr sports hardtop)
H—engine code
0—last digit of model year, R
R—assembly plant code (R-Hamtramck, G-St. Louis) *Not "B"*
100001—consecutive sequence number
Serial number located on plate attached to left side of dash panel, visible through the windshield.

Engine code
H—340 ci 4V V-8 275 hp

Head casting number
340 ci—2531894

Carburetors
340 ci 4V V-8—Carter AVS4933S/manual, AVS4936S/manual w/ECS, AVS4934S/automatic, AVS4937S/automatic w/ECS, AVS4935S/automatic w/ECS, w/AC

Distributors
IBS-4018/manual, 3438325/automatic

Option order codes and retail prices
VS29 2 dr sports coupe	$2,547.00
A01 Light Package	29.60
A04 Basic Group w/bucket seats	82.60
A04 Basic Group w/bench seats	90.90
A35 Trailer Towing Package	14.05
A88 Interior Decor Group	23.90
B41 Disc brakes	Std
B51 Power brakes	42.95
C14 Shoulder belts	26.45
C15 Deluxe seatbelts	13.75
C16 Console (w/bucket seats & D34)	53.35
C65 Foam front seat cushion	8.30
C92 Color-keyed accessory floor mats	10.90
C93 Color-keyed carpets (std w/L2, D2 trim, std w/A88)	18.20
D21 Manual 4 speed transmission (NA w/A35)	187.90
D34 TorqueFlite automatic transmission	216.20
D91 Sure-Grip differential	42.35
F11 50 amp alternator (std w/H51)	11.00

F23 59 amp battery	12.95
G11 Tinted windows	32.75
G15 Tinted windshield	20.40
G31 Manual outside right mirror	6.85
G33 Remote control outside left mirror	10.45
G41 Day-night inside mirror	7.10
H31 Rear window defogger	26.25
H51 Air conditioning/w heater	346.55
J11 Glove box lock	4.10
J25 Variable-speed windshield wipers w/electric washers	10.60
J31 Dual horns	5.15
J41 Pedal dress-up	5.45
J55 Undercoating w/hood insulator pad	16.60
L42 Headlight time delay & warning buzzer	18.20
M05 Door edge protectors	4.65
M25 Custom sill molding	13.15
M26 Wheel lip molding	7.60
M31 Belt molding	13.60
M85 Front & rear bumper guards	23.80
N85 Tachometer	42.35
N95 Evaporative emission control (Calif.)	37.85
R11 Solid-state AM radio	61.55
S77 Power steering	85.15
Vinyl bench seat w/center armrest	64.75
Vinyl bucket seats	112.60
Cloth & vinyl trim	36.85
Vinyl roof	83.95
High-impact paint colors	14.05
Two-tone paint	22.65
Tires—set of 5 (replaces E70x14 BSW fiberglass belted)	
T74 E70x14 WSW fiberglass	26.45
T76 E70x14 RWL fiberglass belted	26.45

Exterior color codes

Ice Blue Metallic	EB3
Blue Fire Metallic	EB5
Jamaica Blue Metallic	EB7
In Violet Metallic	FC7
Rallye Red	FE5
Lime Green Metallic	FF4
Ivy Green Metallic	EF8
Lime Light	FJ5
Vitamin C Orange	EK2
Deep Burnt Orange Metallic	FK5
Sandpebble Beige	BL1
Burnt Tan Metallic	FT6
Tor Red	EV2
Alpine White	EW1
Black Velvet	TX9
Lemon Twist	FY1
Yellow Gold	DY3
Citron Mist Metallic	FY4

Interior trim codes-vinyl

Color	Std bench	Bench-cloth & vinyl	Bench*	Buckets*
Blue	D2B7	L1B7	L4B7	—
Red	—	—	L4E4	—
Green	D2F8	L1F8	L4F8	—
Tan	—	—	L4T5	—
Black	D2X9	L1X9	L4X9	L6X9
White/Blue	—	—	—	L6BW
White/Red	—	—	—	L6EW
White/Black	—	—	—	L6X9

*Optional

Vinyl roof color codes

Green	V1F
White	V1W
Black	V1X

Transverse tape stripe-std

Black	V8X

Facts

Sharing the same front styling as the Plymouth Valiant, the Duster 340 was an economy, compact-sized muscle car. The Duster had a fastback roof design and different taillight treatment. To keep costs down, pop-out rear side windows were used instead of roll-up windows.

The Duster 340 could be identified by its flat-black front grille, longitudinal side stripes and rear tape treatment.

The dash was standard Valiant, but a 150 mph speedometer took the place of the stock unit. An 8000 rpm tachometer was optional. Bench seats were standard; buckets optional.

The suspension consisted of heavy-duty front torsion bars and rear leaf springs with standard manual front disc brakes. The Duster 340 also came with a front anti-sway bar. E70x14 tires mounted on the 14 in. Rallye wheels were also standard.

The 340 ci small-block V-8 engine, rated at 275 hp, was mated to a three-speed manual transmission with a floor-mounted shifter. Optional was a four-speed manual and the TorqueFlite automatic transmission.

1970 Plymouth Valiant Duster 340

Chapter 52

1971 Plymouth Valiant Duster 340

Production

2 dr sports hardtop 8 cyl   10,403

Serial numbers

VS29H1B100001
V—car line, Plymouth Valiant
S—price class (S-special)
29—body type (29-2 dr sports hardtop)
H—engine code
1—last digit of model year
B—assembly plant code (B-Hamtramck)
100001—consecutive sequence number
Serial number located on plate attached to left side of dash panel,
visible through the windshield.

Engine code

H—340 ci 4V V-8 275 hp
(net rating 235 hp)

Head casting number

340 ci—2531894

Carburetors

340 ci 4V V-8—Carter TQ4972S/manual, TQ4973S/automatic

Distributors

340 ci—3438522/manual, 3438517/automatic, 3656151/manual
w/electronic ignition, 3438986/automatic w/electronic ignition

Option order codes and retail prices*

VS29 2 dr sports hardtop	$2,704.00
A01 Light Package	29.15
A04 Basic Group	92.10
A31 High Performance Axle Package	61.40
A88 Interior Decor Group	23.65
B41 Front disc brakes	32.05
B51 Power brakes	42.30
C14 Rear shoulder belts	26.10
C16 Console (w/buckets & D34)	52.55
C65 Front foam seat cushion	8.20
D21 Manual 4 speed transmission	189.80
D34 TorqueFlite automatic transmission	190.60
D91 Sure-Grip differential	41.70
F11 50 amp alternator (std w/H51)	10.85
F23 59 amp battery	13.60
G11 Tinted windows	33.60
G15 Tinted windshield only	22.25
G31 Chrome outside right mirror (requires G33)	6.80

G33 Chrome outside left mirror 10.35
G36 Mirrors, racing left outside remote & right manual color-
keyed (w/A04) 15.55
G36 Mirrors, racing left outside remote & right manual color-
keyed (w/oA04) 25.75
G37 Mirrors, racing left outside remote & right manual chrome
(w/A04) 15.55
G37 Mirrors, racing left outside remote & right manual chrome
(w/oA04) 25.75
G41 Day-night inside mirror 7.05
H31 Rear window defogger 27.35
H51 Air conditioning 384.00
J11 Glove box lock 4.05
J25 Variable-speed windshield wipers w/electric washers 10.60
J31 Dual horns 5.10
J41 Pedal dress-up 5.35
J45 Hood pins 15.20
J55 Undercoating w/hood insulator pad 20.80
J81 Aerodynamic rear spoiler 34.30
M05 Door edge protectors 4.60
M25 Custom sill molding (requires M26) 13.00
M26 Wheel lip molding (requires M25) 7.45
M31 Belt molding 13.40
M85 Front & rear bumper guards 24.90
N25 Engine block heater 13.85
N85 Tachometer 49.45
N95 NOx exhaust emission control (Calif) 11.90
R11 Solid-state AM radio 64.10
R26 AM radio w/stereo cassette player (w/oA04, w/oC16) 210.95
R26 AM radio w/stereo cassette player (w/A04, w/oC16) 147.00
R33 Tape recorder microphone (w/R26) 10.75
S77 Power steering 99.80
S81 Deluxe steering wheel 9.90
S84 Tuff steering wheel (NA w/A88, S77 req'd) 28.85
W11 Deluxe wheel covers 26.75
W15 Wire wheel covers 66.10
W21 Rallye road wheels 6.80
V24 Hood performance paint (w/340 engine callout,
    NA w/two-tone paint) 20.55
High-impact paint colors 13.85
Two-tone paint 28.55
Vinyl roof 88.25
Vinyl side molding 15.50
Vinyl split back bench seat w/center armrest 63.80
Vinyl bucket seat & carpeting 111.00
Tires (replaces E70x14 BSW P/F)
    T76 E70x14 RWL P/F 43.40
*April 1, 1971, revision

Exterior color codes

Winchester Gray Metallic	GA4
Glacial Blue Metallic	GB2
True Blue Metallic	GB5
Evening Blue	B7
Amber Sherwood Metallic	GF3
Sherwood Green Metallic	GF7
Autumn Bronze Metallic	GK6
Tunisian Tan Metallic	GT2
Sno White	GW3
Formal Black	TX9
Gold Leaf Metallic	GY8
Tawny Gold Metallic	GY9
In Violet	FC7
Sassy Grass Green	FV6
Bahama Yellow	EG5
Tor Red	EV2
Curious Yellow	GY3
Lemon Twist	FY1

Interior trim codes

Color	Cloth & vinyl bench	Vinyl bench	Vinyl buckets
Black	B1F6	L4X9	L6X9
Blue	B1B5	L4B7	—
Green	B1F6	L4F8	—
Tan	—	L4T5	—
Gold	—	L4Y3	—
Black/Orange	—	—	L6XV
Black/White	—	—	L6XW

Vinyl roof color codes

Black	V1X
White	V1W
Green	V1F
Gold	V1Y

Side stripe color codes

Black	V9X
White	V9W

Facts

The Duster got a new argent painted grille and a different side stripe treatment that ended with large 340 lettering on the rear quarter panels.

Although the engine and transmission options remained the same from 1970, the Duster 340 was downgraded to the extent that certain standard features became optional, such as the manual front disc brakes and the Rallye wheels. Tire size remained unchanged—E70x14.

Performance options included a tachometer, front disc brakes, the Rallye wheels, Tuff steering wheel, rear wing spoiler, hood pins and a blacked-out performance hood with large 340 lettering.

A rare option was the manual folding sunroof.

Chapter 53

1972 Plymouth Valiant Duster 340

Production
2 dr sports hardtop8 cyl   14,132

Serial numbers
VS29H2B100001
V—car line, Plymouth Valiant
S—price class (S-special)
29—body type (29-2 dr sports hardtop)
H—engine code
2—last digit of model year
B—assembly plant code (B-Hamtramck)
100001—consecutive sequence number
Serial number located on plate attached to left side of dash panel,
visible through the windshield.

Engine code
H—340 ci 4V V-8   240 hp

Head casting number
340 ci—3418915

Carburetors
340 ci 4V V-8—Carter TQ6138S/manual, TQ6139S/automatic

Distributors
3656278/manual, 3656283/manual & automatic

Option order codes and retail prices
VS29 2 dr sports hardtop	$2,784.00
A01 Light Package	30.50
A04 Basic Group	119.35
A21 Custom Exterior Package	21.10
A25 Interior Convenience Group	19.55
A88 Interior Decor Group (w/L1, C4, C6 trim)	19.85
A88 Interior Decor Group, others	38.25
B41 Power disc brakes	65.95
B51 Power drum brakes	42.80
C16 Console (buckets & D34 req'd)	54.00
D21 Manual 4 speed transmission	195.25
D34 TorqueFlite automatic transmission	220.55
D91 Sure-Grip differential	43.05
F23 59 amp battery	14.10
G11 Tinted glass, all windows	37.95
G15 Tinted windshield	25.80
G31 Manual chrome outside right mirror (G33 req'd)	7.00

G33 Remote control chrome outside left mirror (std w/A04)	12.30
G36 Dual racing mirrors, remote left, manual right (body color w/A04)	14.30
G36 Dual racing mirrors, remote left, manual right (body color w/oA04)	26.60
G37 Remote outside left racing mirrors & manual chrome right (w/A04)	14.30
G37 Remote outside left racing mirrors & manual chrome right (w/oA04)	26.60
G41 Day-night inside mirror (std w/A04)	7.25
H31 Rear window defogger	28.10
H51 Air conditioning	374.40
J11 Glove box lock (std w/A04)	4.20
J25 Variable-speed wipers w/electric washers (std w/A04)	10.95
J52 Inside hood release	10.05
J55 Undercoating w/hood insulator pad	21.45
M05 Door edge protectors	4.80
M31 Belt molding	13.80
M85 Front & rear bumper guards	25.65
N23 Electronic ignition system	32.55
N95 Emission control system & testing (req'd Calif)	27.05
R11 Solid-state AM radio	62.90
R21 AM/FM radio (w/A04)	68.95
R21 AM/FM radio (w/oA04)	131.80
R31 Rear seat speaker	14.25
S77 Power steering	97.65
S84 Tuff steering wheel (NA w/A25, S77 req'd)	29.65
S84 Tuff steering wheel (w/A25, S77 req'd)	19.50
V21 Performance hood paint	18.35
W11 Deluxe wheel covers	25.95
W21 Rallye road wheels, set of 4 w/std spare (w/A04)	30.00
W21 Rallye road wheels, set of 4 w/std spare (w/oA04)	55.90
High-impact paint colors	14.25
Two-tone paint	29.35
Vinyl roof	79.85
Sunroof (NA w/vinyl roof)	236.40
Vinyl side molding	14.75
Vinyl bench seat	24.40
Vinyl split back bench seat w/center armrest & carpets	78.90
Vinyl bucket seat & carpeting	127.25
Tires (replaces E70x14 BSW bias belted)	
T76 E70x14 RWL	39.50

Exterior color codes

Winchester Gray Metallic	GA4
Blue Sky	HB1
Basin Street Blue	TB3
True Blue Metallic	GB5
Rallye Red	FE5
Amber Sherwood Metallic	GF3
Mojave Tan Metallic	HT6

Chestnut Metallic			HT8
Spinnaker White			EW1
Honeydew			GY4
Gold Leaf Metallic			GY8
Tawny Gold Metallic			GY9
Formal Black			TX9
Tor Red			EV2
Lemon Twist			FY1

Interior trim codes

Color	Buckets	Cloth & vinyl Bench	Split Bench	Vinyl split Bench
Blue	—	D2B5	B1B5	C4B5
Green	—	D2F6	B1F6	C4F6
Black	C6X9	D2X9	B1X9	C4X9
White	C6XW	—	—	C4XW
Gold	—	—	—	C4Y3

Vinyl roof color codes

Black	V1X
White	V1W
Gold	V1Y
Green	V1F

Tape stripe codes

Black	V6X
White	V6W

Facts

The 1972 Duster 340's changes were mostly under the hood. The 340 ci V-8 engine was now rated at 240 hp. Compression ratio dropped to 8.5:1, and the 340 now used the same cylinder heads as the 360 ci V-8, which had smaller intake valves measuring 1.88 in.

Transmissions, suspension and brake availability remained unchanged from 1971.

The folding sunroof was still on the option list, but only a few were ever sold.

Chapter 54

1973 Plymouth Valiant Duster 340

Production
2 dr sports hardtop 8 cyl   13,862

Serial Numbers
VS29H3B100001
V—car line, Plymouth Valiant
S—price class (S-special)
29—body type (29-2 dr sports hardtop)
H—engine code
3—last digit of model year
B—assembly plant code (B-Hamtramck)
100001—consecutive sequence number
Serial number located on plate attached to left side of dash panel,
visible through the windshield.

Engine code
H—340 ci 4V V-8 240 hp

Head casting number
340 ci—3671587

Carburetors
340 ci 4V V-8—Carter TQ6318S/manual, TQ6339S/manual (Calif),
TQ6319S/automatic, TQ6340S/automatic (Calif)

Option order codes and retail prices
S29 2 dr sports hardtop V-8	$2,443.00
A01 Light Package	28.80
A04 Basic Group	112.70
A21 Custom Exterior Group	34.35
A25 Interior Convenience Group	18.45
A33 Heavy-duty Package (std w/A35)	35.65
A34 Trailer Towing Wiring Package	36.15
A35 Trailer Towing Package (requires D34)	83.60
A88 Interior Decor Group	36.15
B41 Front power disc brakes (req'd w/340 ci)	40.45
C16 Console (D34 req'd)	51.60
C73 Spacemaker Pak-folding rear seat	84.35
C93 Carpets (std w/A88)	17.45
D21 Manual 4 speed transmission	184.50
D34 TorqueFlite automatic transmission	208.40
D91 Sure-Grip differential	40.65
F23 375 amp battery	13.30
G01 Electric rear window defogger	48.20
G11 Tinted glass, all windows	35.85

Option order codes and retail prices *(continued)*

G15 Tinted windshield only	24.35
G33 Remote control chrome left mirror	11.60
G36 Body-color dual racing mirrors, remote left, manual right (w/A04)	13.50
G36 Body-color dual racing mirrors, remote left, manual right (w/oA04)	25.10
G37 Remote outside left racing mirrors & manual chrome right (w/A04)	13.50
G37 Remote outside left racing mirrors & manual chrome right (w/oA04)	25.10
G41 Day-night inside mirror (std w/A04)	5.65
H31 Rear window defogger	26.55
H51 Air conditioning	353.80
J25 3-speed windshield wipers w/electric washers	10.35
J52 Inside hood release	9.50
J55 Undercoating w/hood insulator pad	20.25
M52 Manually operated sunroof	139.80
M85 Front & rear bright bumper guards	14.50
N95 Emission control system & testing (req'd Calif)	25.55
R11 AM radio	59.40
R21 AM/FM radio (w/A04)	65.15
R21 AM/FM radio (w/oA04)	124.55
R31 Rear seat speaker (requires R11 or R21, NA w/C73)	13.45
S77 Power steering	92.25
V21 Hood performance paint	17.30
W11 Deluxe wheel covers	24.50
W21 Rallye road wheels (w/A04)	28.35
W21 Rallye road wheels (w/oA04)	52.80
High-impact paint colors	13.45
Canopy vinyl roof	60.10
Full vinyl roof	75.45
Bodyside tape stripe	13.90
Vinyl bench seat	27.85
Vinyl split back bench seat w/center armrest & carpets	74.55
Vinyl bucket seat & carpeting	120.25
Tires (replaces 5 E70x14 BSW bias belted)	
T76 E70x14 RWL bias belted	37.30

Exterior color codes

Silver Frost Metallic	JA5
Sky Blue	HB1
Basin Street Blue	TB3
True Blue Metallic	GB5
Rallye Red	FE5
Mist Green	JF1
Forest Green Metallic	JF8
Autumn Bronze Metallic	GK6
Sahara Beige	HL4
Honey Gold	JY3
Golden Haze Metallic	JY6

Exterior color codes *(continued)*

Tahitian Gold Metallic	JY9
Spinnaker White	EW1
Formal Black	TX9
Lemon Twist	FY1
Amber Sherwood Metallic	GF3

Interior trim codes

Color	Vinyl Split-back Bench	Vinyl Split-back Bench w/armrest	Cloth & vinyl Split-back Bench	Vinyl Buckets
Blue	D2B5	C4B5	A1B5	—
Green	D2F6	C4F6	A1F6	—
Parchment	D2L3	C4L3	—	—
Black	D2X9	C4X9	A1X9	C6X9
Gold	D2Y4	—	—	—
White	—	—	—	C6XW

Vinyl roof color codes

Color	Full	Canopy
Black	V1X	V4X
White	V1W	V4W
Gold	V1Y	—
Green	V1F	—

Standard side stripes

Color	Bodyside	Lower Deck
Black	V6X	V8X
White	V6W	V8W

Facts

For 1973, Dusters got new front end styling with a different grille design and stronger bumpers. The taillight treatment was similar to 1972, but the taillight bezels were smaller.

There were some new items on the option list. The folding sunroof was replaced by a manual metal sunroof, the rear defogger heated the rear window electrically and the Spacemaker Pak, a fold-down rear seat, was now available.

Power disc brakes were now standard equipment on the Duster.

In addition to the regular full vinyl roof, a canopy roof was available. The 340 engine was unchanged from 1972.

Chapter 55

1986 Shelby GLHS

Production
4 dr hatchback 4 cyl   500

Serial numbers
1B34Z48LXGD100001
1—country, U.S.A.
B—make, Dodge
3—vehicle type, passenger car
4—restraint system, manual seatbelt
Z—line, Omni
4—trim level, high
8—body style, 4 dr hatchback
L—engine, EDL 2.2l TC II
X—check digit, 0 thru 9 or X
G—model year, 1986
D—assembly plant code (D-Belvedere)
100001—consecutive sequence number

Engine code
L—2.2l 4 cyl EFI TC II 75 hp

Options and retail prices
4 dr Dodge Omni GLH hatchback	$7,918.00
2.2l turbocharged engine	898.00
Rear window defroster	137.00
Air conditioning	663.00
Shelby GLH-S Package	1,379.00

Exterior color code
Black   PX8

Interior trim code
Gray   B5A3

Facts
The first car to be modified at the Shelby facility in Whittier, California, was the Dodge Omni GLHS four-door. GLHS reportedly stood for "Goes Like Hell Somemore."

Based on the four-door Omni GLH, the GLHS came only with the five-speed manual transmission, high-back cloth covered buckets, AM/FM stereo radio and other GLH options.

What made the GLHS go was the Shelby-modified 2.2 liter turbo engine. The increased horsepower came from a Shelby ram-type manifold, larger 46 mm throttle body (vs. 42 mm stock), larger fuel lines and injectors and a modified logic computer. Turbo boost pressure was also increased to 12 psi (from 9 psi).

Also unique to the GLHS was the Shelby-installed intercooler setup, which would later be used by Dodge also. In addition, a heated O2 was used. The result was the Turbo II engine rated at 175 hp and 175 ft.-lbs. torque. Quarter mile times were in the mid-14 second range and top speed is about 130 mph.

Shelby modifications included Koni struts up front and Koni shocks in the rear. Shelby left the factory front and rear sway bars on, which measured 1 in. front and 5/8 in. rear, but did make adjustments to the front and rear alignment specifications. Special Shelby Centurion aluminum wheels and Goodyear Gatorback 205/50VR-15 tires were used.

Shelby body modifications included a front spoiler, sideskirts and Shelby tape graphics, which used white tape rather than the stock GLH red, and a white Shelby decal on the top of the windshield.

In the interior, a leather-wrapped steering wheel and shift knob were installed. Replacing the standard Omni emblem was a special Shelby dash plaque which indicated what number the GLHS was. A clear sticker overlay was added to the unpegged speedometer which extended its readout to 135 mph.

Most, if not all, GLHSs were built with the options listed above. However, several were built with a roll bar and an engine oil cooler. According to Dempsey Bowling, cars 001 (Shelby's personal car), 007, 008, 010, 047 and 048 had the roll bar.

Chapter 56

1987 Shelby CSX

Production
2 dr hatchback 4 cyl   750

Serial numbers
1B3BS44EXHN100001
1—country, U.S.A.
B—make, Dodge
3—vehicle type, passenger car
4—restraint system, manual seatbelt
S—line, Shadow
4—trim level, high
4—body style, 2 dr hatchback
E—engine, EDG 2.2l TC
X—check digit, 0 thru 9 or X
H—model year, 1987
D—assembly plant, (D-Belvedere, N-Sterling)
100001—consecutive sequence number

Engine code
E—EDG 2.2l 4 cyl turbocharged 175 hp

Retail price
2 dr hatchback $13,495.00

Engine code
E—2.2l 4 cyl turbocharged 175 hp

Exterior color code
Black   DX8

Interior trim code
Gray   R7A3

Facts
The fourth Shelby-modified car was the Shelby CSX, which was based on the Dodge Shadow ES Turbo. Using the 2.2 liter Turbo I engine modified to Turbo II specs, the horsepower rating was the same as for the other Shelby offerings, 175 hp.

The Shelby CSX was considerably more hospitable than the Omni- or Charger-based GLHS. Standard equipment included full instrumentation, reclining front seats, 60/40 rear split fold-down seats, air conditioning, AM/FM cassette stereo, tinted glass and rear defogger.

Shelby modifications were similar to the ones made on the 1987 Shelby Lancer. These included Monroe Formula GP gas struts/shocks, high-rate coil springs, 1.06 in. front/1.13 in. rear sway bars and four-wheel disc brakes. There was only one transmission, a five-speed manual. Final drive ratio was 3.56:1.

Wheels were Shelby Centurion II and tires were Goodyear Gatorback, 205/50VR-15.

On the exterior, front and rear airdams were used along with matching sideskirts. The stock grille was replaced with a larger one.

Shelby graphics consisted of Shelby CSX lettering on the lower part of the doors, intercooled decals on the power bulge hood, a large circular Shelby logo in the center of the rear hatch deck lid, a CSX decal on the grill, and a Shelby decal at the top of the windshield. Each CSX was also identified by a serial number plate on the dash which had Carroll Shelby's signature. There was a unique boost gauge in the dash with blue SHELBY TURBO lettering.

An underhood plate stated that the CSX was manufactured by Shelby Automobiles, Inc.

In all, 750 Shelby CSXs were produced, and all were equipped identically. Of these, 165 cars, without options, were sold to Thrifty Car Rental.

Chapter 57

1987 Shelby GLHS

Production
2 dr hatchback 4 cyl   1,000

Serial numbers
1B3BZ44AXAD100001
1—country, U.S.A.
B—make, Dodge
3—vehicle type, passenger car
B—restraint system, manual seatbelt
Z—line, Charger
4—trim level, high
4—body style, 2 dr hatchback
E—engine, EDG 2.2l TC
X—check digit, 0 thru 9 or X
G—model year, 1987
D—assembly plant code (D-Belvedere)
100001—consecutive sequence number

Engine code
E—2.2l 4 cyl turbocharged 175 hp

Options and retail prices
2 dr hatchback $12,995.00

Exterior color code
Black   PX8

Interior trim code
Gray   B5A3

Facts
    The second Dodge vehicle to be modified by Shelby was based on the Dodge Charger. The fastback body was more appropriate for the image Shelby wanted to convey. Again, there was only one color choice, black. The black was a special-order color which did not have a silver stripe down the center of the car.
    The suspension was modified with Koni adjustable shocks and struts and the wheel alignment was changed as well.
Shelby identification included GLHS decals on the hood and rear. The hood got a power bulge treatment. Shelby Centurion aluminum alloy wheels were used with Goodyear Gatorback 205/50VR-15 tires.
    Standard GLHS features included AM/FM stereo cassette, front airdam and rear spoiler, 14:1 quick ratio power steering, removable glass sunroof, five-speed manual transmission (no automatic available) and Rallye cluster instrumentation which consisted of a tachometer, oil pressure, temperature gauges and trip

odometer. The speedometer received an overlay which showed a higher top speed, 125 mph.

Interestingly, the GLHS did not have the rear window louver, which was standard equipment on all 1987 Dodge Shelby Chargers.

The 2.2L engine was the same one used on the 1986 GLHS, rated at 175 hp. The stock Turbo I was converted by Shelby to Turbo II specs and included a specially tuned intake manifold, a larger throttle body and an intercooler.

In the interior, a leather-wrapped steering wheel and shift knob were installed as was a numbered dash plaque. The dash plaque, as well as the speedometer overlay, was different from those used on the 1986 GLHS.

On the exterior, a small silver tape stripe was used on the sides of the body along with Shelby lettering behind the front wheels, GLHS C-pillar decals and a Shelby windshield decal.

1987 Shelby GLHS

Chapter 58

1987 Shelby Lancer

Production
4 dr hatchback 4 cyl   780

Serial numbers
1B3BX68EXHD100001
1—country, U.S.A.
B—make, Dodge
3—vehicle type, passenger car
B—restraint system, manual seatbelt
X—line, Lancer
6—trim level, special
8—body style, 4 dr hatchback
E—engine, EDG 2.2l 4 cyl TC
X—check digit, 0 thru 9 or X
H—model year, 1987
D—assembly plant code (D-Belvedere, N-Sterling)
100001—consecutive sequence number

Engine code
E—2.2l 4 cyl turbo 175 hp

Options and retail prices
2 dr hatchback $16,995.00
Leather interior   1,000.00

Exterior color code
Graphic Red   PR5

Interior trim code
Gray leather   HLS8
Gray cloth   E7S8

Facts
The third car to be modified at Shelby's facility was the Dodge Lancer. The same Turbo II engine was used on the Lancer. However, the Lancer received more suspension modifications.

Standard features on the Lancer included air conditioning, a full-length console with armrest, overhead console with compass, outside temperature and courtesy lights, dual illuminated vanity mirrors, full instrumentation, premium sound insulation, power mirrors, power windows, power door locks, driver's side power seat, rear defroster, split folding rear seat and tilt steering with signature steering wheel.

The sound system, a bit ahead of its time, was a 120 watt Pioneer DEX77 AM/FM stereo CD player with an integrated nine-band equalizer and anti-theft coding capability. It utilized two amps and featured 10 speakers.

The suspension was lowered 1/2 in., firmer springs were installed and Monroe Formula GP shocks were installed. Kelsey Hayes 10.6 in. rear disc brakes replaced the stock rear drum brakes. Aluminum Shelby CSS wheels and Goodyear Gatorback 205/60VR15 tires were installed to complete the suspension package.

Externally, the Lancer got Shelby Lancer decals on the front doors, while Intercooled Turbo lettering was located on each side of the front airdam in front of the wheels. The Lancer also came with sideskirts.

Of the 780 Lancers produced, 380 came with the five-speed manual transmission and 400 with the automatic transmission. The manual-equipped cars came with the cloth interior, while the automatics were equipped with leather (except for five cars that got cloth instead).

Not to be confused with the Shelby Lancer was the availability of the Dodge Shelby Lancer that was produced by Dodge in 1987. Using the Shelby name, the Dodge version did not have the four-wheel disc brakes, engine modifications and other unique Shelby modifications.

1987 Shelby Lancer

Chapter 59

1988 Shelby CSX-T

Production
2 dr hatchback 4 cyl   1,000

Serial Numbers
1B3BS44EXJN100001
1—country, U.S.A.
B—make, Dodge
3—vehicle type, passenger car
4—restraint system, manual seatbelt
S—line, Shadow
4—trim level, high
4—body style, 2 dr hatchback
E—engine, EDG 2.2l TC
X—check digit, 0 thru 9 or X
J—model year, 1988
N—assembly plant (D-Belvedere, N-Sterling)
100001—consecutive sequence number

Engine code
E – 2.2l 4 cyl turbo 145 hp

Exterior color code
White   FW9

Interior trim code
Gray   R7A3

Facts
In 1988, Shelby built 1,000 CSX-Ts for Thrifty Car Rental. These cars were all painted white and carried the same suspension modifications as the 1987 Shelby CSX, but they did not receive any of the engine modifications. However, they did get the Shelby engine valve cover.

The 2.2 liter turbo engine was not intercooled, but it did have a new one-piece intake manifold, which was used on all 1988 Dodge 2.2l turbo engines.

Standard equipment included full instrumentation, reclining front seats, 60/40 rear split fold-down seats, air conditioning, AM/FM cassette stereo, tinted glass and rear defogger.

Shelby modifications were similar to the ones made on the 1987 Shelby CSX. These included Monroe Formula GP gas struts/shocks, high-rate coil springs, 1.06 in. front/1.13 in. rear sway bars and four-wheel disc brakes. There was only one transmission, a five-speed manual. The final drive ratio was 3.56:1. The wheels were a polished aluminum five-spoke design with the inlets painted white to match the body. The tires were Goodyear Gatorbacks, 205/50VR-15.

The CSX-T used different wheels. These were a new five-spoke polished aluminum design measuring 15x6.5 in. The wheel's cutouts were painted white, matching the body color.

On the exterior, front and rear airdams were used along with matching sideskirts. The stock grille was replaced with a larger one.

Shelby graphics consisted of Shelby CSX lettering on the lower part of the doors, intercooled decals on the power bulge hood, a large circular Shelby logo in the center of the rear hatch deck lid, a CSX-T decal on the grille and a Shelby decal at the top of the windshield. Each CSX-T was also identified by a serial number plate on the dash which had the Thrifty logo instead of Shelby's signature. There was also a unique boost gauge in the dash with blue SHELBY TURBO lettering.

An underhood plate stated that the CSX-T was manufactured by Shelby Automobiles, Inc.

One thousand CSX-Ts were produced. All were identically equipped except for two. The first was equipped with the 175 hp Turbo II intercooled engine and given to Thrifty's president. The other CSX-T got a sunroof and was given to Thrifty's president's daughter and did not have an intercooled engine.

Chapter 60

1989 Shelby CSX-VNT

Production
2 dr hatchback 4 cyl 500

Serial numbers
1B3BP44A5XKN100001
1—country, U.S.A.
B—make, Dodge
3—vehicle type, passenger car
B—restraint system, manual seatbelt
P—line, Shadow
4—trim level, high
4—body style, 2 dr hatchback
A—engine, EDR 2.2l TC II I/C
X—check digit, 0 thru 9 or X
K—model year, 1989
N—assembly plant (D-Belvedere, N-Sterling)
100001—consecutive sequence number

Engine code
A—2.2l 4 cyl Turbo II 175 hp

Exterior color code
Exotic Red   PR1

Options and retail prices
2 dr hatchback	$14,100.00
Recaro seats	895.00
Z50 tires	540.00

Facts
The last Shelby-modified Shadow came out as a 1989 model. Based on the Shadow, the Shelby CSX-VNT came with some very unique features.

The 175 hp Turbo II engine came with VNT, Variable Nozzle Turbocharging. This system reduces turbo lag by as much as 50 percent. Although horsepower is the same as previous Shelby engines, torque was up to 210 lbs. at 3200 rpm, greatly boosting low rpm performance.

The CSX-VNT was also the first car to come with composite wheels. The wheels, made of fiberglass by Motor Wheel Corporation, are lighter, stronger and are supposed to require less maintenance than aluminum wheels. Tire size was increased to Goodyear 225/50VR15 Eagles with Z rated tires optional.

In the interior, there was a Shelby signature steering wheel and Shelby charcoal cloth inserts. On the exterior, the CSX-VNT came with a new aero package complete with an airdam, sideskirts, rear wing and a rear skirt.

Although 500 cars were built, only 498 were sold. The other two were prototypes. Seventeen CSXs were equipped with the optional Z rated tires. Fifteen of these also got the Recaro seats.

Chapter 61

1989 Shelby Dakota

Production
2WD pickup   1,475

Serial numbers
1B7GN16YXKS100001
1—country, U.S.A.
B—make, Dodge
7—vehicle type, truck
G—other, 5,001–6,000 lb.
N—line, Dakota Sport, 4x2
1—series, 150 job rated
6—conventional cab
Y—engine, ELG- 5.2l EFI
X—check digit, 0 thru 9 or X
K—model year, 1989
S—assembly plant code (K-Pillette Road, M-Lago Alberto, S-Dodge City)
100001—consecutive sequence number

Engine code
Y—5.2l V-8 175 hp

Options and retail prices
2WD shortbed pickup
$15,813.00

Exterior color code
Graphic Red   DR5
Bright White   GW7

Interior trim code
Gray/Red

Facts
Shelby's Dakota was based on the production two-wheel drive shortbed Dakota Sport model. The biggest change was the substitution of the standard 3.9l V-6 with the 5.2l (318 ci) V-8. Because of space limitations, the factory engine fan was removed and replaced by two radiator-mounted electric fans. Output was 175 hp at 4000 rpm with 270 ft.-lbs. torque at 2000 rpm. A Shelby decal on the air cleaner identified the engine.

The four-speed automatic was the only transmission available, with a 3.91:1 Sure-Grip rear differential.

Complementing the V-8 engine was the Dakota Sport heavy-duty suspension. Shelby five-spoke aluminum wheels were used shod with 225/70HR-15 Goodyear Eagle GT+4 tires.

An airdam, with integrated driving lights, was painted black along with the bumper and grille. The grille had a Shelby emblem mounted on it. The rear bumper, along with various trim pieces, was also painted black. A distinctive light bar was located behind the cab. Shelby decals were placed on each side of the truck, and a V-8 decal was located next to each turn signal light on the front fenders. A large Shelby decal was also used on top of the windshield.

The interior featured a leather-wrapped steering wheel. The standard bench seat was finished in special gray/red cloth with Shelby imprint; the same cloth was also used on the door panel inserts. Two Shelby plaques were located on the dash. Rounding out the package was an AM/FM cassette stereo system.

Of the 1,475 built, 480 were white and 995 were red. Some sources indicate that a total of 1,500 units were built.

1989 Shelby Dakota